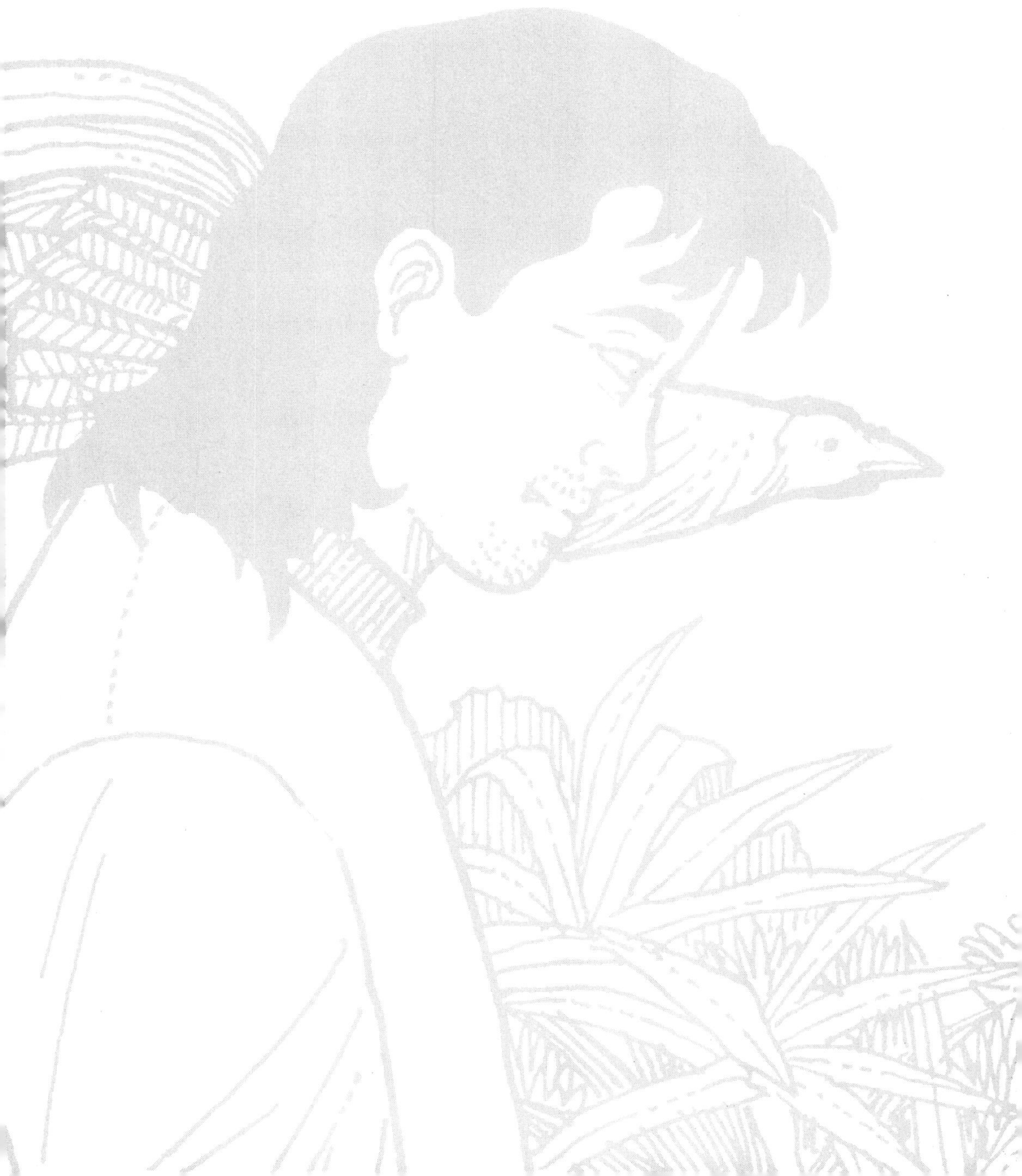

ELMER

Written and Drawn by
Gerry Alanguilan

Book Design by Gerry Alanguilan

Published by SLG Publishing, P.O. Box 26427,
San Jose, CA 95159

www.slgcomic.com
gerry.alanguilan.com

ISBN-13: 978-1-59362-204-6
First Printing: October 2010

ELMER

written & illustrated by
Gerry Alanguilan

for my parents

OCTOBER 6, 2003.
I woke up at 4:30 am. I had been dreaming. I remember being chased. People with knives. A forest and a sea full of hidden, dangerous creatures. It was terrifying.

I **HATE** waking up so early. It's still so dark that it makes me feel like everybody's still asleep except me.

My interview wasn't until 9:00am, but I couldn't sleep anymore.

I sat down to write my dream, but I've forgotten most of it. I used to get a lot of my great ideas from dreams. Some of them, I'm sure, would make great movies.

Speaking of movies, I really should call my brother. But it's hard to get in touch with him sometimes. It's hard to convince HIS IDIOT PEOPLE THAT I'M NOT SOME GOD DAMNED *FAN*.

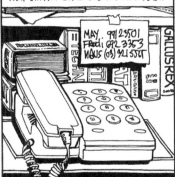

AND IT'S HARD TO CONVINCE HIM THAT IT'S NOT JUST GOD DAMNED MONEY I WANT. JEEZ! CAN'T A BROTHER JUST *CALL*?!

I checked some email and surfed a little bit. I read some news.

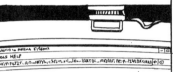

BIRD FLU: SHOULD WE PANIC?
By Ritchie Patrick

5 October, 2003

Scientists have warned that the strain could cause a lethal pandemic if it develops into a form that can be spread from human-to-human, but many stress that the risk remains low.

Bird Flu was thought only to infect birds until the first human cases were seen in Hong Kong in 1997. Since then, according to the World Health Organisation, 77 people have died in countries mostly located in South Asia - until now.

So as the disease moves ever closer, how worried should we be and what can be done to ensure it doesn't become a pandemic?

A Bird Flu pandemic is a global threat, which ignores borders and requires a co-ordinated international response. Only this week the world's third-largest bank, the HSBC announced contingency plans to deal with an outbreak which, it fears, could leave up to half of its staff off work.

Given the trans-national nature of this disease we need member states in the European Union to work together to ensure that Avian Flu does not spread.

Back in October of last year Greece became the first EU country to confirm a case of Bird Flu and since then the European Commission has taken the issue very seriously. European Commission surveillance

But I didn't read them too much because they were just too damned depressing.

PENDING PANDEMIC!

Smut surfed instead. Much to my amazement, I discovered that little child star ANNA ROSIE has now grown up to be a bonafide *BOLDIE!!*

OH my *GOD!* she has *REALLY* grown. And I do mean *GROWN.* Lordy! God have mercy!

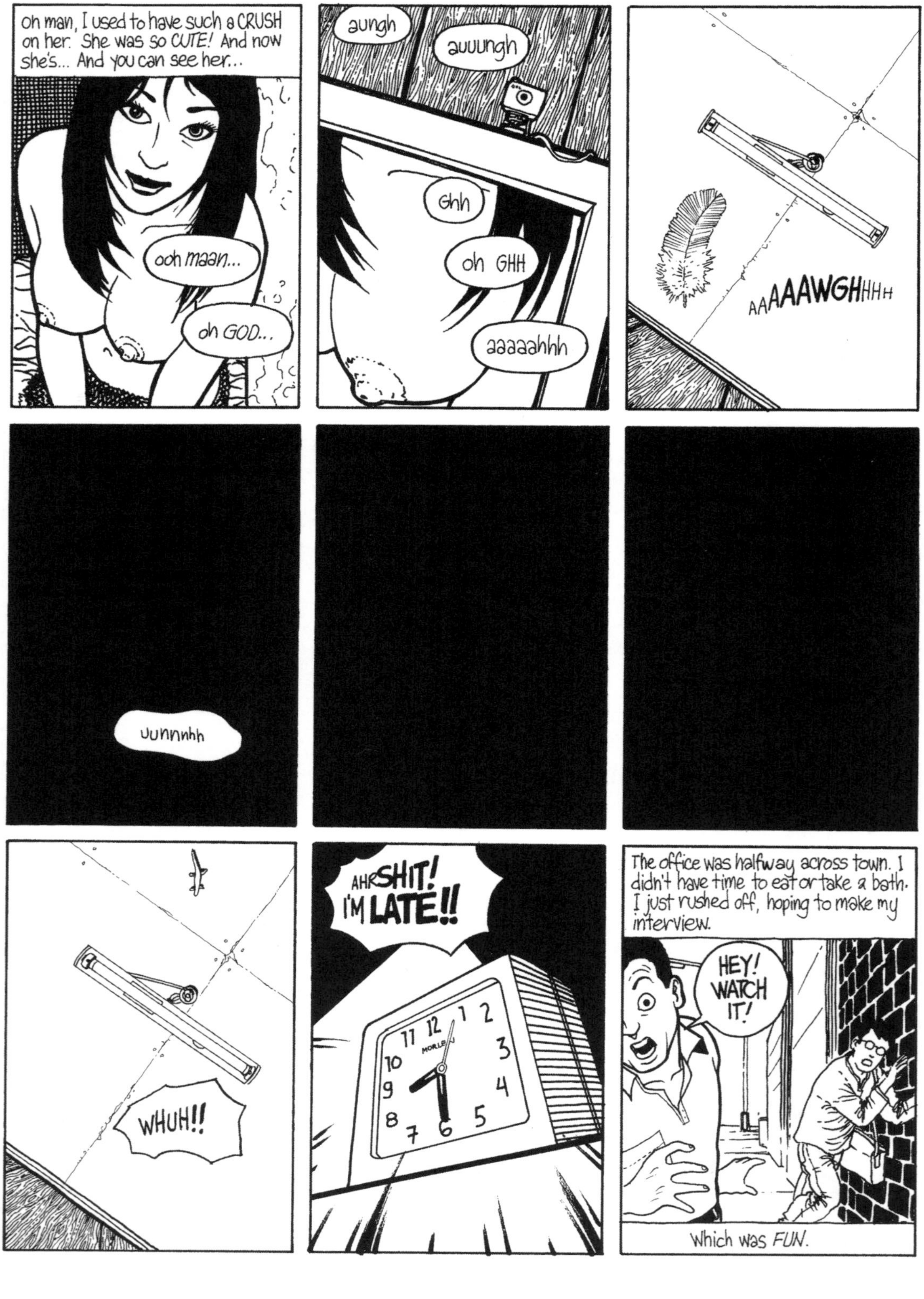
oh man, I used to have such a CRUSH on her. She was so CUTE! And now she's... And you can see her...
ooh maan...
oh GOD...
aungh
auuungh
Ghh
oh GHH
aaaaahhh
AAAAAWGHHHH
uunnnhh
WHUH!!
AHRSHIT! I'M LATE!!
The office was halfway across town. I didn't have time to eat or take a bath. I just rushed off, hoping to make my interview.
HEY! WATCH IT!
Which was FUN.

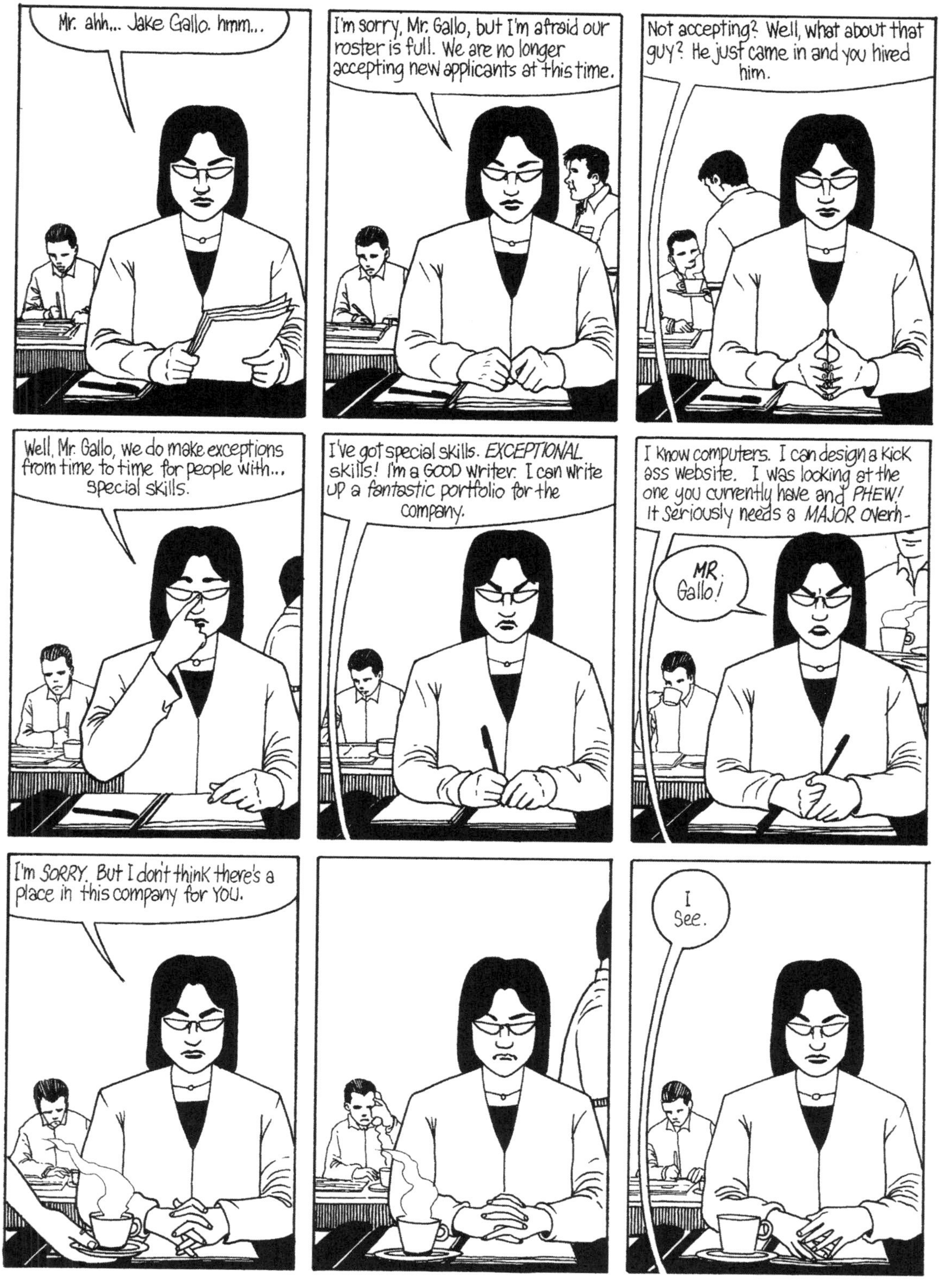
Mr. ahh... Jake Gallo. hmm...
I'm sorry, Mr. Gallo, but I'm afraid our roster is full. We are no longer accepting new applicants at this time.
Not accepting? Well, what about that guy? He just came in and you hired him.
Well, Mr. Gallo, we do make exceptions from time to time for people with... special skills.
I've got special skills. EXCEPTIONAL skills! I'm a GOOD writer. I can write up a fantastic portfolio for the company.
I know computers. I can design a kick ass website. I was looking at the one you currently have and PHEW! It seriously needs a MAJOR overh-
MR. Gallo!
I'm SORRY. But I don't think there's a place in this company for YOU.
I see.

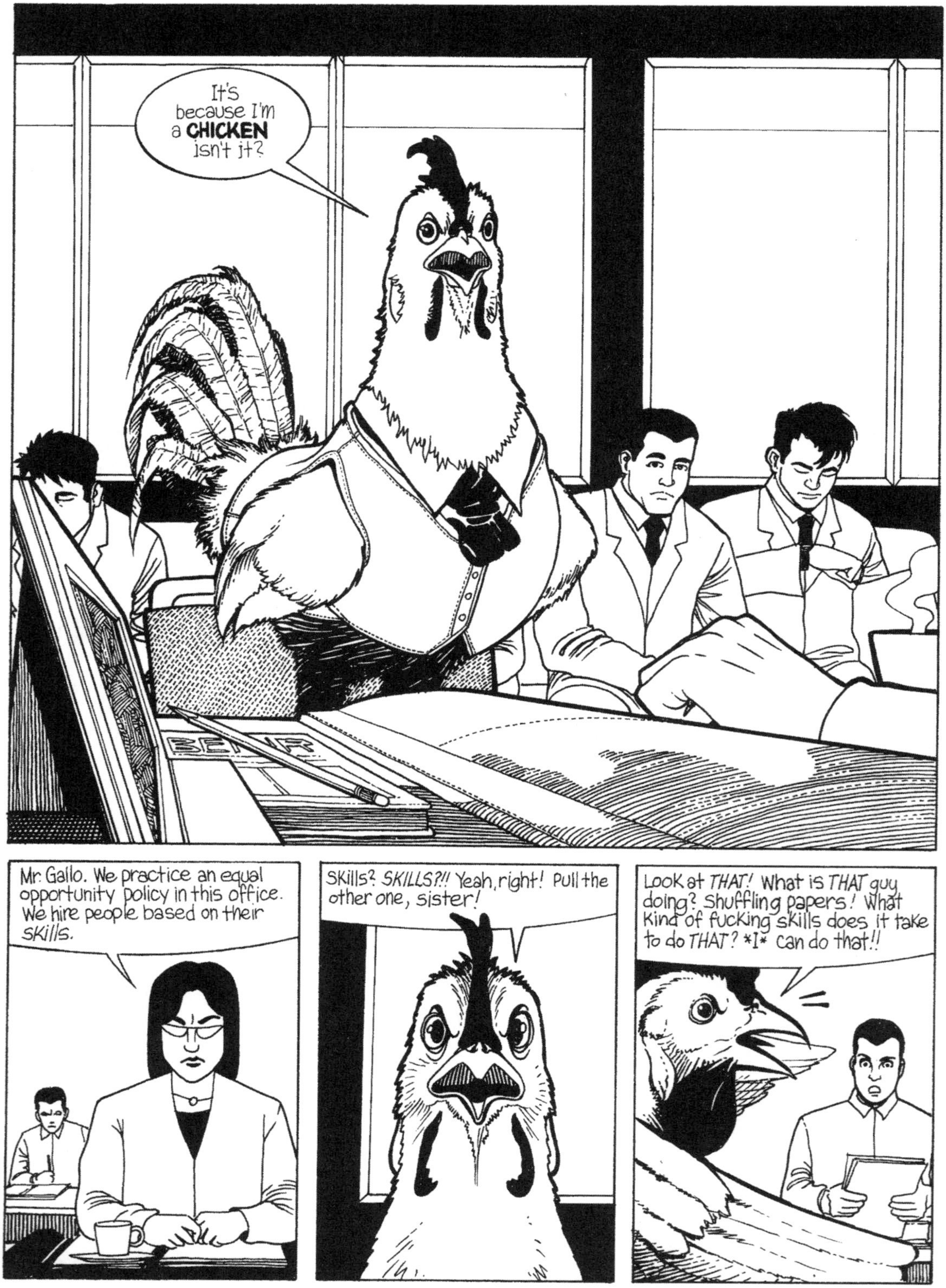
It's because I'm a **CHICKEN** isn't it?
Mr. Gallo. We practice an equal opportunity policy in this office. We hire people based on their *skills*.
Skills? *SKILLS?!!* Yeah, right! Pull the other one, sister!
Look at *THAT*! What is *THAT* guy doing? Shuffling papers! What kind of fucking skills does it take to do *THAT*? *I* can do that!!

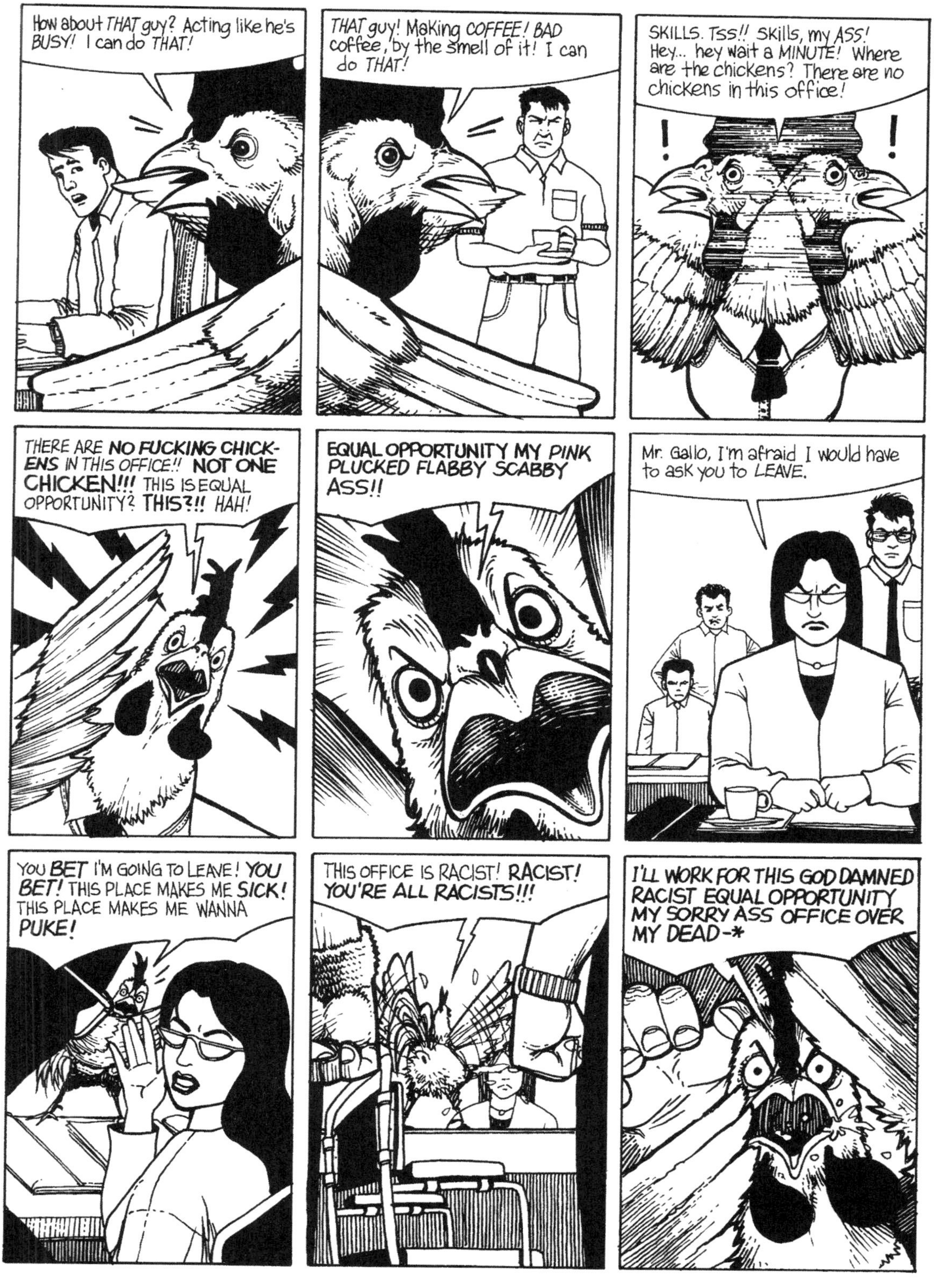
How about THAT guy? Acting like he's BUSY! I can do THAT!
THAT guy! Making COFFEE! BAD coffee, by the smell of it! I can do THAT!
SKILLS. Tss!! Skills, my ASS! Hey... hey wait a MINUTE! Where are the chickens? There are no chickens in this office!
!
!
THERE ARE NO FUCKING CHICKENS IN THIS OFFICE!! NOT ONE CHICKEN!!! THIS IS EQUAL OPPORTUNITY? THIS?!! HAH!
EQUAL OPPORTUNITY MY PINK PLUCKED FLABBY SCABBY ASS!!
Mr. Gallo, I'm afraid I would have to ask you to LEAVE.
YOU BET I'M GOING TO LEAVE! YOU BET! THIS PLACE MAKES ME SICK! THIS PLACE MAKES ME WANNA PUKE!
THIS OFFICE IS RACIST! RACIST! YOU'RE ALL RACISTS!!!
I'LL WORK FOR THIS GOD DAMNED RACIST EQUAL OPPORTUNITY MY SORRY ASS OFFICE OVER MY DEAD-*

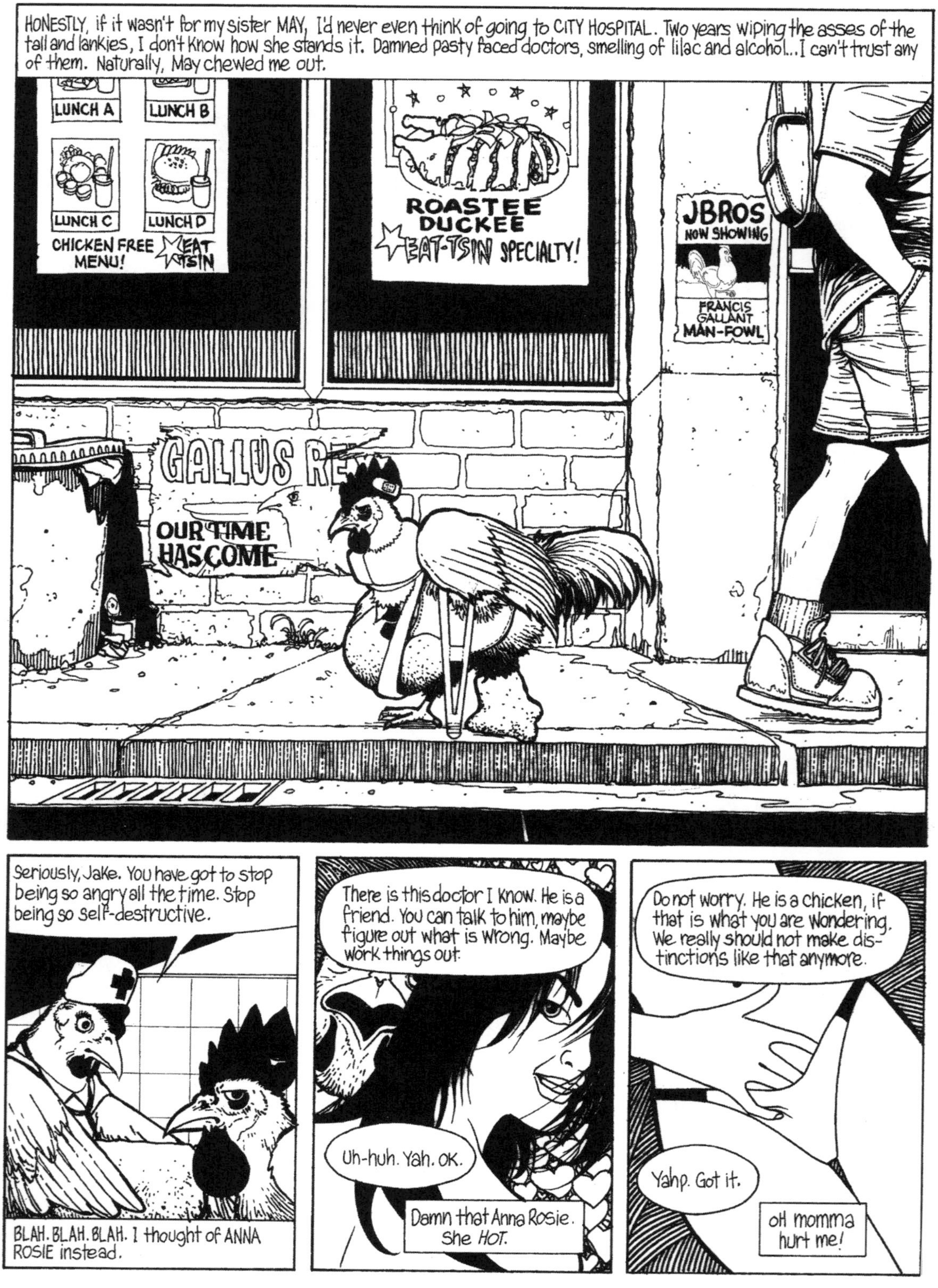
HONESTLY, if it wasn't for my sister MAY, I'd never even think of going to CITY HOSPITAL. Two years wiping the asses of the tall and lankies, I don't know how she stands it. Damned pasty faced doctors, smelling of lilac and alcohol... I can't trust any of them. Naturally, May chewed me out.
LUNCH A
LUNCH B
LUNCH C
LUNCH D
CHICKEN FREE MENU!
EAT TSIN
ROASTEE DUCKEE
EAT-TSIN SPECIALTY!
JBROS
NOW SHOWING
FRANCIS GALLANT
MAN-FOWL
GALLUS RE
OUR TIME HAS COME
Seriously, Jake. You have got to stop being so angry all the time. Stop being so self-destructive.
BLAH. BLAH. BLAH. I thought of ANNA ROSIE instead.
There is this doctor I know. He is a friend. You can talk to him, maybe figure out what is wrong. Maybe work things out.
Uh-huh. Yah. OK.
Damn that Anna Rosie. She *HOT*.
Do not worry. He is a chicken, if that is what you are wondering. We really should not make distinctions like that anymore.
Yahp. Got it.
OH momma hurt me!

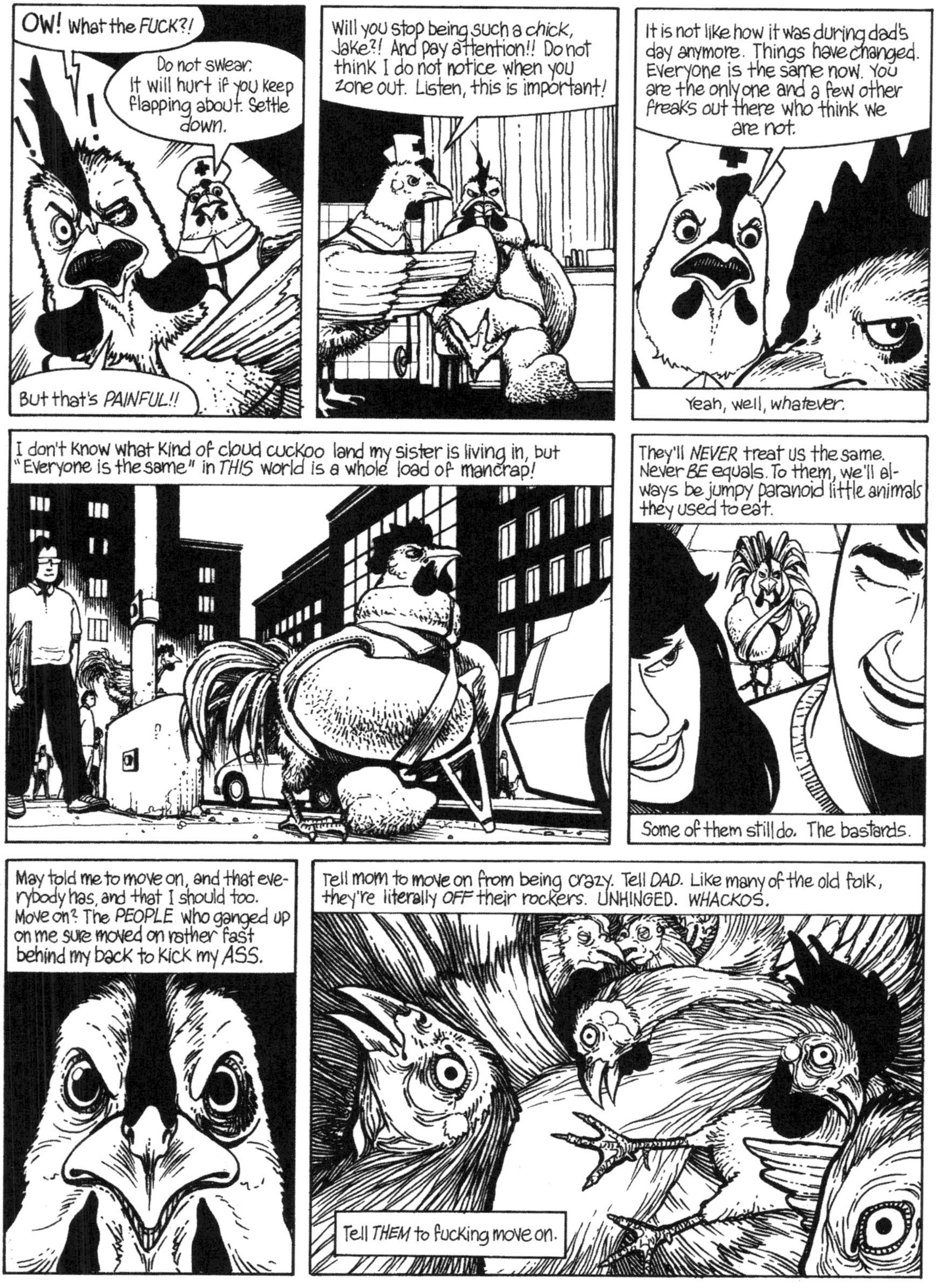
OW! What the FUCK?!
Do not swear. It will hurt if you keep flapping about. Settle down.
But that's PAINFUL!!
Will you stop being such a chick, Jake?! And pay attention!! Do not think I do not notice when you zone out. Listen, this is important!
It is not like how it was during dad's day anymore. Things have changed. Everyone is the same now. You are the only one and a few other freaks out there who think we are not.
Yeah, well, whatever.
I don't know what kind of cloud cuckoo land my sister is living in, but "Everyone is the same" in THIS world is a whole load of mancrap!
They'll NEVER treat us the same. Never BE equals. To them, we'll always be jumpy paranoid little animals they used to eat.
Some of them still do. The bastards.
May told me to move on, and that everybody has, and that I should too. Move on? The PEOPLE who ganged up on me sure moved on rather fast behind my back to kick my ASS.
Tell mom to move on from being crazy. Tell DAD. Like many of the old folk, they're literally OFF their rockers. UNHINGED. WHACKOS.
Tell THEM to fucking move on.

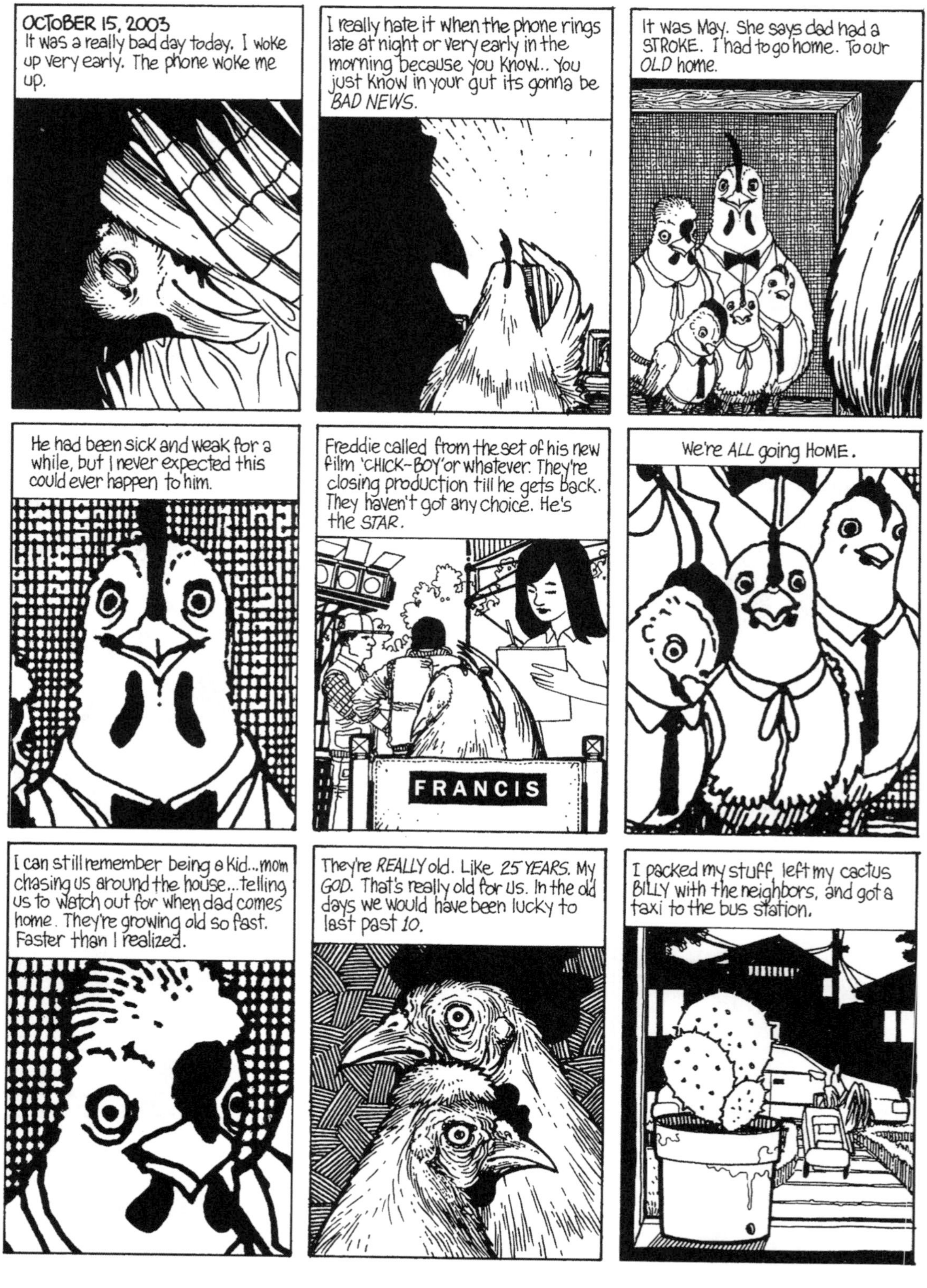
OCTOBER 15, 2003
It was a really bad day today. I woke up very early. The phone woke me up.
I really hate it when the phone rings late at night or very early in the morning because you know... You just know in your gut its gonna be BAD NEWS.
It was May. She says dad had a STROKE. I had to go home. To our OLD home.
He had been sick and weak for a while, but I never expected this could ever happen to him.
Freddie called from the set of his new film 'CHICK-BOY' or whatever. They're closing production till he gets back. They haven't got any choice. He's the STAR.
FRANCIS
We're ALL going HOME.
I can still remember being a kid...mom chasing us around the house...telling us to watch out for when dad comes home. They're growing old so fast. Faster than I realized.
They're REALLY old. Like 25 YEARS. My GOD. That's really old for us. In the old days we would have been lucky to last past 10.
I packed my stuff, left my cactus BILLY with the neighbors, and got a taxi to the bus station.

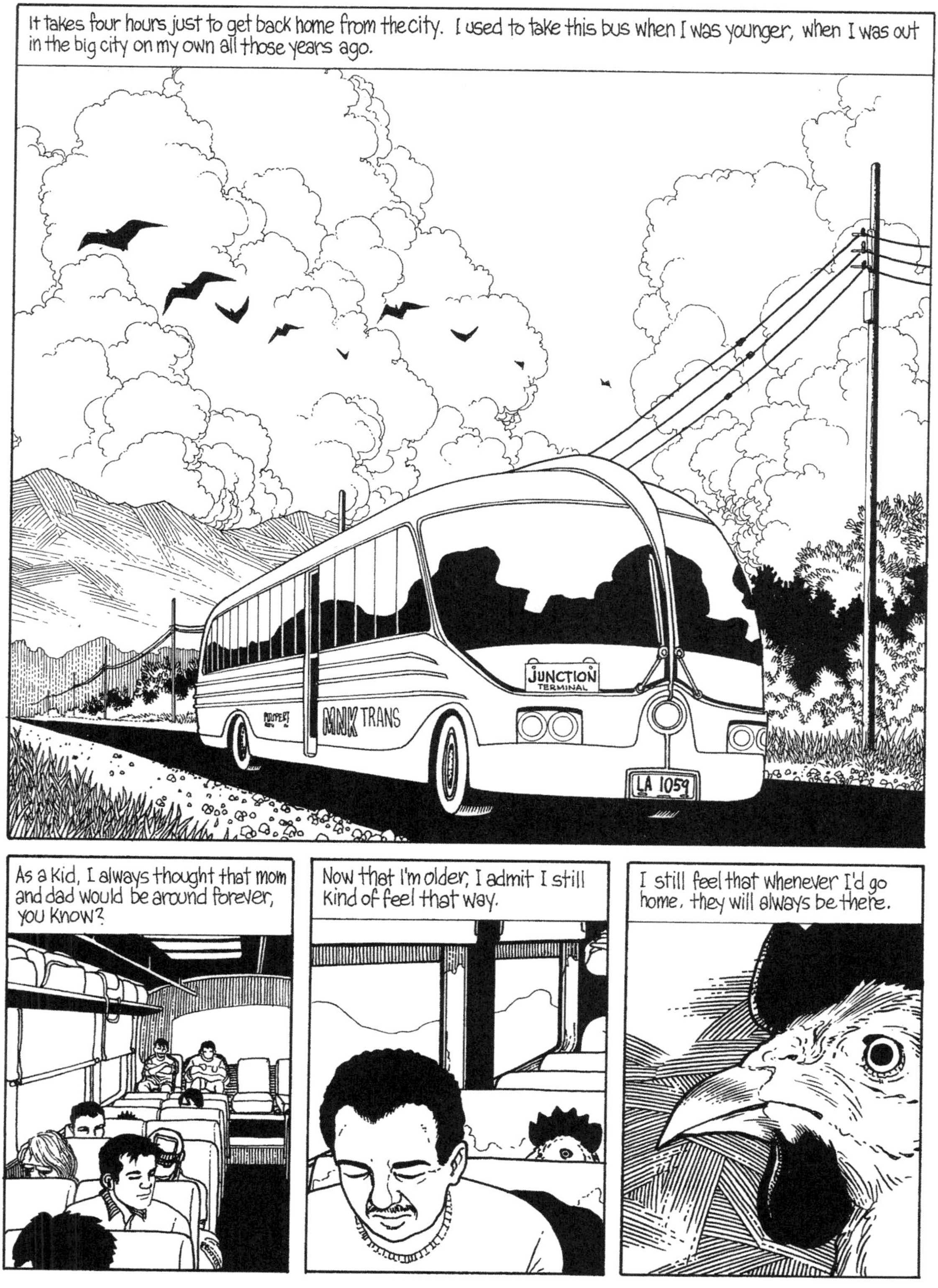

It takes four hours just to get back home from the city. I used to take this bus when I was younger, when I was out in the big city on my own all those years ago.
JUNCTION TERMINAL
MNK TRANS
LA 1059
As a kid, I always thought that mom and dad would be around forever, you know?
Now that I'm older, I admit I still kind of feel that way.
I still feel that whenever I'd go home, they will always be there.

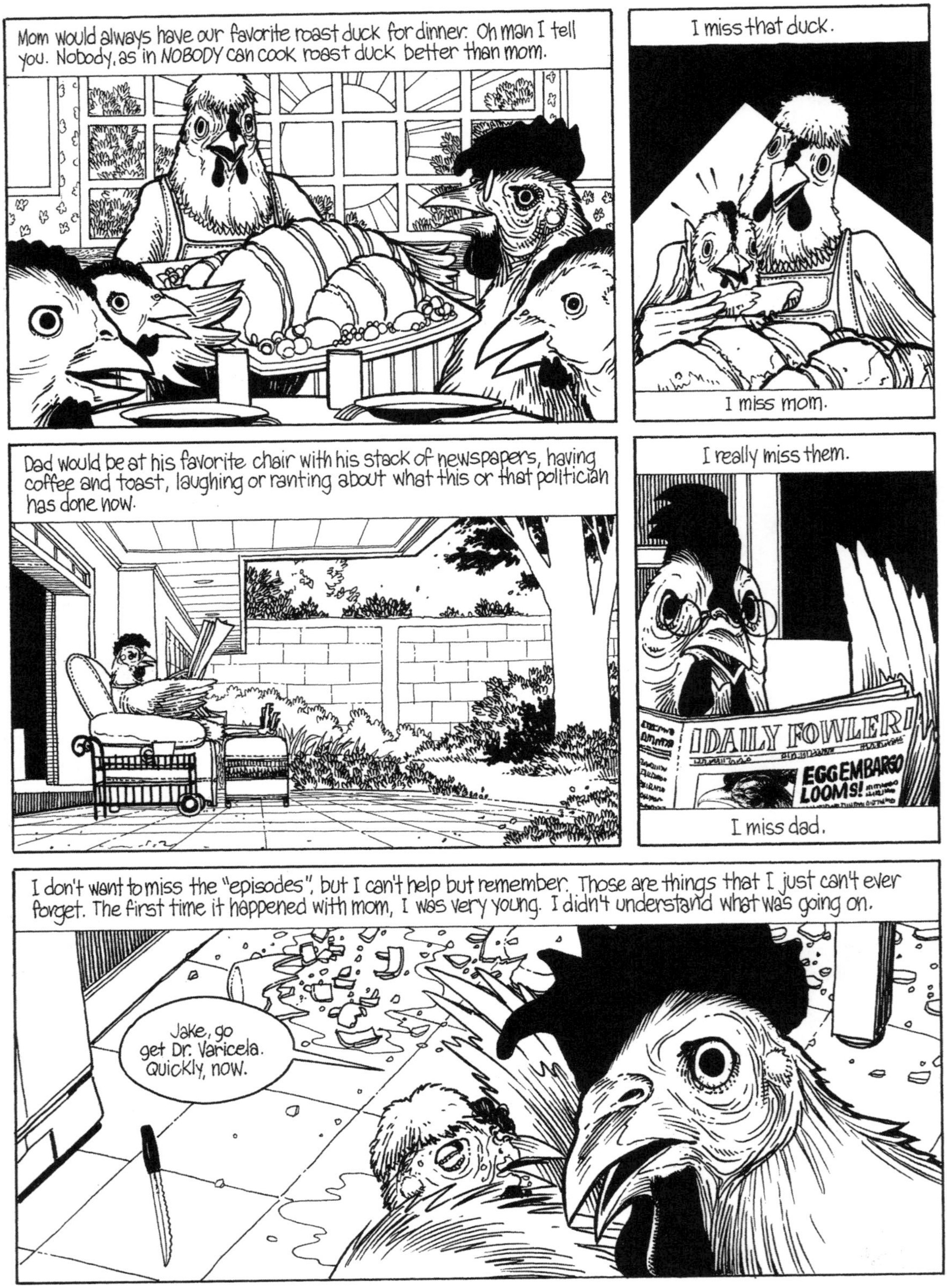
Mom would always have our favorite roast duck for dinner. Oh man I tell you. Nobody, as in NOBODY can cook roast duck better than mom.
I miss that duck.
I miss mom.
Dad would be at his favorite chair with his stack of newspapers, having coffee and toast, laughing or ranting about what this or that politician has done now.
I really miss them.
DAILY FOWLER
EGG EMBARGO LOOMS!
I miss dad.
I don't want to miss the "episodes", but I can't help but remember. Those are things that I just can't ever forget. The first time it happened with mom, I was very young. I didn't understand what was going on.
Jake, go get Dr. Varicela. Quickly, now.

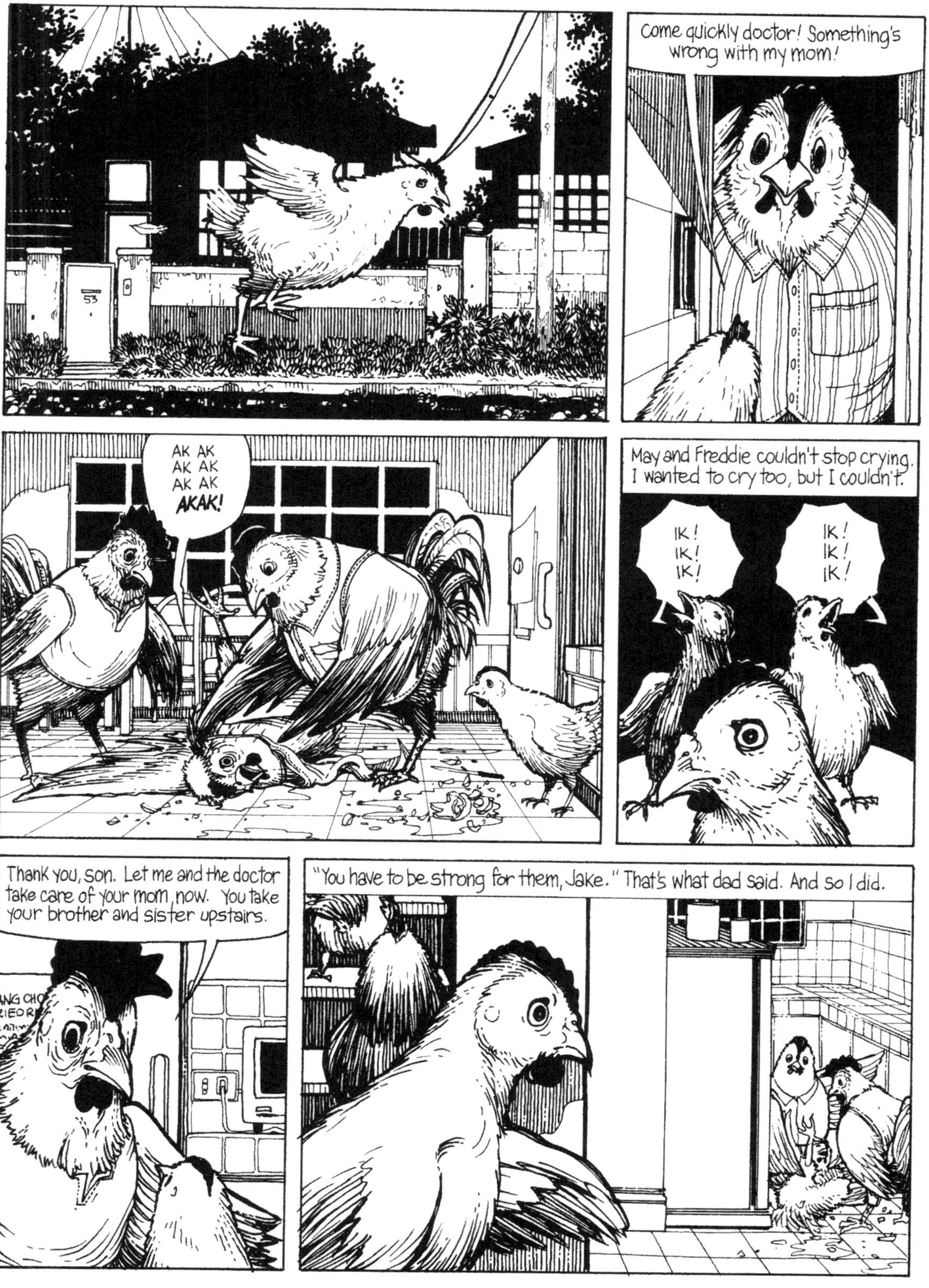
53
Come quickly doctor! Something's wrong with my mom!
AK AK
AK AK
AK AK
AKAK!
May and Freddie couldn't stop crying. I wanted to cry too, but I couldn't.
IK! IK! IK!
IK! IK! IK!
Thank you, son. Let me and the doctor take care of your mom, now. You take your brother and sister upstairs.
"You have to be strong for them, Jake." That's what dad said. And so I did.

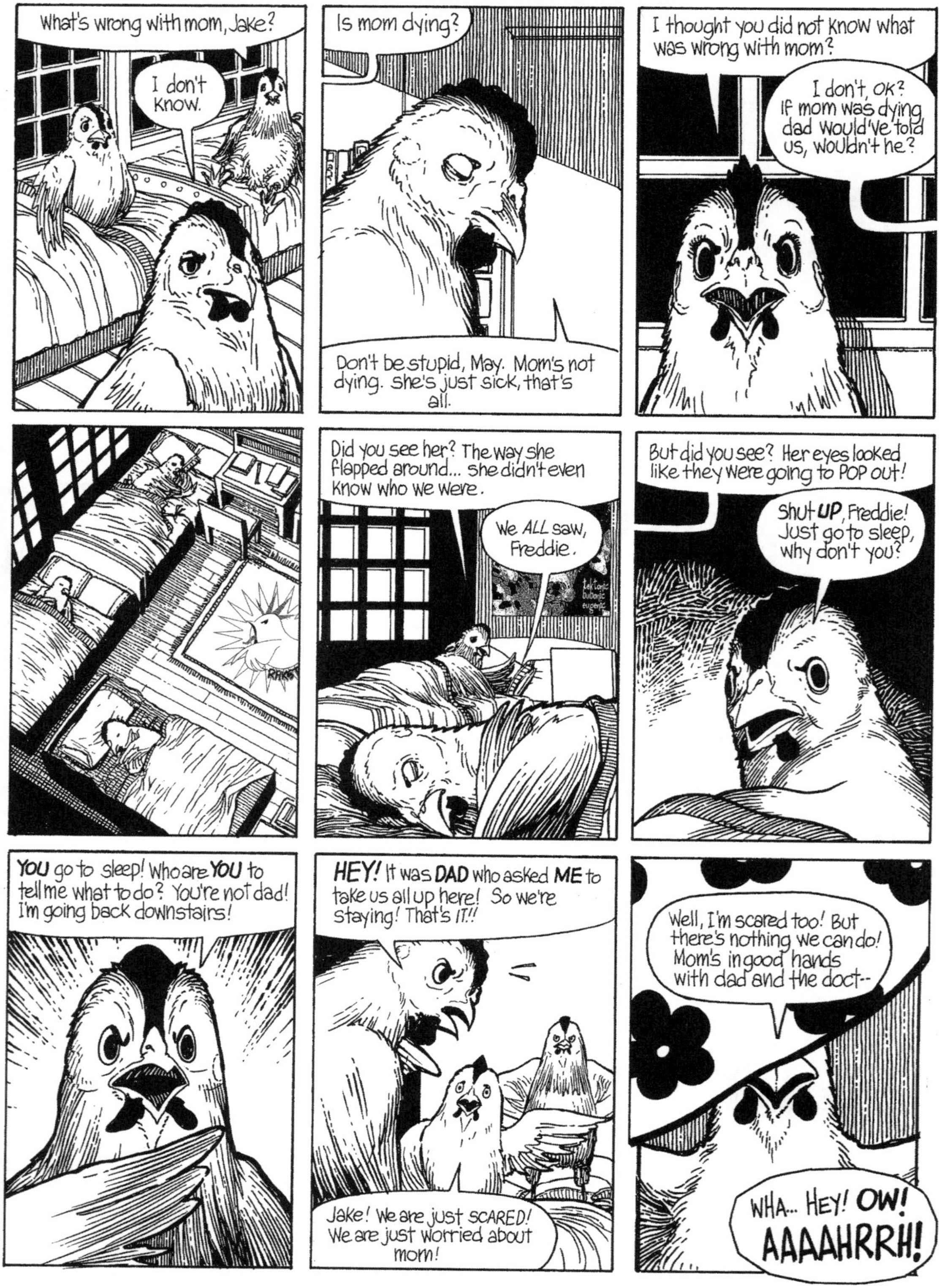

What's wrong with mom, Jake?
I don't know.
Is mom dying?
Don't be stupid, May. Mom's not dying. she's just sick, that's all.
I thought you did not know what was wrong with mom?
I don't, OK? If mom was dying dad would've told us, wouldn't he?
Did you see her? The way she flapped around... she didn't even know who we were.
We ALL saw, Freddie.
But did you see? Her eyes looked like they were going to POP out!
Shut UP, Freddie! Just go to sleep, why don't you?
YOU go to sleep! Who are YOU to tell me what to do? You're not dad! I'm going back downstairs!
HEY! It was DAD who asked ME to take us all up here! So we're staying! That's IT!!
Jake! We are just SCARED! We are just worried about mom!
Well, I'm scared too! But there's nothing we can do! Mom's in good hands with dad and the doct--
WHA... HEY! OW! AAAAHRRH!

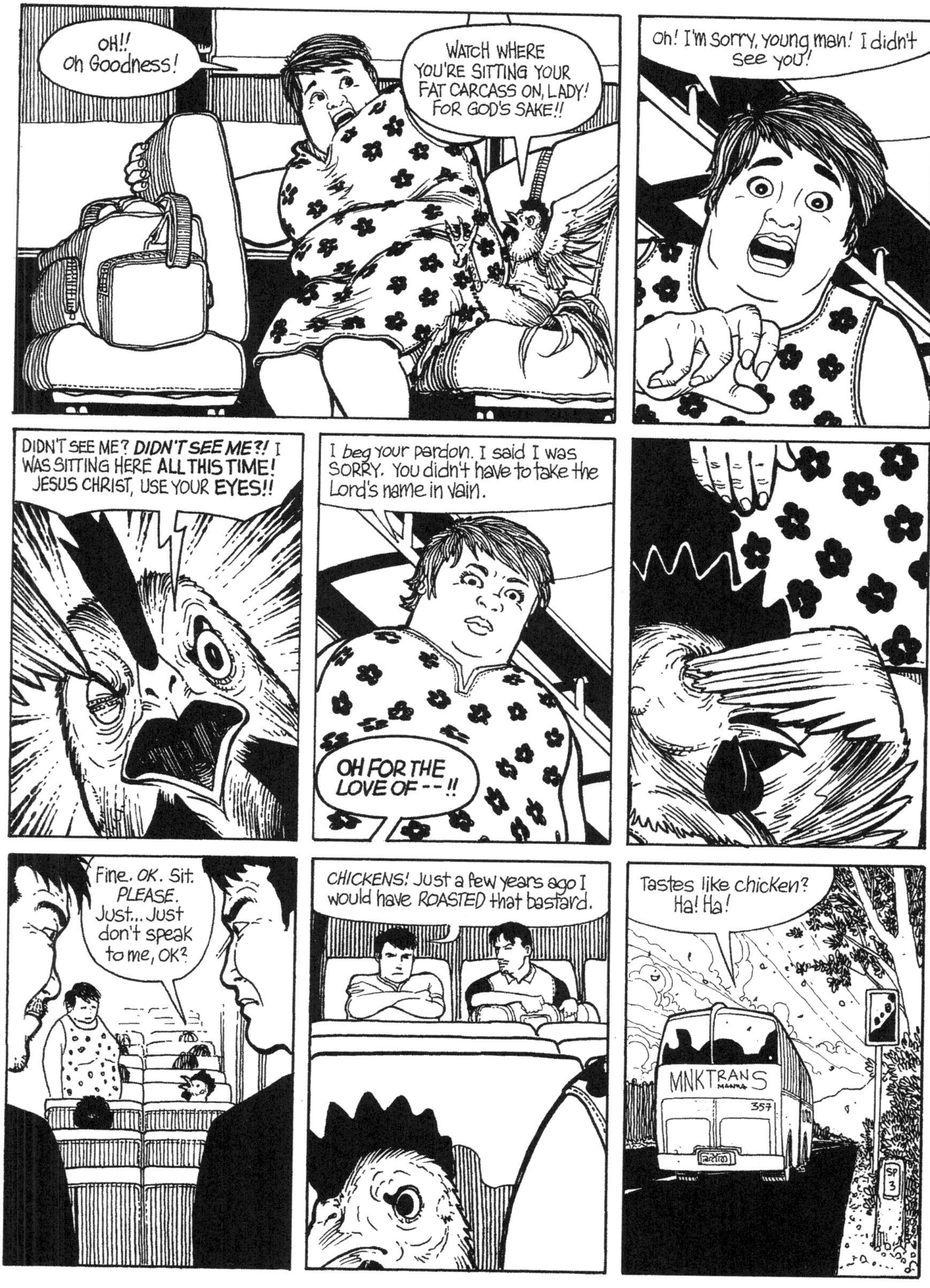
OH!! Oh Goodness!
WATCH WHERE YOU'RE SITTING YOUR FAT CARCASS ON, LADY! FOR GOD'S SAKE!!
Oh! I'm sorry, young man! I didn't see you!
DIDN'T SEE ME? DIDN'T SEE ME?! I WAS SITTING HERE ALL THIS TIME! JESUS CHRIST, USE YOUR EYES!!
I beg your pardon. I said I was SORRY. You didn't have to take the Lord's name in vain.
OH FOR THE LOVE OF --!!
Fine. OK. Sit. PLEASE. Just... Just don't speak to me, OK?
CHICKENS! Just a few years ago I would have ROASTED that bastard.
Tastes like chicken? Ha! Ha!
MNKTRANS
357
SP 3

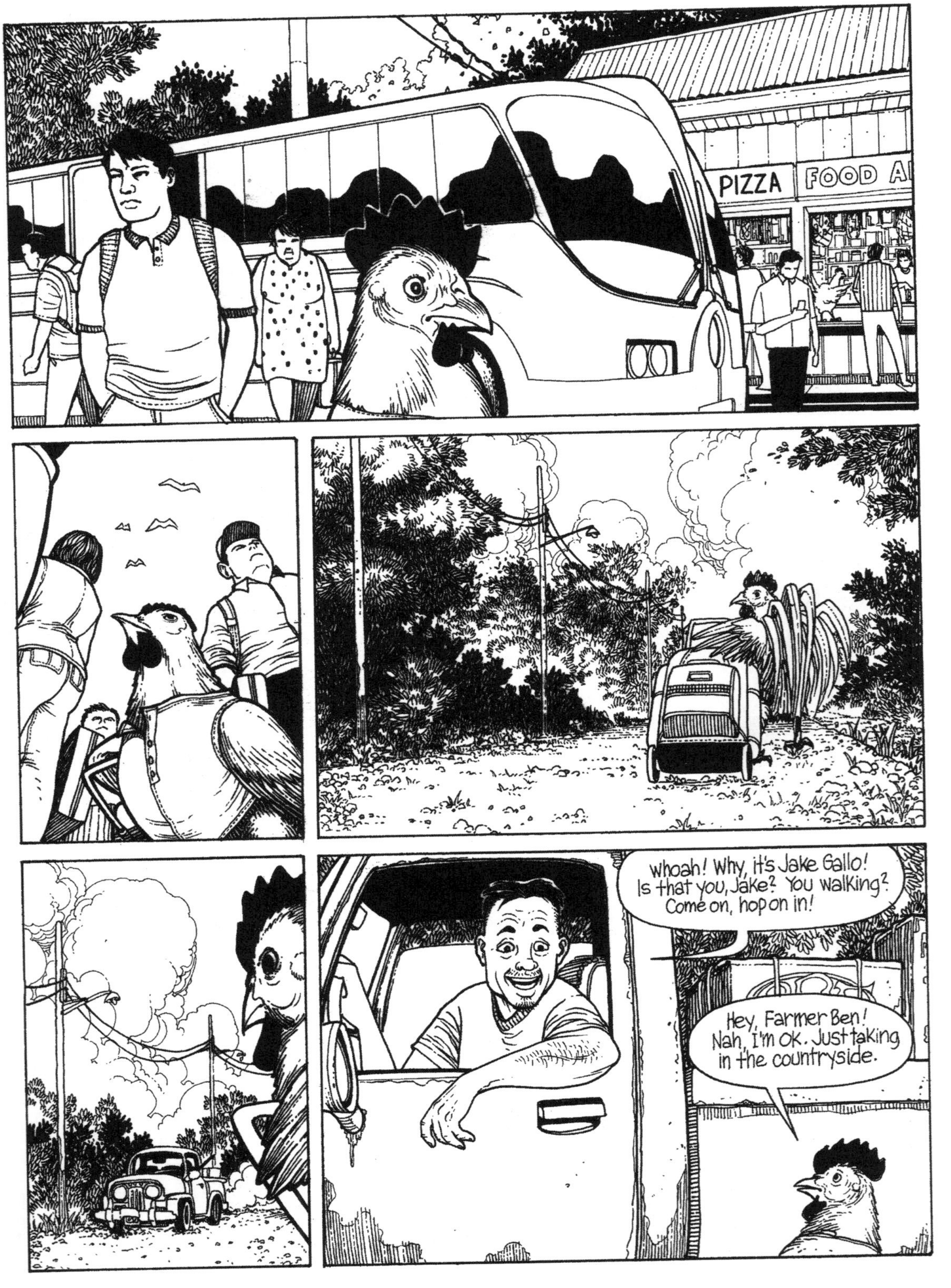
PIZZA
FOOD A
Whoah! Why, it's Jake Gallo! Is that you, Jake? You walking? Come on, hop on in!
Hey, Farmer Ben! Nah, I'm OK. Just taking in the countryside.

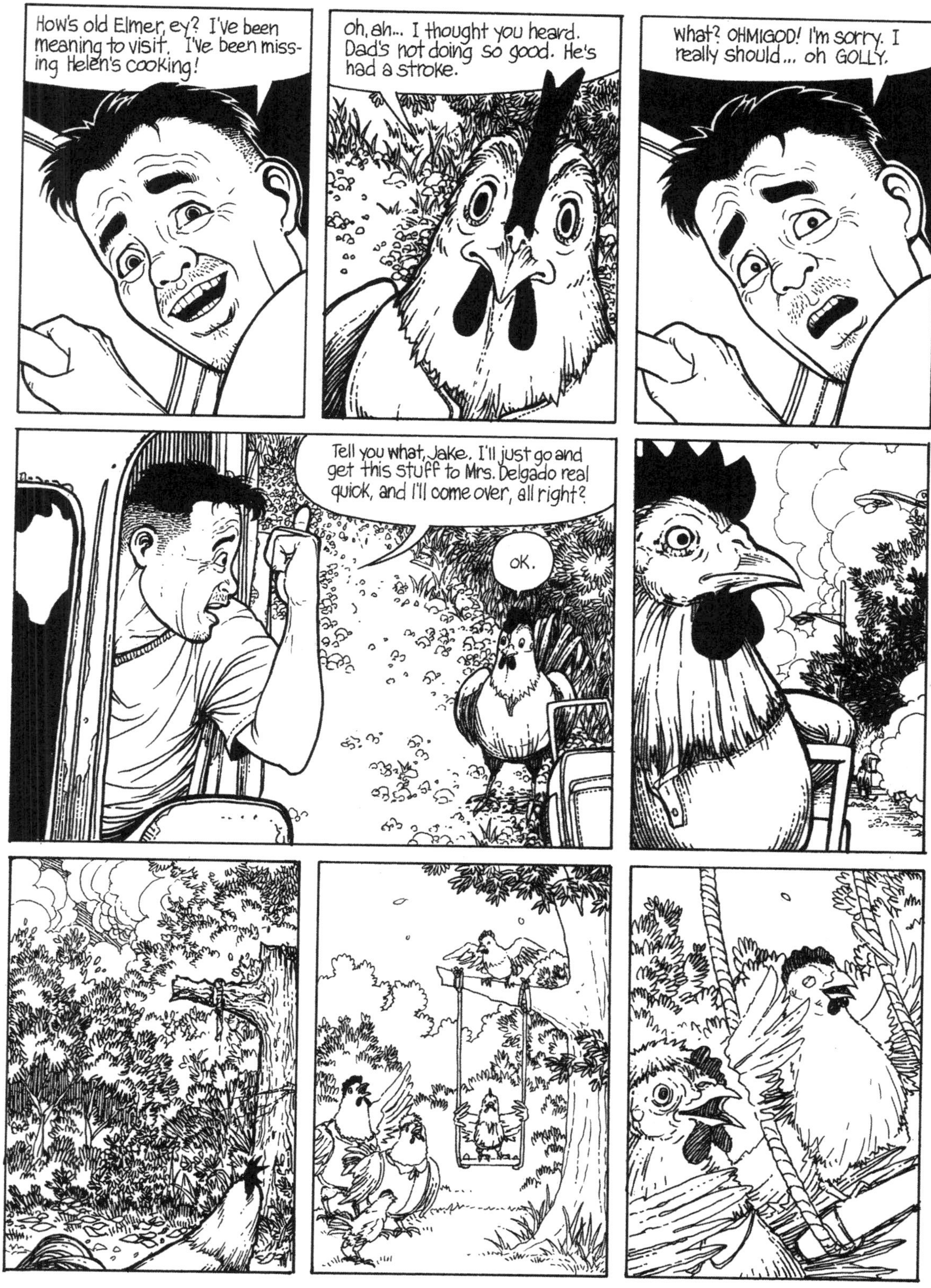
How's old Elmer, ey? I've been meaning to visit. I've been missing Helen's cooking!
Oh, ah... I thought you heard. Dad's not doing so good. He's had a stroke.
What? OHMIGOD! I'm sorry. I really should... oh GOLLY.
Tell you what, Jake. I'll just go and get this stuff to Mrs. Delgado real quick, and I'll come over, all right?
OK.

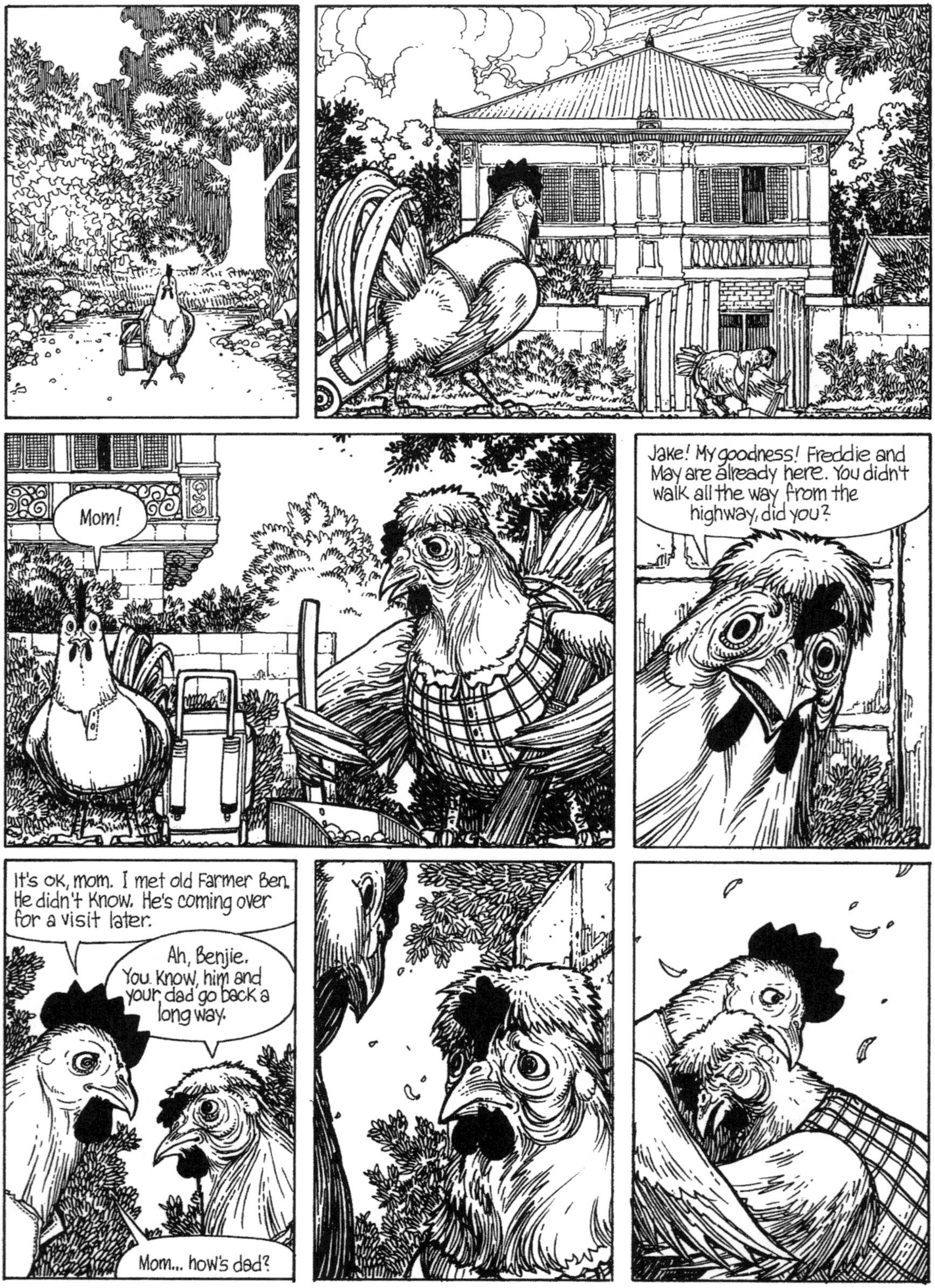
Mom!
Jake! My goodness! Freddie and May are already here. You didn't walk all the way from the highway, did you?
It's ok, mom. I met old Farmer Ben. He didn't know. He's coming over for a visit later.
Ah, Benjie. You know, him and your dad go back a long way.
Mom... how's dad?

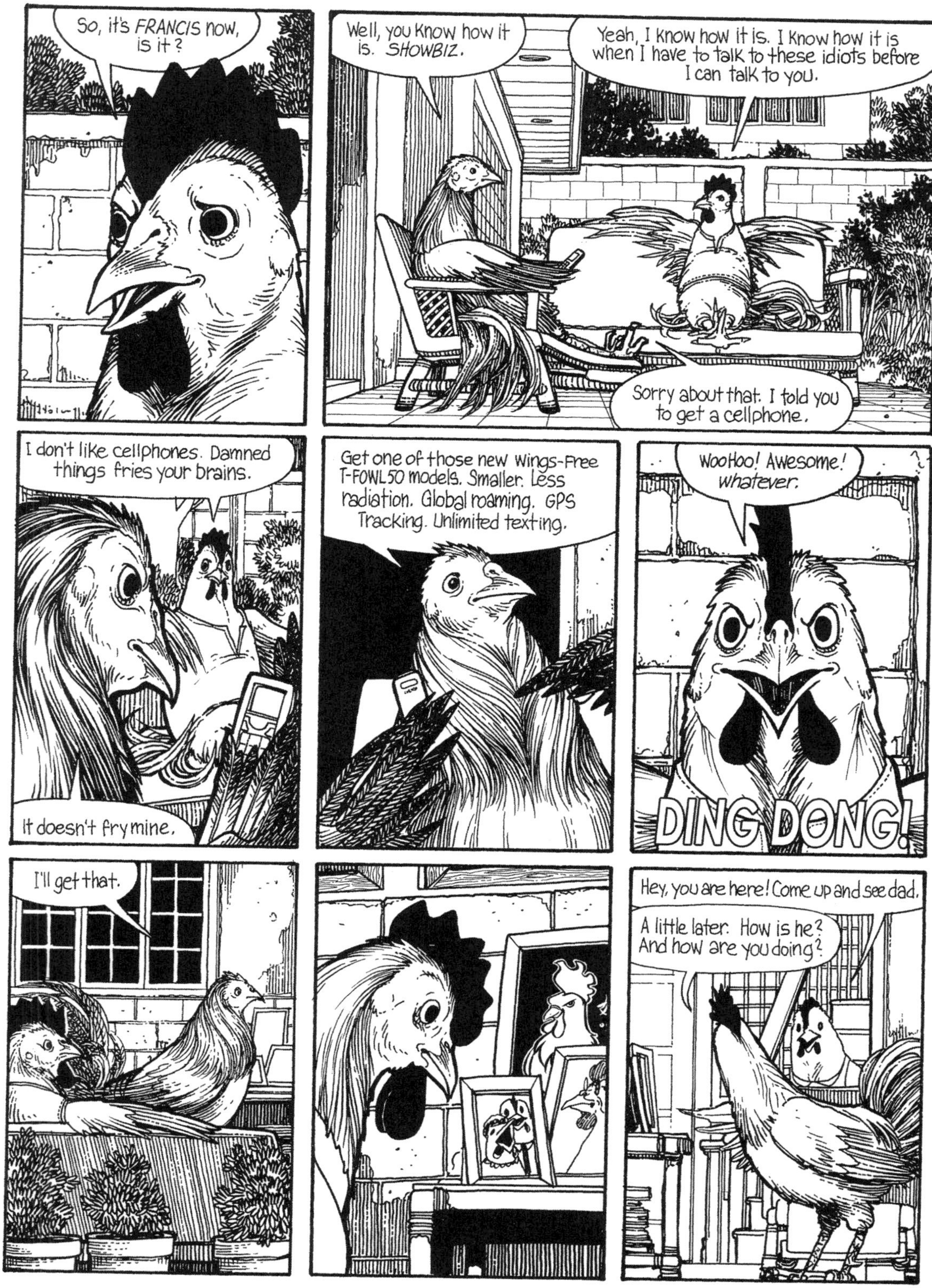
So, it's FRANCIS now, is it?
Well, you know how it is. SHOWBIZ.
Yeah, I know how it is. I know how it is when I have to talk to these idiots before I can talk to you.
Sorry about that. I told you to get a cellphone.
I don't like cellphones. Damned things fries your brains.
It doesn't fry mine.
Get one of those new Wings-Free T-FOWL50 models. Smaller. Less radiation. Global roaming. GPS Tracking. Unlimited texting.
WooHoo! Awesome! whatever.
DING DONG!
I'll get that.
Hey, you are here! Come up and see dad.
A little later. How is he? And how are you doing?

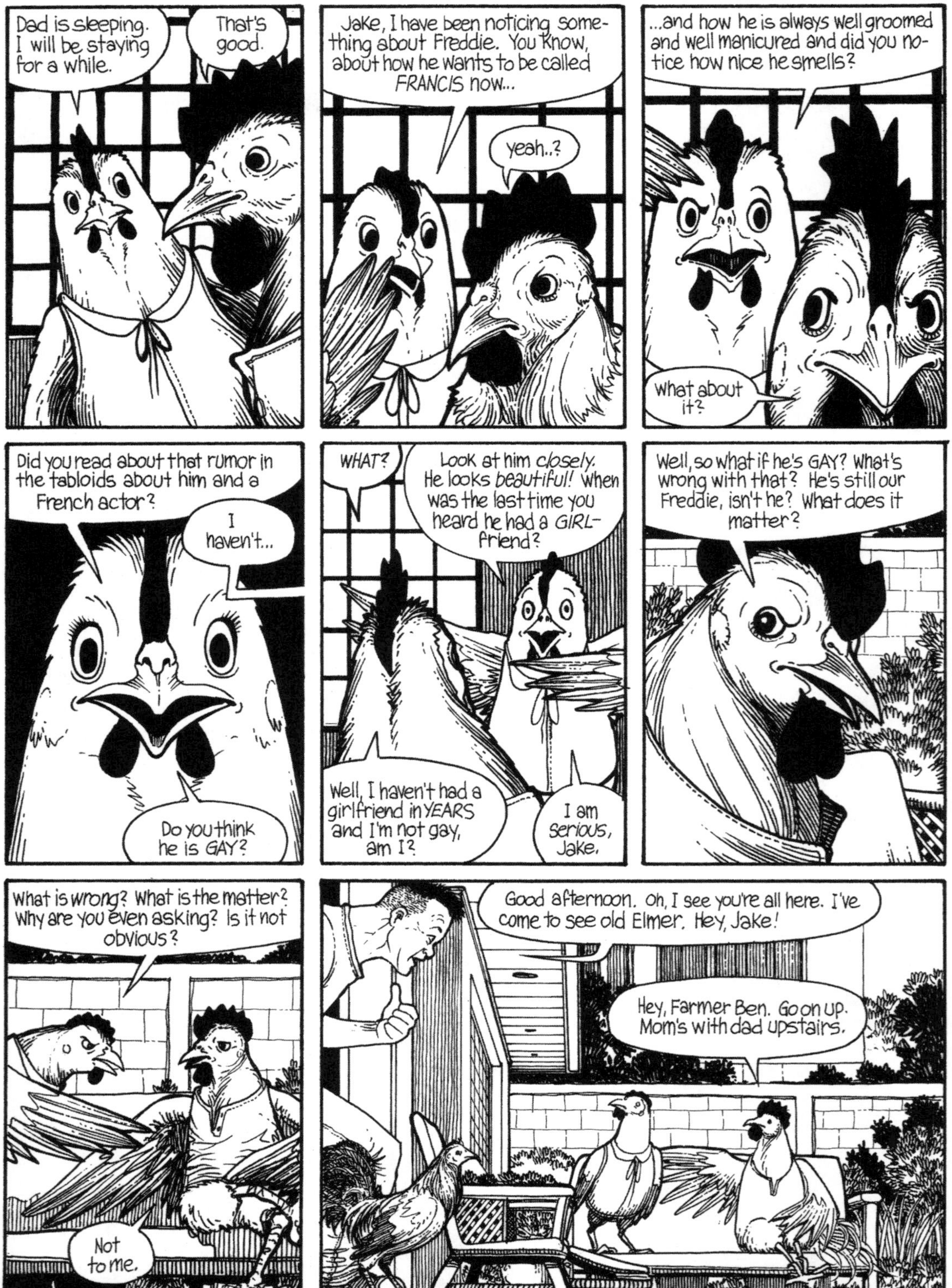
Dad is sleeping. I will be staying for a while.
That's good.
Jake, I have been noticing something about Freddie. You know, about how he wants to be called FRANCIS now...
yeah..?
...and how he is always well groomed and well manicured and did you notice how nice he smells?
What about it?
Did you read about that rumor in the tabloids about him and a French actor?
I haven't...
Do you think he is GAY?
WHAT?
Look at him closely. He looks beautiful! When was the last time you heard he had a GIRLfriend?
Well, I haven't had a girlfriend in YEARS and I'm not gay, am I?
I am serious, Jake.
Well, so what if he's GAY? What's wrong with that? He's still our Freddie, isn't he? What does it matter?
What is wrong? What is the matter? Why are you even asking? Is it not obvious?
Not to me.
Good afternoon. Oh, I see you're all here. I've come to see old Elmer. Hey, Jake!
Hey, Farmer Ben. Go on up. Mom's with dad upstairs.

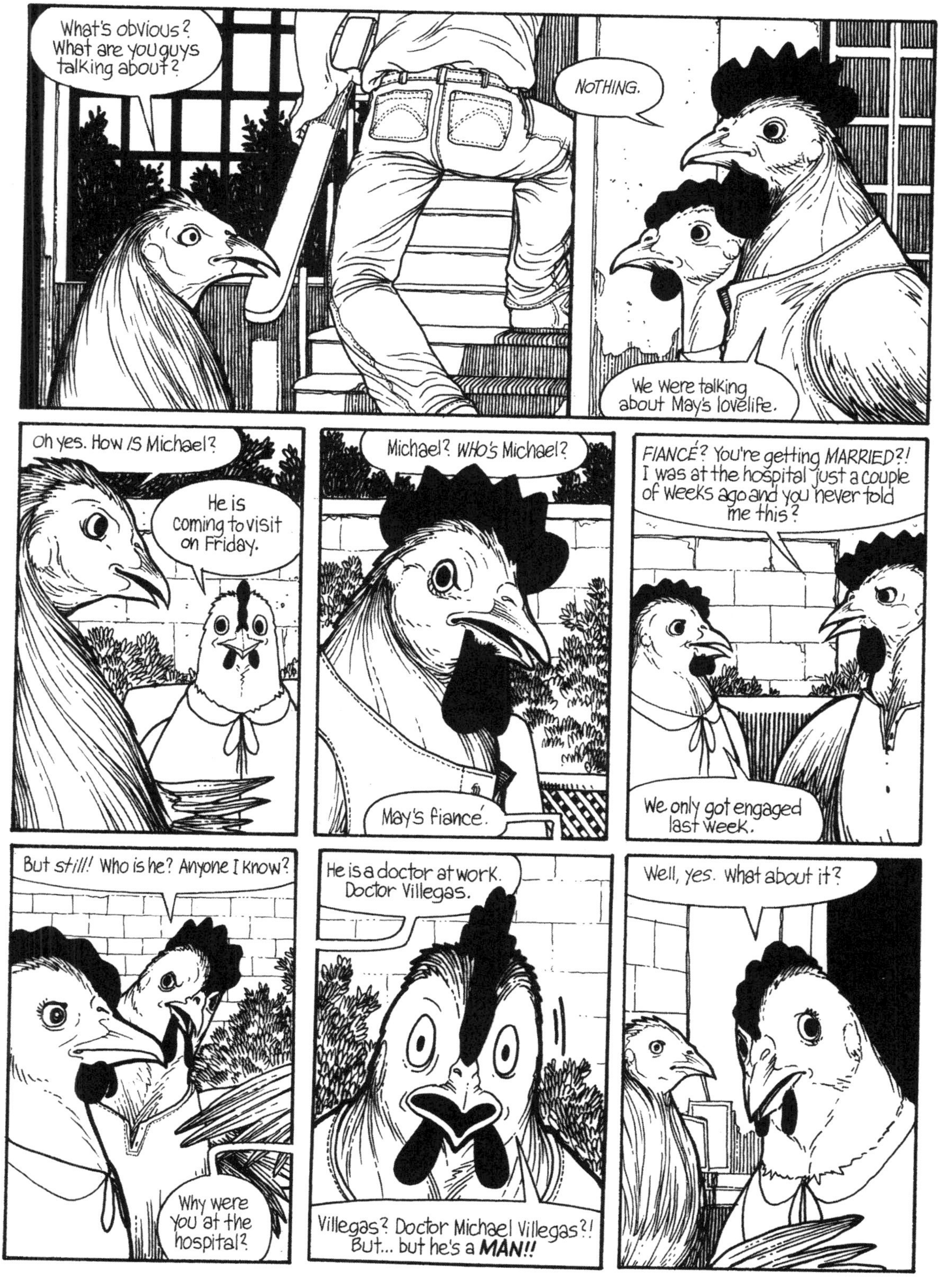
What's obvious? What are you guys talking about?
NOTHING.
We were talking about May's lovelife.
Oh yes. How IS Michael?
He is coming to visit on Friday.
Michael? WHO's Michael?
May's fiancé.
FIANCÉ? You're getting MARRIED?! I was at the hospital just a couple of weeks ago and you never told me this?
We only got engaged last week.
But still! Who is he? Anyone I know?
Why were you at the hospital?
He is a doctor at work. Doctor Villegas.
Villegas? Doctor Michael Villegas?! But... but he's a MAN!!
Well, yes. What about it?

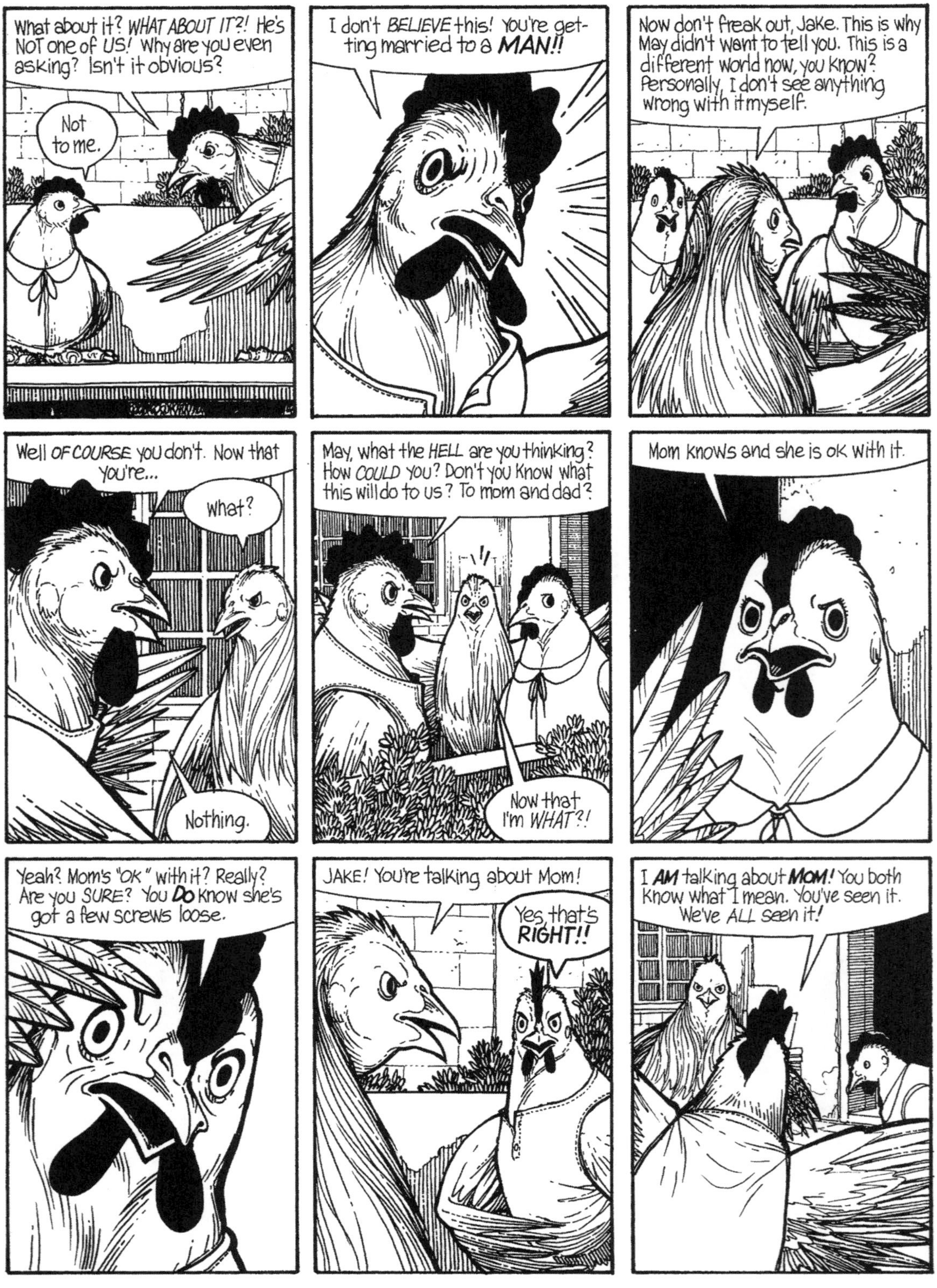
What about it? WHAT ABOUT IT?! He's NOT one of US! Why are you even asking? Isn't it obvious?
Not to me.
I don't BELIEVE this! You're getting married to a MAN!!
Now don't freak out, Jake. This is why May didn't want to tell you. This is a different world now, you know? Personally, I don't see anything wrong with it myself.
Well OF COURSE you don't. Now that you're...
What?
Nothing.
May, what the HELL are you thinking? How COULD YOU? Don't you know what this will do to us? To mom and dad?
Now that I'm WHAT?!
Mom knows and she is OK with it.
Yeah? Mom's "OK" with it? Really? Are you SURE? You DO know she's got a few screws loose.
JAKE! You're talking about Mom!
Yes, that's RIGHT!!
I AM talking about MOM! You both know what I mean. You've seen it. We've ALL seen it!

You're all forgetting what happened to mom and dad... to ALL of us! They herded our parents like cattle into DEATH CAMPS!

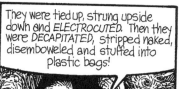

They were tied up, strung upside down and ELECTROCUTED. Then they were DECAPITATED, stripped naked, disemboweled and stuffed into plastic bags!

JAKE!

And did you know what happened NEXT? They were EATEN.

Yes, EATEN!

CRISPY FRIED, STEAMED, BARBECUED, ROASTED, and BAKED! You name it! With ketchup! Don't forget the fucking banana ketchup!

Your precious Doctor Villegas is a LIAR if he says he hasn't eaten us as well!!

STOP IT, JAKE! STOP IT!!

What the hell's the matter with you, Jake?! The past is OVER. Get over it!

Yeah. Get over it. It's so fucking easy to say.

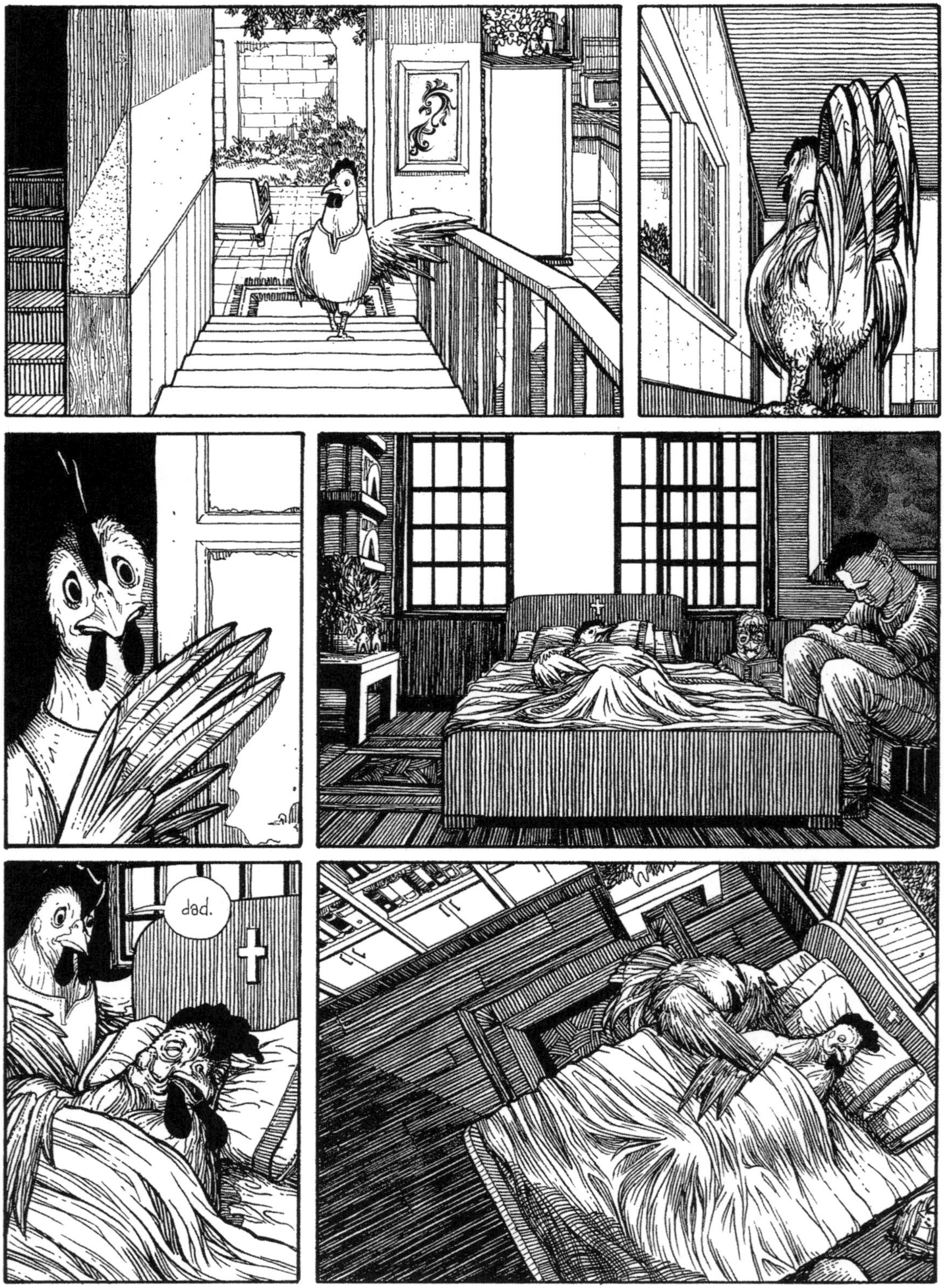
dad.

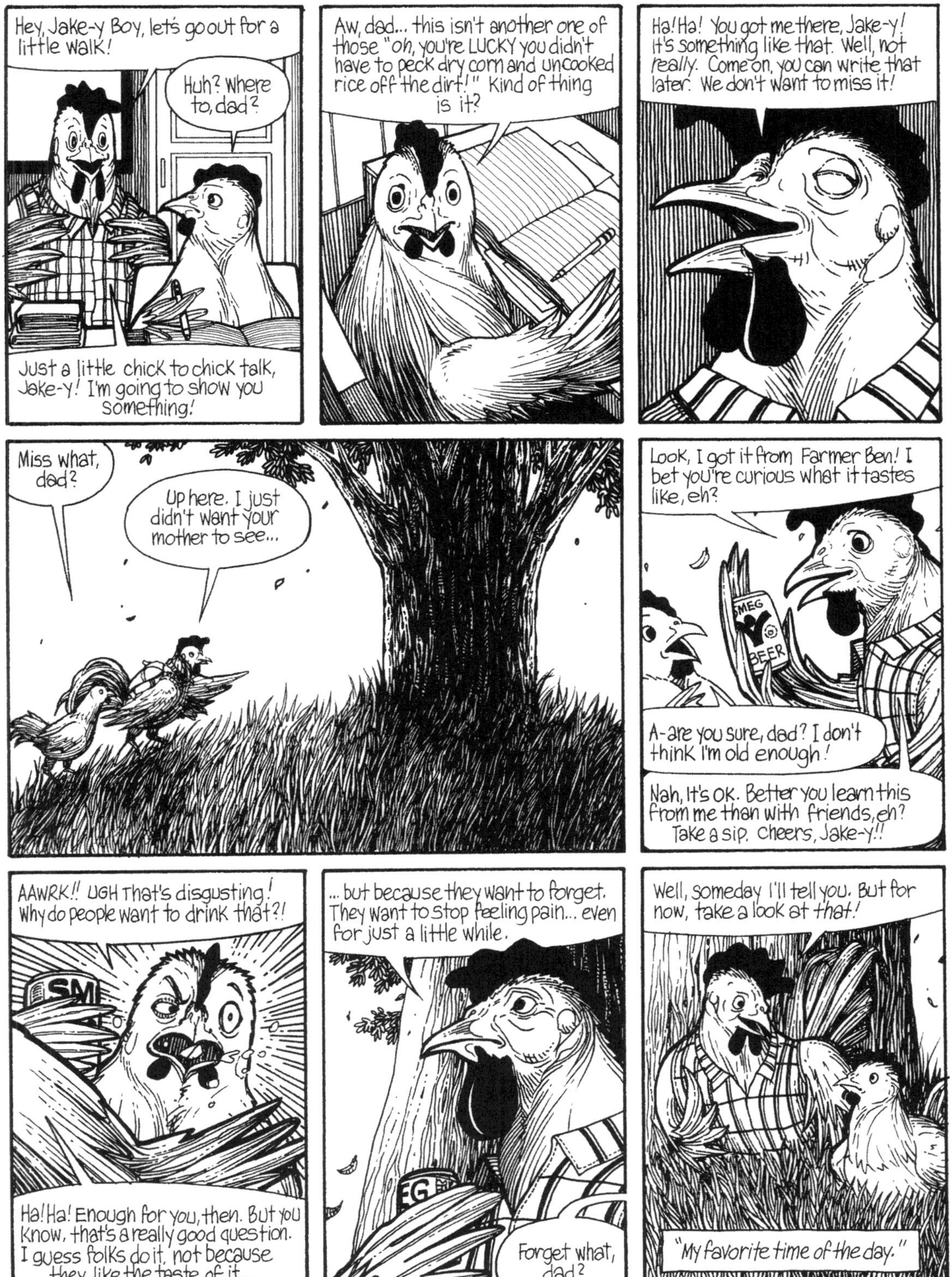

Hey, Jake-y Boy, let's go out for a little walk!
Huh? Where to, dad?
Just a little chick to chick talk, Jake-y! I'm going to show you something!
Aw, dad... this isn't another one of those "oh, you're LUCKY you didn't have to peck dry corn and uncooked rice off the dirt!" kind of thing is it?
Ha! Ha! You got me there, Jake-y! It's something like that. Well, not really. Come on, you can write that later. We don't want to miss it!
Miss what, dad?
Up here. I just didn't want your mother to see...
Look, I got it from Farmer Ben! I bet you're curious what it tastes like, eh?
SMEG
BEER
A-are you sure, dad? I don't think I'm old enough!
Nah, It's OK. Better you learn this from me than with friends, eh? Take a sip. Cheers, Jake-y!!
AAWRK!! UGH That's disgusting! Why do people want to drink that?!
Ha! Ha! Enough for you, then. But you know, that's a really good question. I guess folks do it, not because they like the taste of it...
... but because they want to forget. They want to stop feeling pain... even for just a little while.
Forget what, dad?
Well, someday I'll tell you. But for now, take a look at that!
"My favorite time of the day."

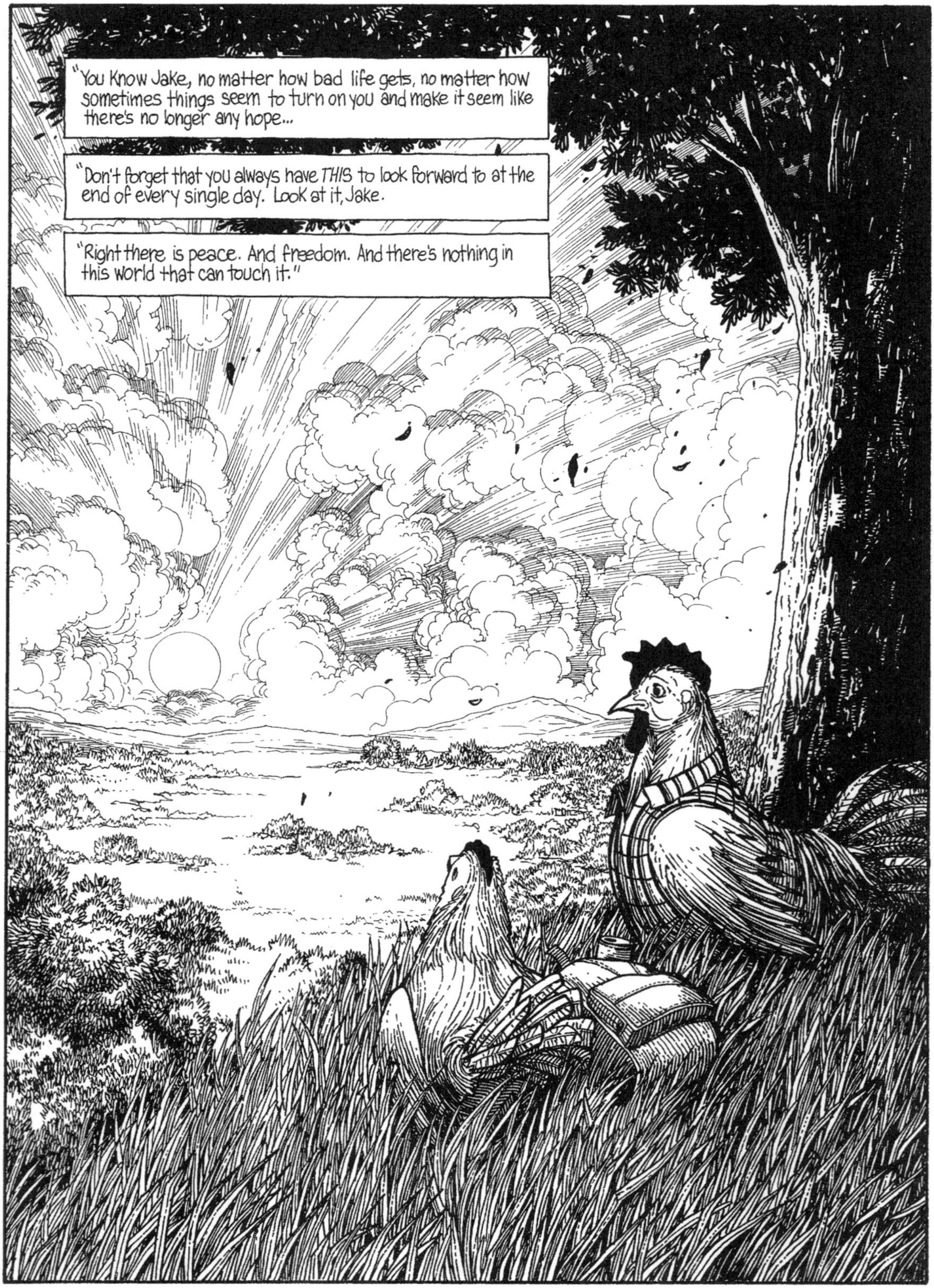
"You Know Jake, no matter how bad life gets, no matter how sometimes things seem to turn on you and make it seem like there's no longer any hope...
"Don't forget that you always have THIS to look forward to at the end of every single day. Look at it, Jake.
"Right there is peace. And freedom. And there's nothing in this world that can touch it."

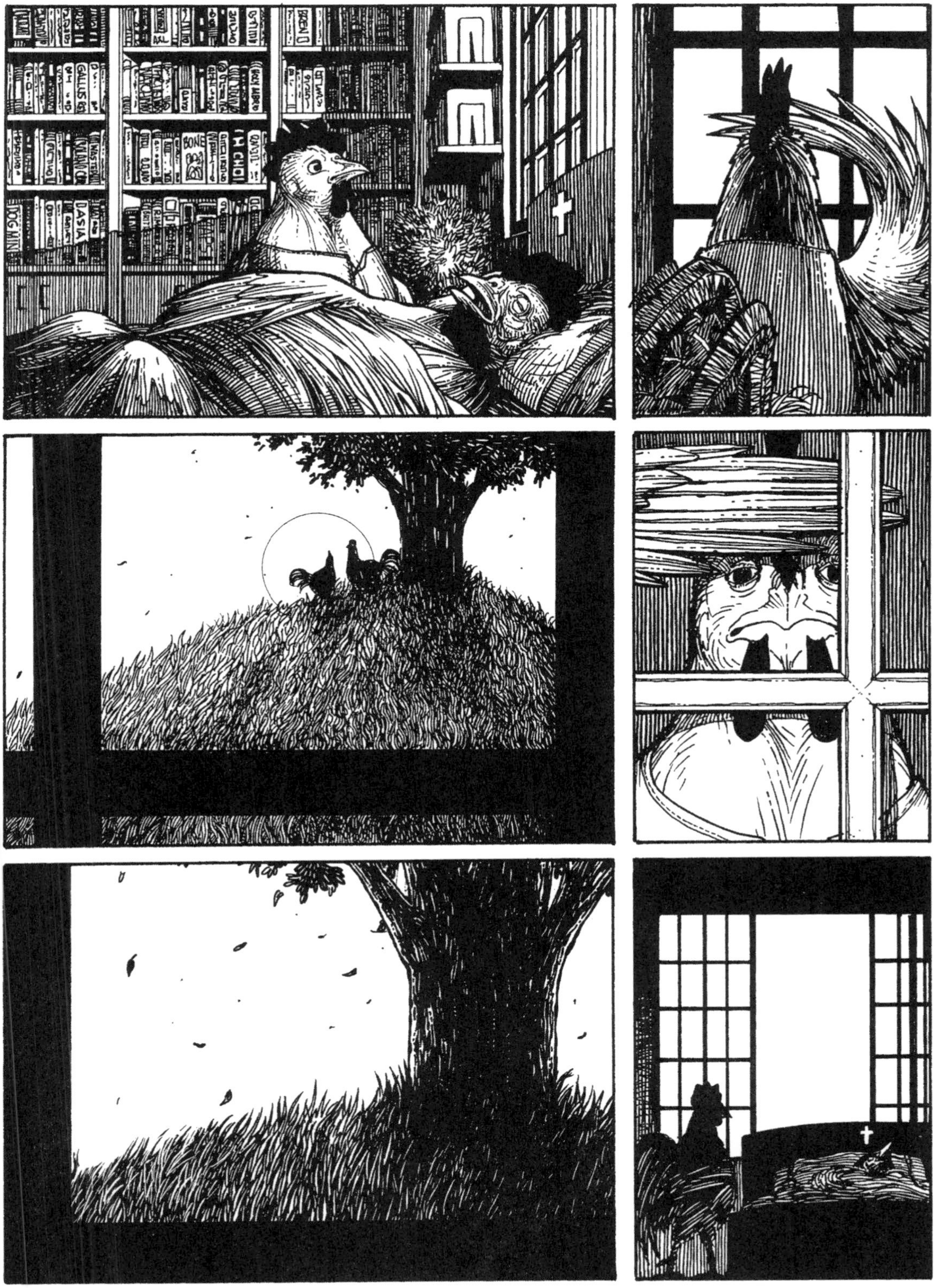

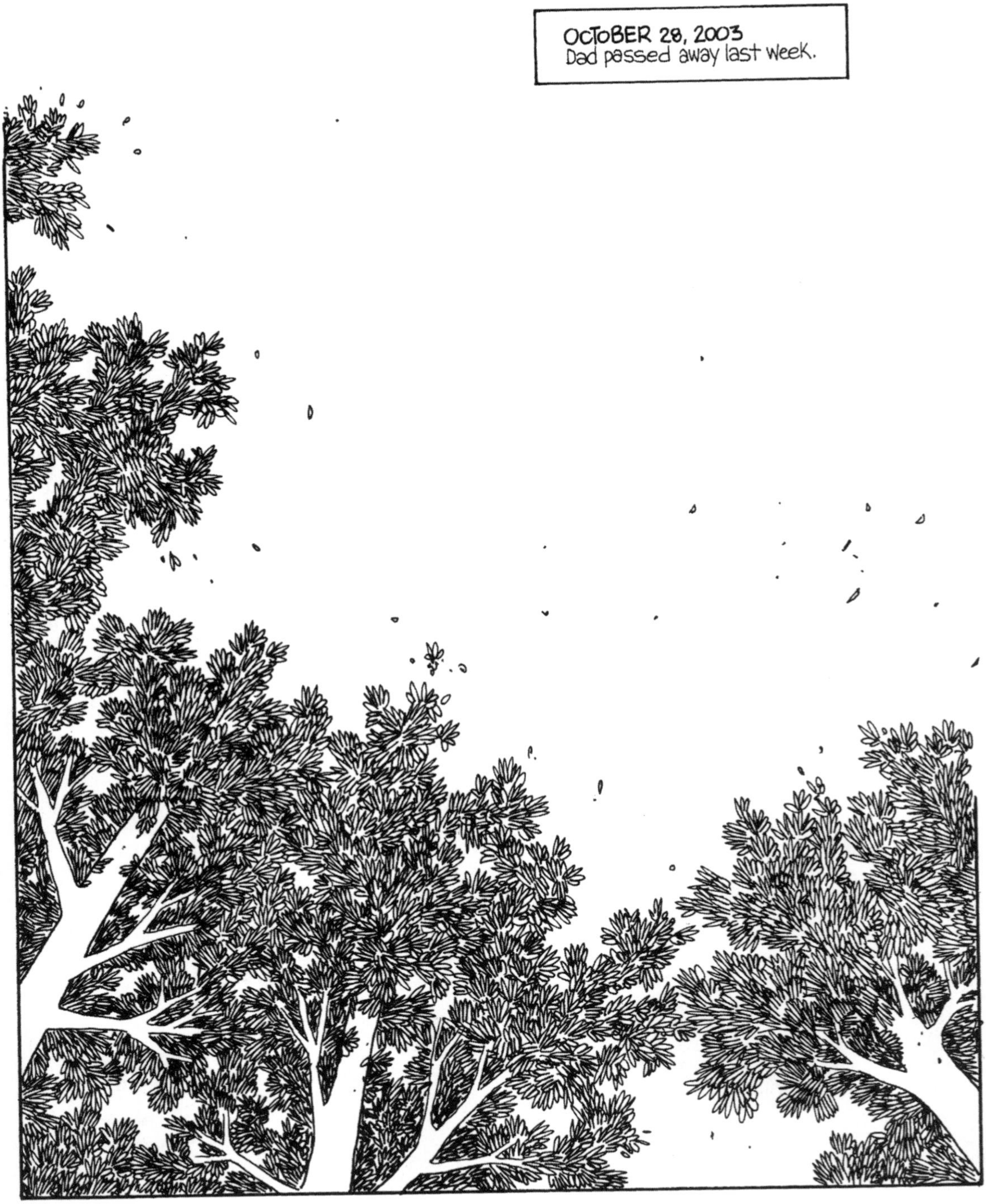
OCTOBER 28, 2003
Dad passed away last week.

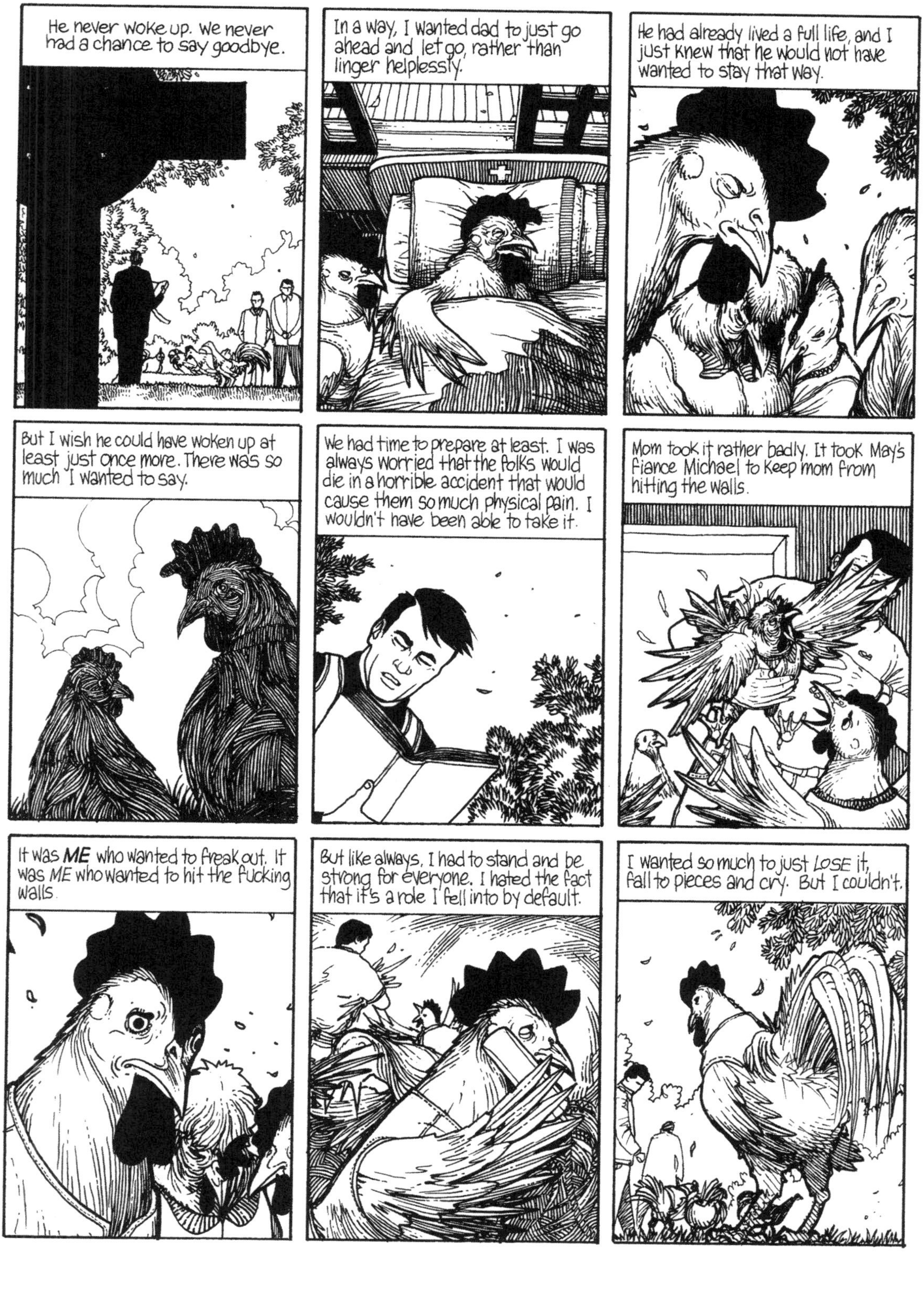
He never woke up. We never had a chance to say goodbye.
In a way, I wanted dad to just go ahead and let go, rather than linger helplessly.
He had already lived a full life, and I just knew that he would not have wanted to stay that way.
But I wish he could have woken up at least just once more. There was so much I wanted to say.
We had time to prepare at least. I was always worried that the folks would die in a horrible accident that would cause them so much physical pain. I wouldn't have been able to take it.
Mom took it rather badly. It took May's fiance Michael to keep mom from hitting the walls.
It was ME who wanted to freak out. It was ME who wanted to hit the fucking walls.
But like always, I had to stand and be strong for everyone. I hated the fact that it's a role I fell into by default.
I wanted so much to just LOSE it, fall to pieces and cry. But I couldn't.

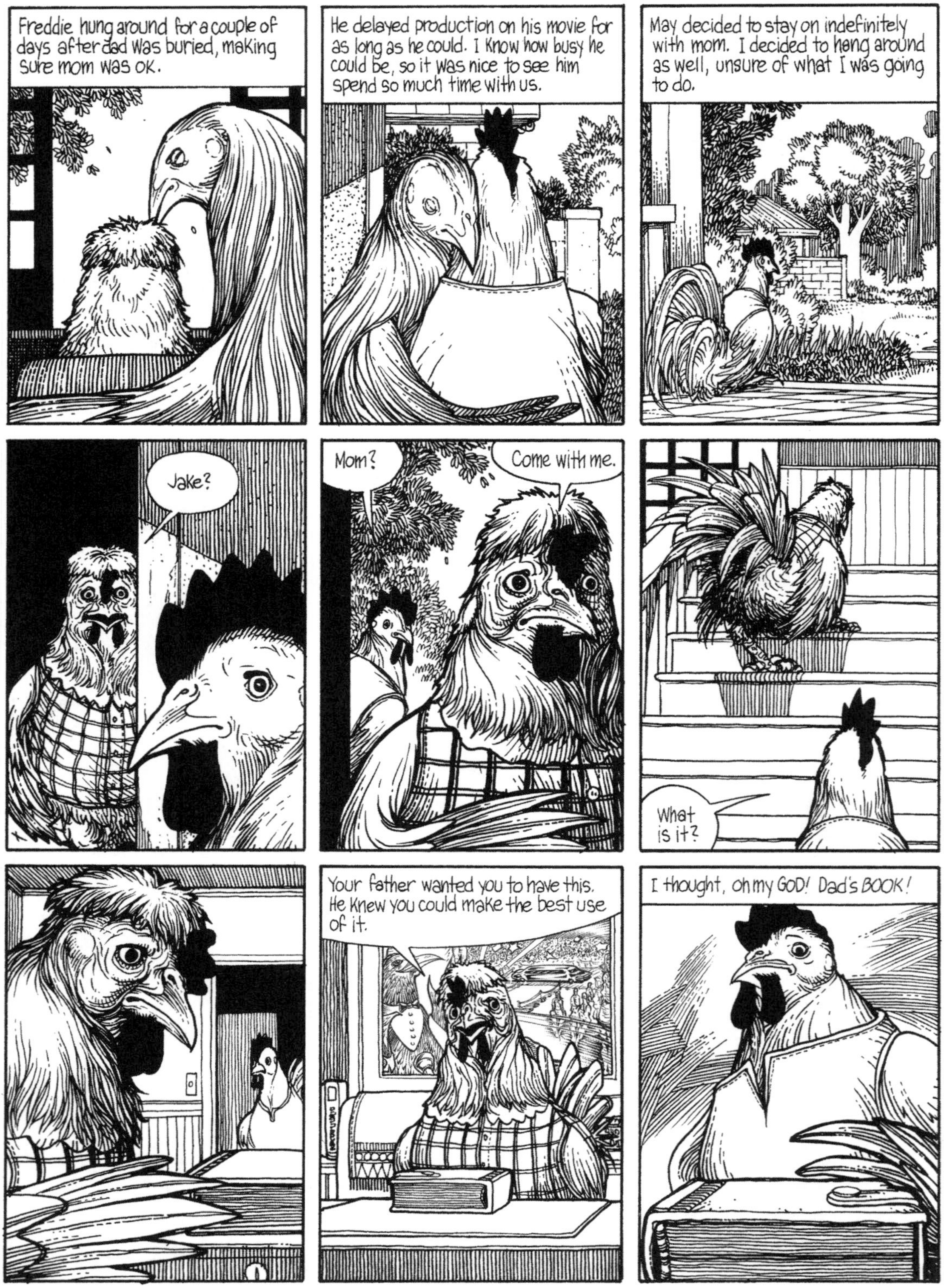

Freddie hung around for a couple of days after dad was buried, making sure mom was OK.
He delayed production on his movie for as long as he could. I know how busy he could be, so it was nice to see him spend so much time with us.
May decided to stay on indefinitely with mom. I decided to hang around as well, unsure of what I was going to do.
Jake?
Mom?
Come with me.
What is it?
Your father wanted you to have this. He knew you could make the best use of it.
I thought, oh my GOD! Dad's BOOK!

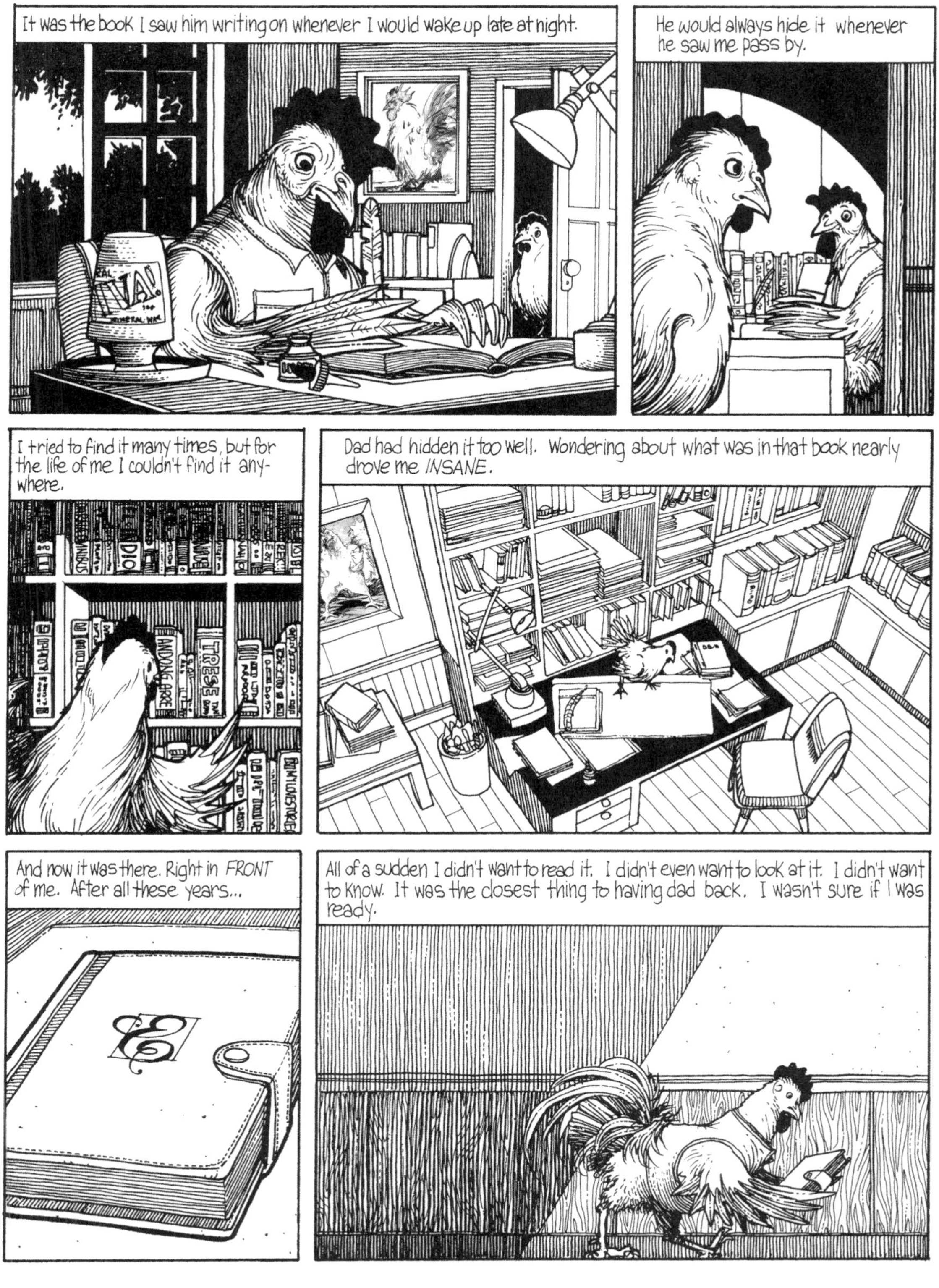
It was the book I saw him writing on whenever I would wake up late at night.
He would always hide it whenever he saw me pass by.
I tried to find it many times, but for the life of me I couldn't find it any-where.
Dad had hidden it too well. Wondering about what was in that book nearly drove me INSANE.
And now it was there. Right in FRONT of me. After all these years...
All of a sudden I didn't want to read it. I didn't even want to look at it. I didn't want to know. It was the closest thing to having dad back. I wasn't sure if I was ready.

I had the book for a couple of days. I tried to keep myself busy with other things just to keep myself from opening it. After waking up from a nap one afternoon, I walked over to my table, opened the book and I read.

WRITING. ONLY THE WAY. REMEMBER IT. TRYING NOT BE FORGET. FORGOT SOME ALREADY, NOTHING BLANK IN MIND.

BACK OF MIND. WRITING HAPPENING BACK OF MIND NOT BE FORGET.

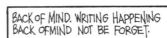

REMEMBER BACK BRIGHT LIGHT. VERY HURT CANT LOOK BURNING AND HOT. STAND NOT STAND WET ON FACE. WAS DEW I THINK.

STILL DARK BUT VERY BRIGHT AND HOT QUICK. NOT LONG. THEN DARK. LIKE OK. LIKE NORMAL. USUAL. MAYBE RIGHT. MAYBE DREAM THINK SO.

STANDING AGAIN. THE SUN... WELCOME THE SUN. BREATH I TAKE AND WELCOME THE SUN.

I thought, what the fuck? Was it a kind of code? I flipped to the middle of the book and read from there.

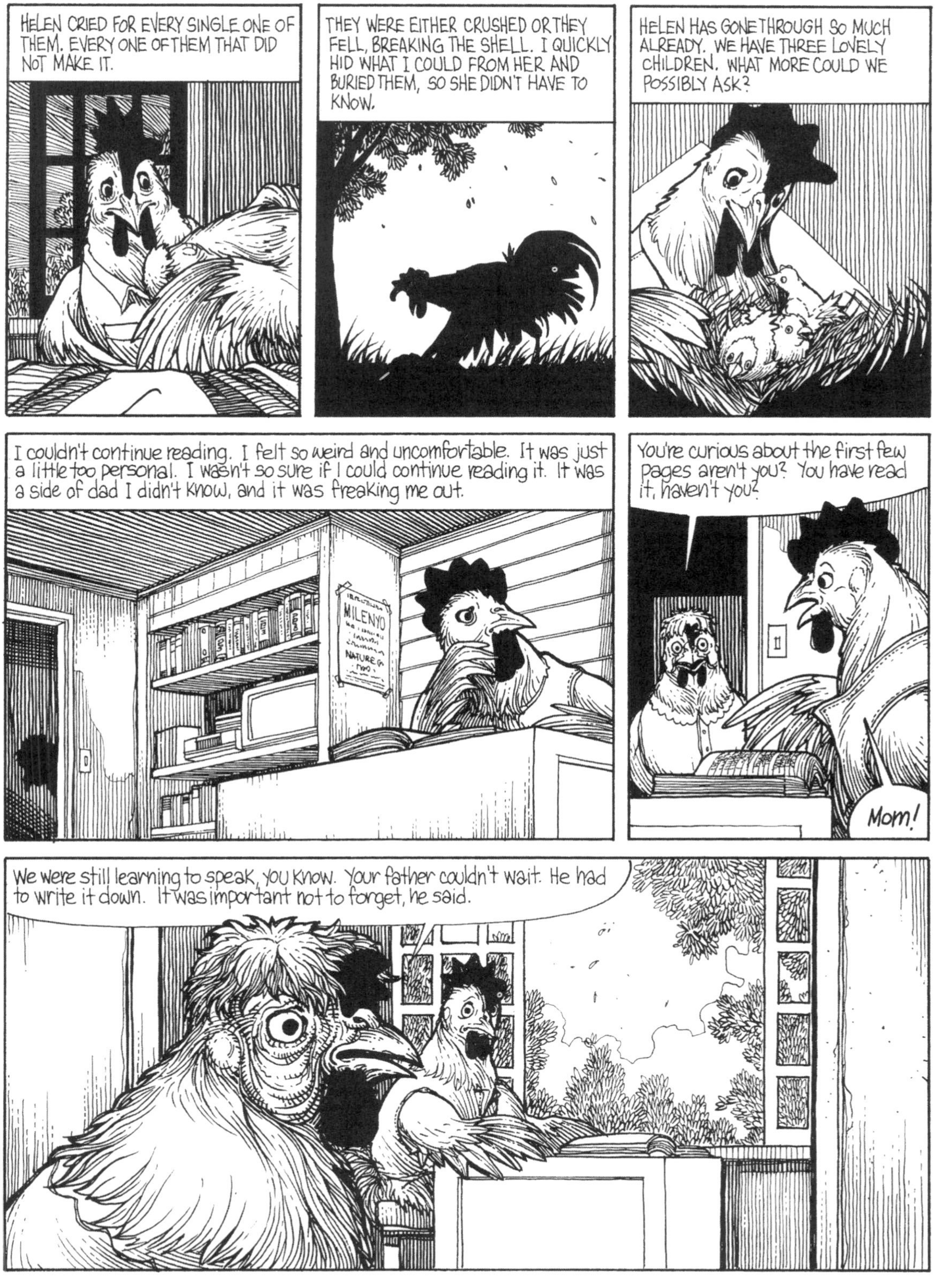
HELEN CRIED FOR EVERY SINGLE ONE OF THEM. EVERY ONE OF THEM THAT DID NOT MAKE IT.
THEY WERE EITHER CRUSHED OR THEY FELL, BREAKING THE SHELL. I QUICKLY HID WHAT I COULD FROM HER AND BURIED THEM, SO SHE DIDN'T HAVE TO KNOW.
HELEN HAS GONE THROUGH SO MUCH ALREADY. WE HAVE THREE LOVELY CHILDREN. WHAT MORE COULD WE POSSIBLY ASK?
I couldn't continue reading. I felt so weird and uncomfortable. It was just a little too personal. I wasn't so sure if I could continue reading it. It was a side of dad I didn't know, and it was freaking me out.
MILENYO
NATURE
You're curious about the first few pages aren't you? You have read it, haven't you?
Mom!
We were still learning to speak, you know. Your father couldn't wait. He had to write it down. It was important not to forget, he said.

Important not to forget.

Mom? Are you OK?

Benjie. Him and your father were friends. Good idea to talk to him.

Farmer Ben. I've always wondered about him. He was always nice to us, but I just couldn't help but think it was out of guilt than anything else.

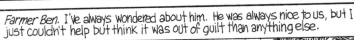

He always had that look in his eye that I just couldn't trust.

I don't know how my dad and someone like _him_ were ever FRIENDS. Dad never talked about it.

Mom seemed to think _him_ being here was the most natural thing in the world. I mean... what the _FUCK?_

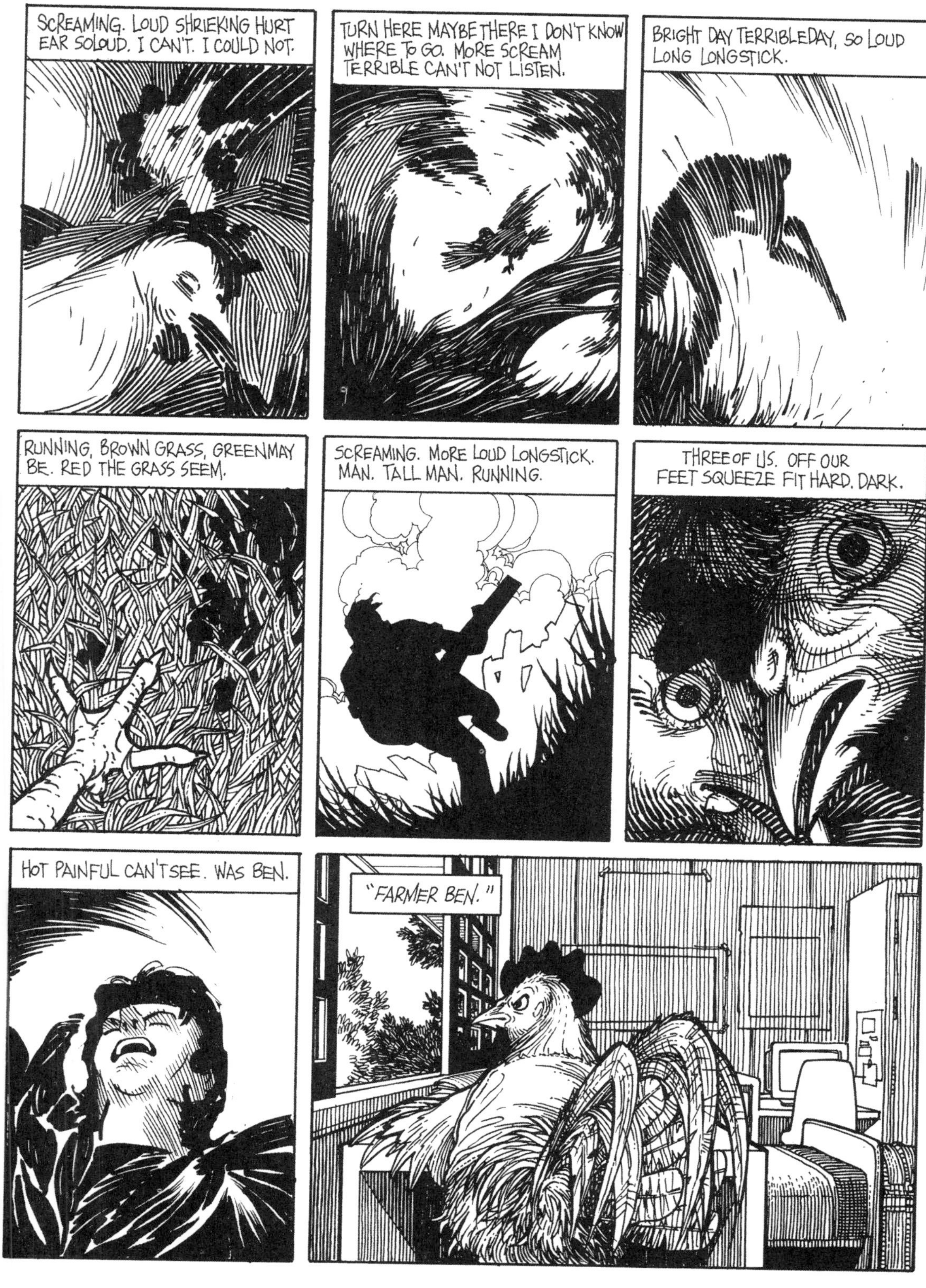
SCREAMING. LOUD SHRIEKING HURT EAR SOLOUD. I CAN'T. I COULD NOT.
TURN HERE MAYBE THERE I DON'T KNOW WHERE TO GO. MORE SCREAM TERRIBLE CAN'T NOT LISTEN.
BRIGHT DAY TERRIBLEDAY, SO LOUD LONG LONGSTICK.
RUNNING, BROWN GRASS, GREENMAY BE. RED THE GRASS SEEM.
SCREAMING. MORE LOUD LONGSTICK. MAN. TALL MAN. RUNNING.
THREE OF US. OFF OUR FEET SQUEEZE FIT HARD. DARK.
HOT PAINFUL CAN'TSEE. WAS BEN.
"FARMER BEN."

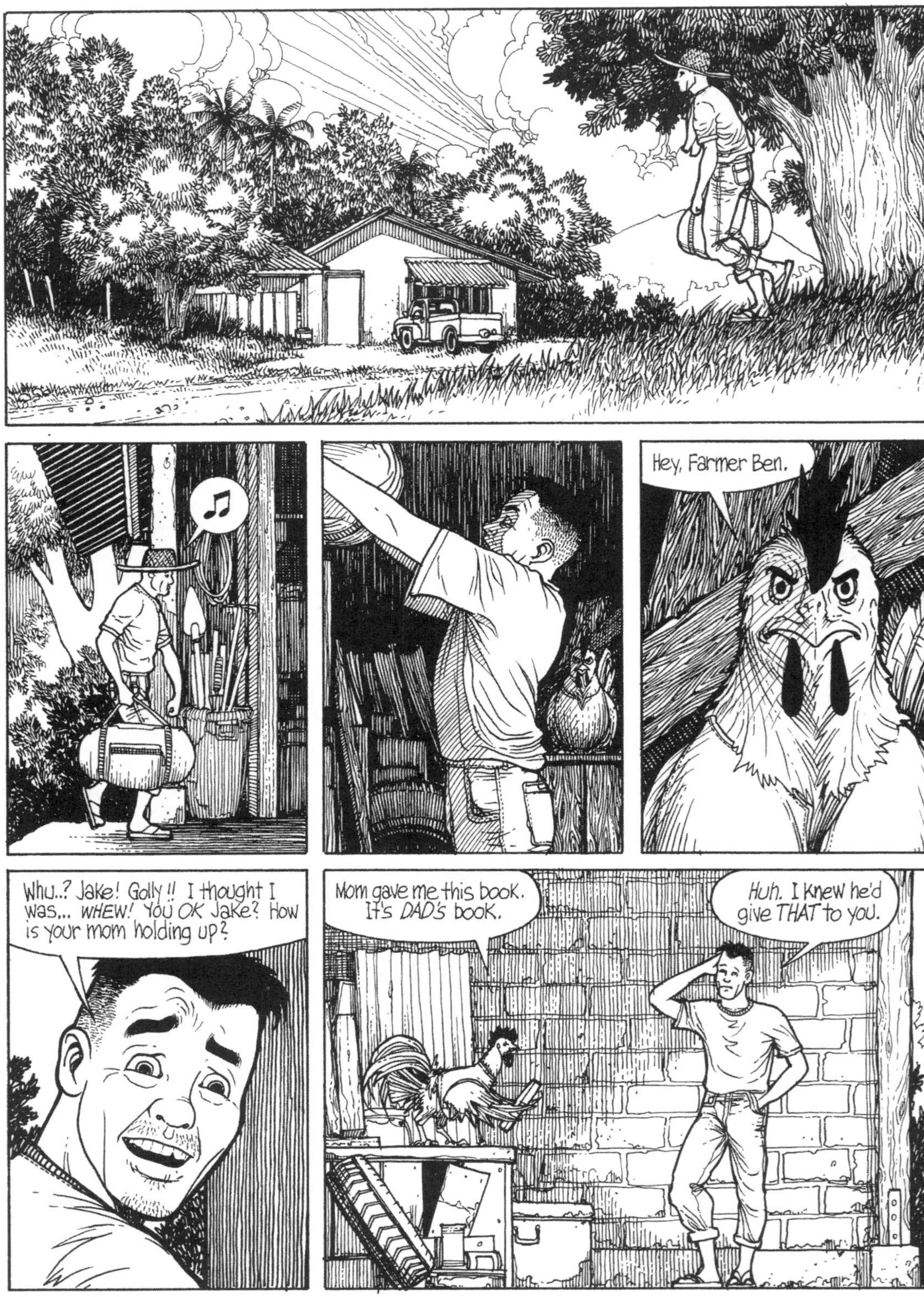
♫
Hey, Farmer Ben.
Whu..? Jake! Golly!! I thought I was... WHEW! You OK Jake? How is your mom holding up?
Mom gave me this book. It's DAD's book.
Huh. I knew he'd give THAT to you.

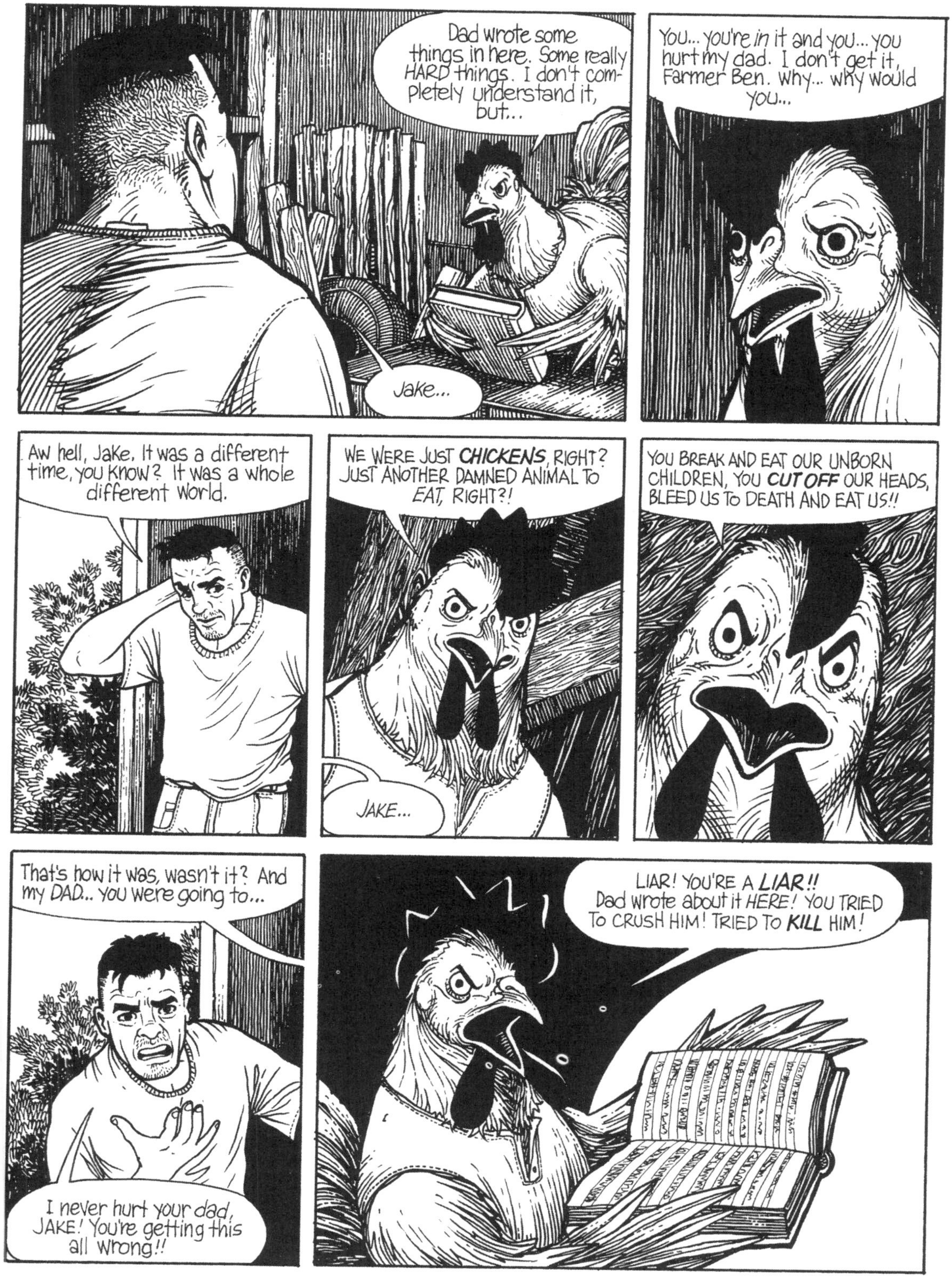
Dad wrote some things in here. Some really HARD things. I don't completely understand it, but...
Jake...
You... you're in it and you... you hurt my dad. I don't get it, Farmer Ben. Why... why would you...
Aw hell, Jake. It was a different time, you know? It was a whole different world.
WE WERE JUST CHICKENS, RIGHT? JUST ANOTHER DAMNED ANIMAL TO EAT, RIGHT?!
JAKE...
YOU BREAK AND EAT OUR UNBORN CHILDREN, YOU CUT OFF OUR HEADS, BLEED US TO DEATH AND EAT US!!
That's how it was, wasn't it? And my DAD... you were going to...
I never hurt your dad, JAKE! You're getting this all wrong!!
LIAR! YOU'RE A LIAR!! Dad wrote about it HERE! YOU TRIED TO CRUSH HIM! TRIED TO KILL HIM!

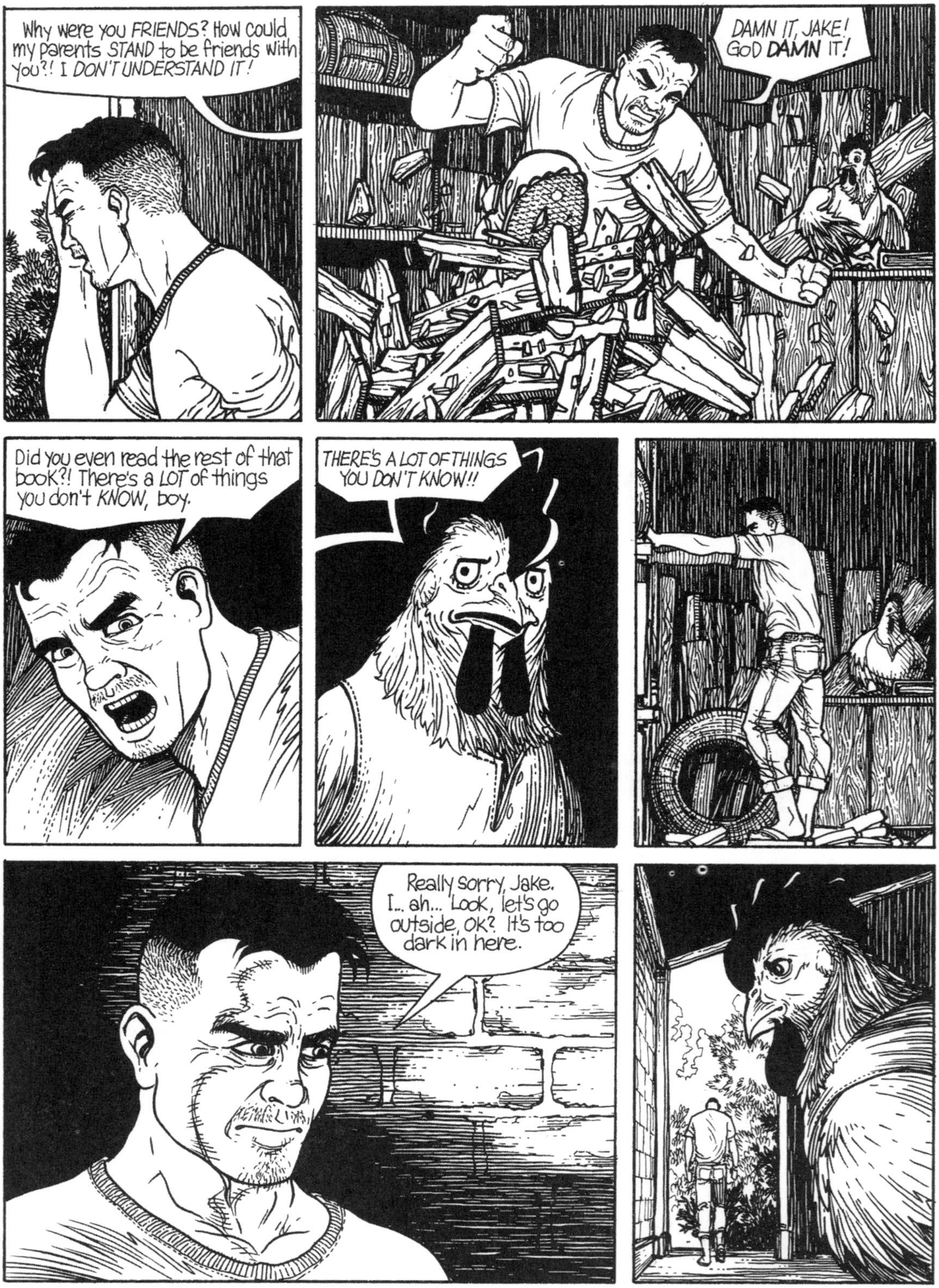
Why were you FRIENDS? How could my parents STAND to be friends with you?! I DON'T UNDERSTAND IT!
DAMN IT, JAKE! GOD DAMN IT!
Did you even read the rest of that book?! There's a LOT of things you don't KNOW, boy.
THERE'S A LOT OF THINGS YOU DON'T KNOW!!
Really sorry, Jake. I... ah... Look, let's go outside, OK? It's too dark in here.

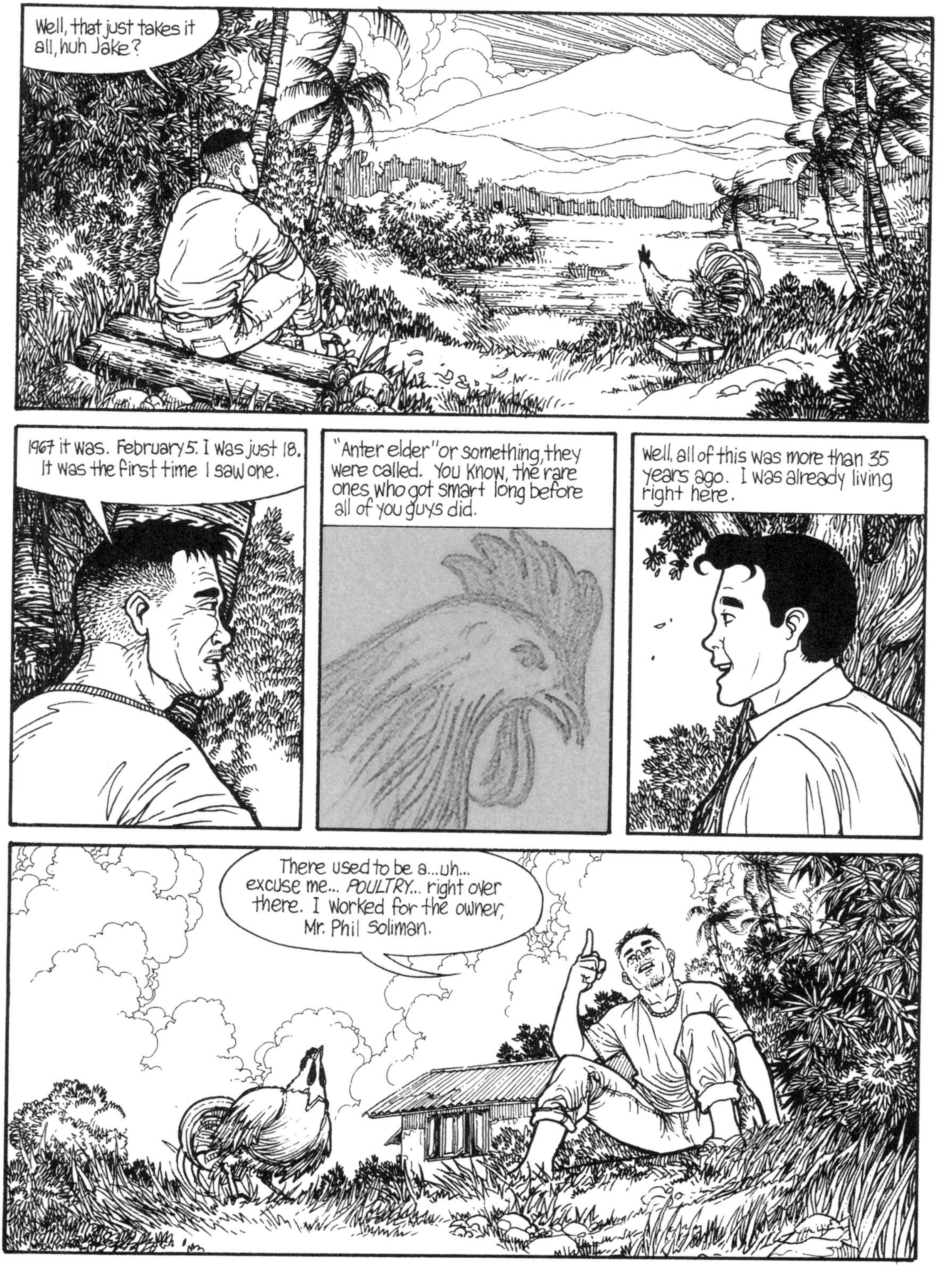
Well, that just takes it all, huh Jake?
1967 it was. February 5. I was just 18. It was the first time I saw one.
"Anter elder" or something, they were called. You know, the rare ones who got smart long before all of you guys did.
Well, all of this was more than 35 years ago. I was already living right here.
There used to be a...uh... excuse me... POULTRY... right over there. I worked for the owner, Mr. Phil Soliman.

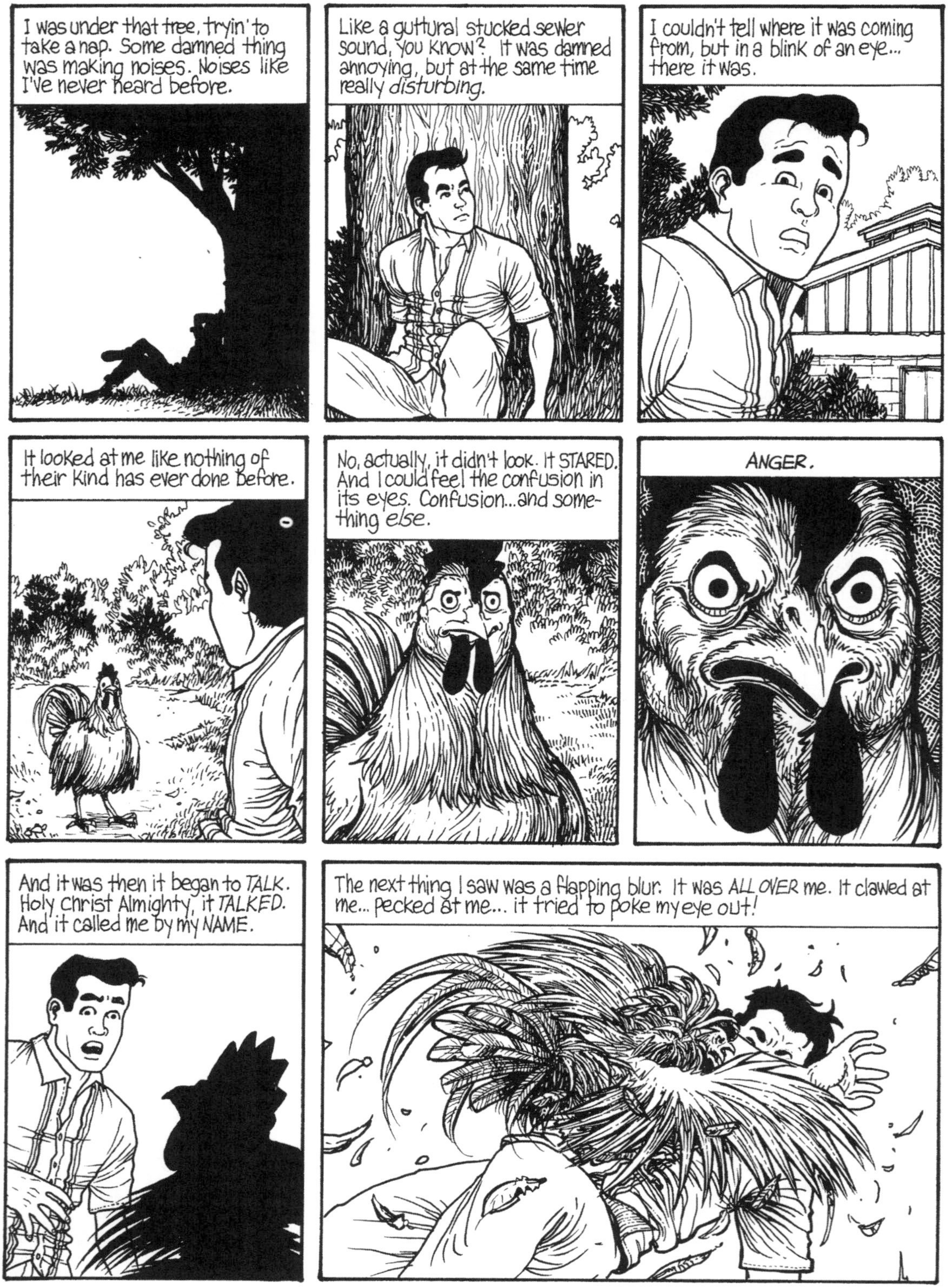
I was under that tree, tryin' to take a nap. Some damned thing was making noises. Noises like I've never heard before.
Like a guttural stucked sewer sound, you know? It was damned annoying, but at the same time really *disturbing*.
I couldn't tell where it was coming from, but in a blink of an eye... there it was.
It looked at me like nothing of their kind has ever done before.
No, actually, it didn't look. It STARED. And I could feel the confusion in its eyes. Confusion...and something *else*.
ANGER.
And it was then it began to *TALK*. Holy christ Almighty, it *TALKED*. And it called me by my *NAME*.
The next thing I saw was a flapping blur. It was *ALL OVER* me. It clawed at me... pecked at me... it tried to poke my eye out!

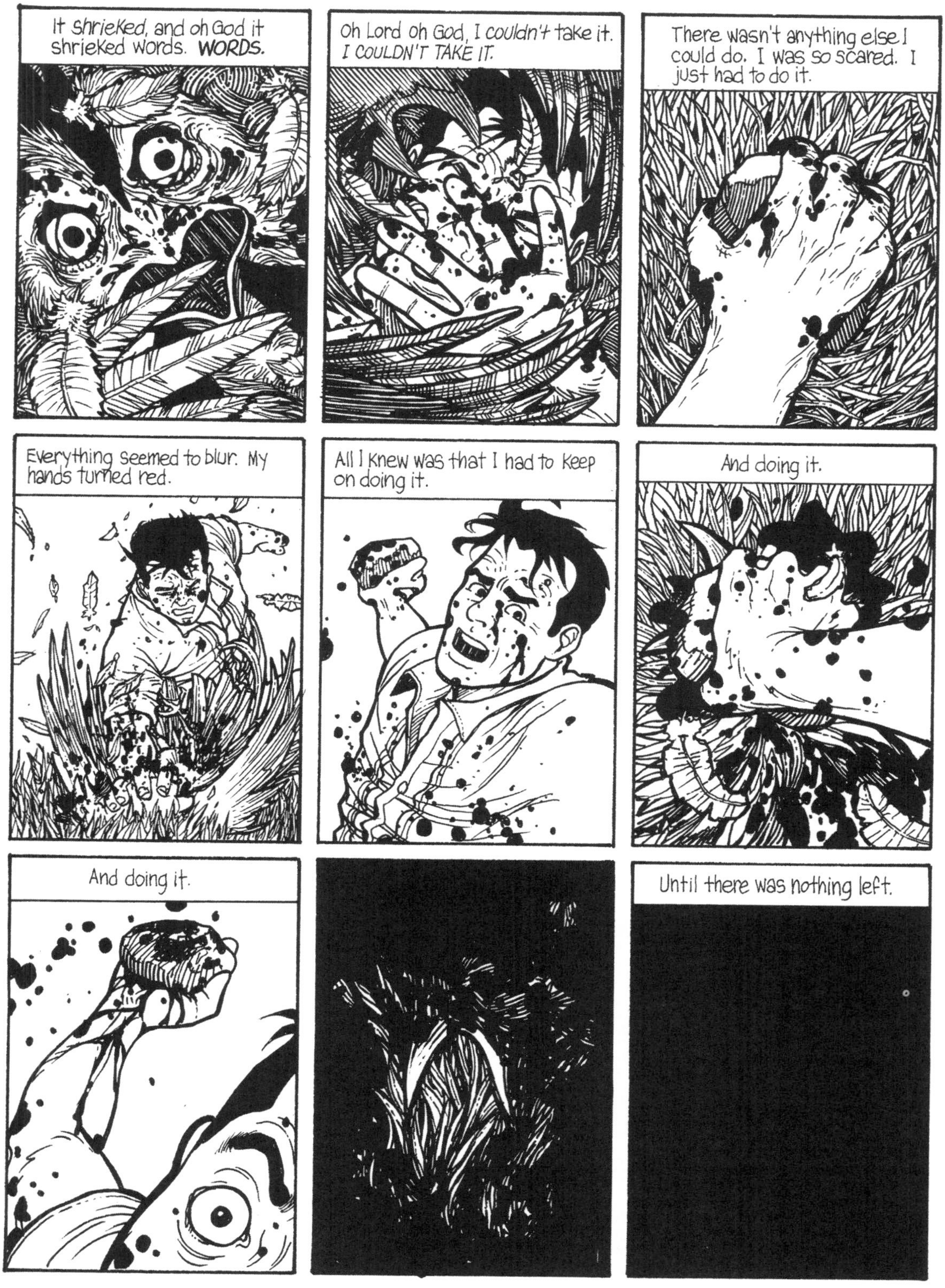
It shrieked, and oh God it shrieked words. **WORDS.**
Oh Lord oh God, I *couldn't* take it. *I COULDN'T TAKE IT.*
There wasn't anything else I could do. I was so scared. I just had to do it.
Everything seemed to blur. My hands turned red.
All I knew was that I had to keep on doing it.
And doing it.
And doing it.
Until there was nothing left.

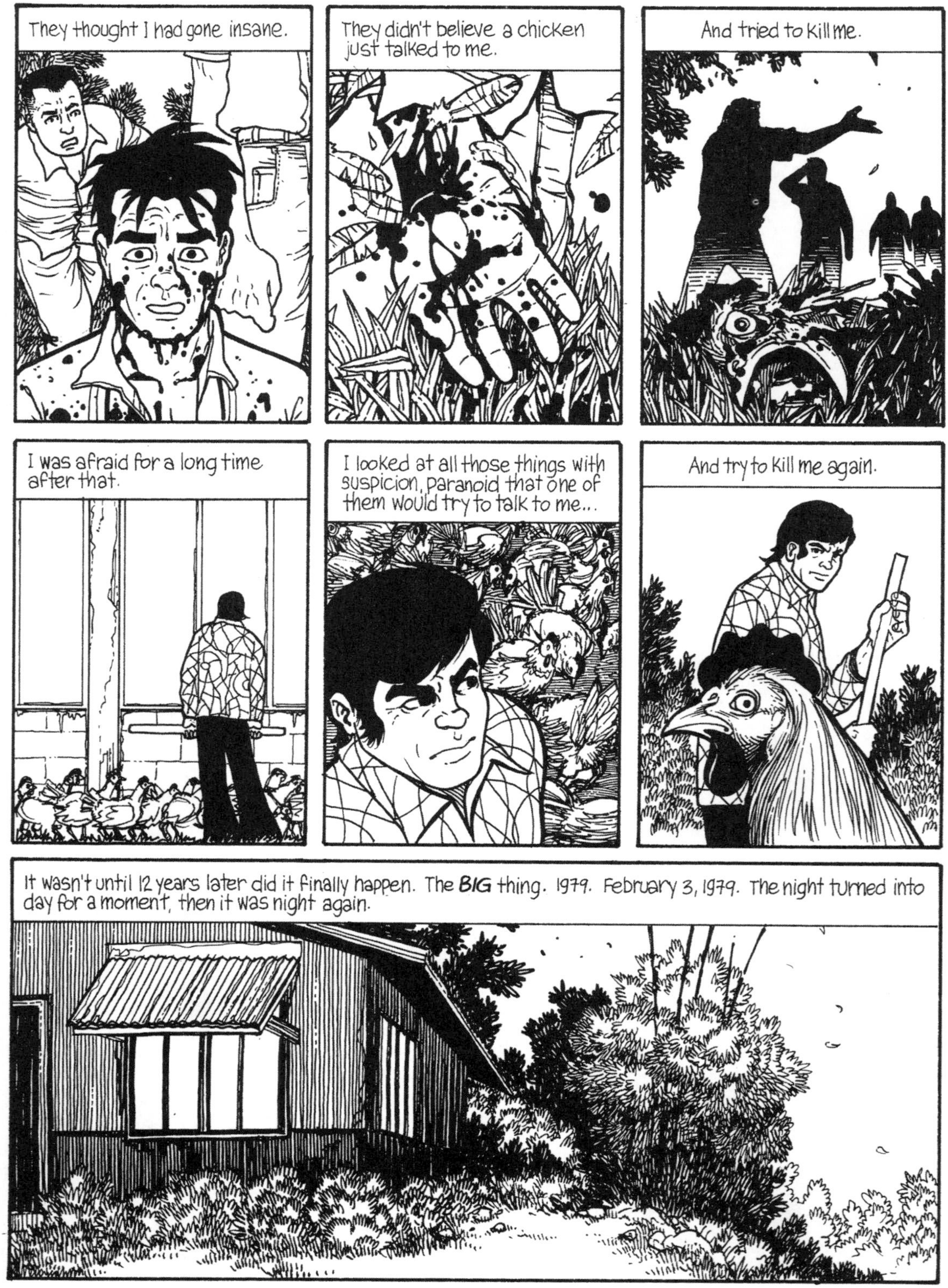
They thought I had gone insane.
They didn't believe a chicken just talked to me.
And tried to kill me.
I was afraid for a long time after that.
I looked at all those things with suspicion, paranoid that one of them would try to talk to me...
And try to kill me again.
It wasn't until 12 years later did it finally happen. The BIG thing. 1979. February 3, 1979. The night turned into day for a moment, then it was night again.

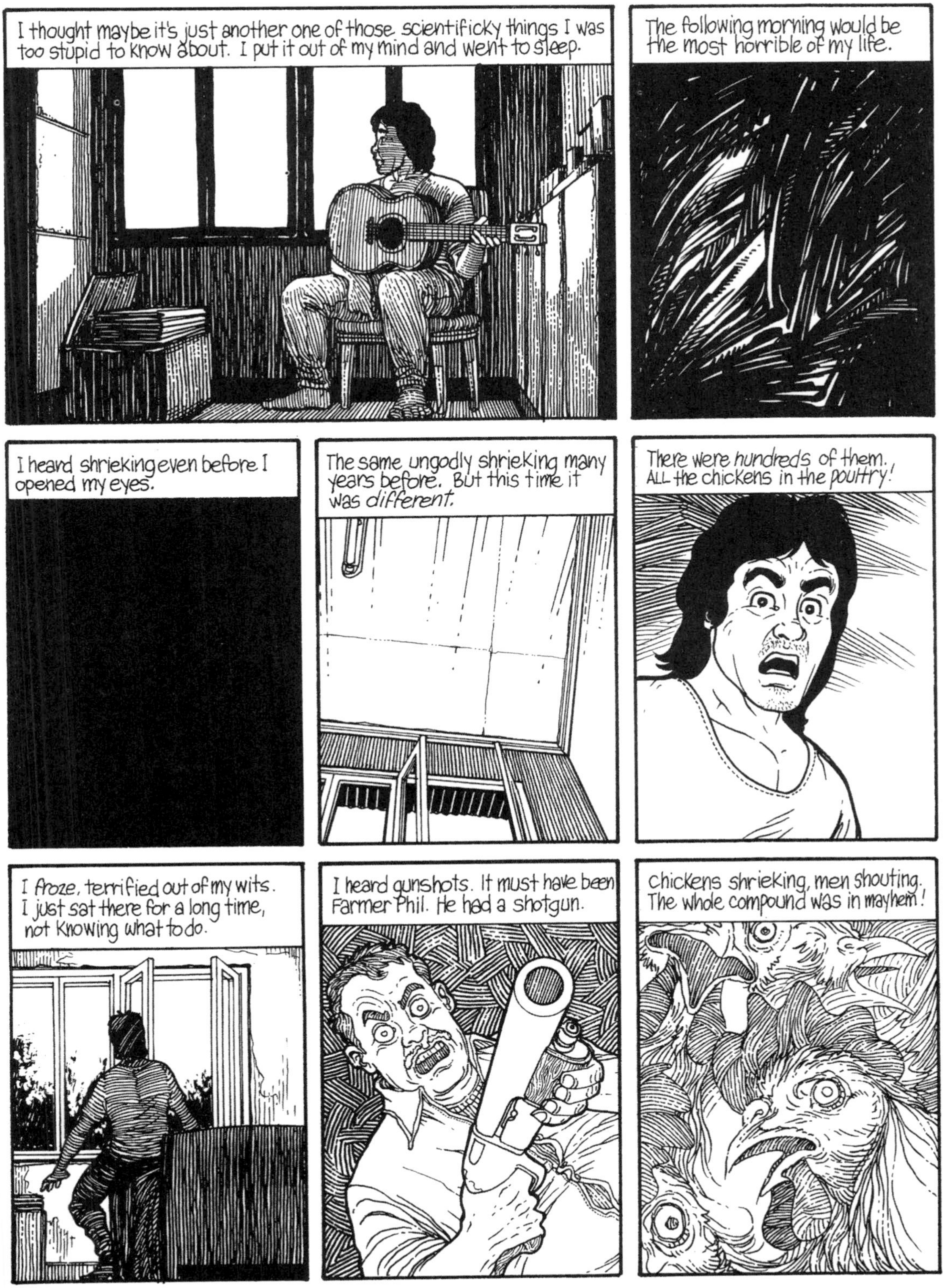
I thought maybe it's just another one of those scientificky things I was too stupid to know about. I put it out of my mind and went to sleep.
The following morning would be the most horrible of my life.
I heard shrieking even before I opened my eyes.
The same ungodly shrieking many years before. But this time it was *different.*
There were *hundreds* of them. ALL the chickens in the *poultry!*
I froze, terrified out of my wits. I just sat there for a long time, not knowing what to do.
I heard gunshots. It must have been Farmer Phil. He had a shotgun.
Chickens shrieking, men shouting. The whole compound was in mayhem!

I rushed towards the window. I saw the poultry start to burn.

In the distance I saw the chickens... and they were all on fire.

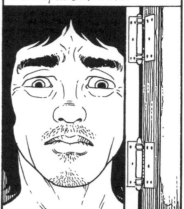

I stood there and I did NOTHING. Part of me was horrified. But a part of me was glad the bastards were burning. If only one of them could do so much harm, how much more could a whole gang of them do?

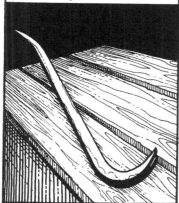

I wished I had a gun. I had a crowbar in one of the back rooms so I ran to get it.

As soon as I got there, one of them was waiting for me.

Seeing it stare at me like that other one did many years before nearly killed me right there.

It was either him or me. I was just about to pound the ungodly thing into the ground when it said something. Something I didn't expect.

Help

help me

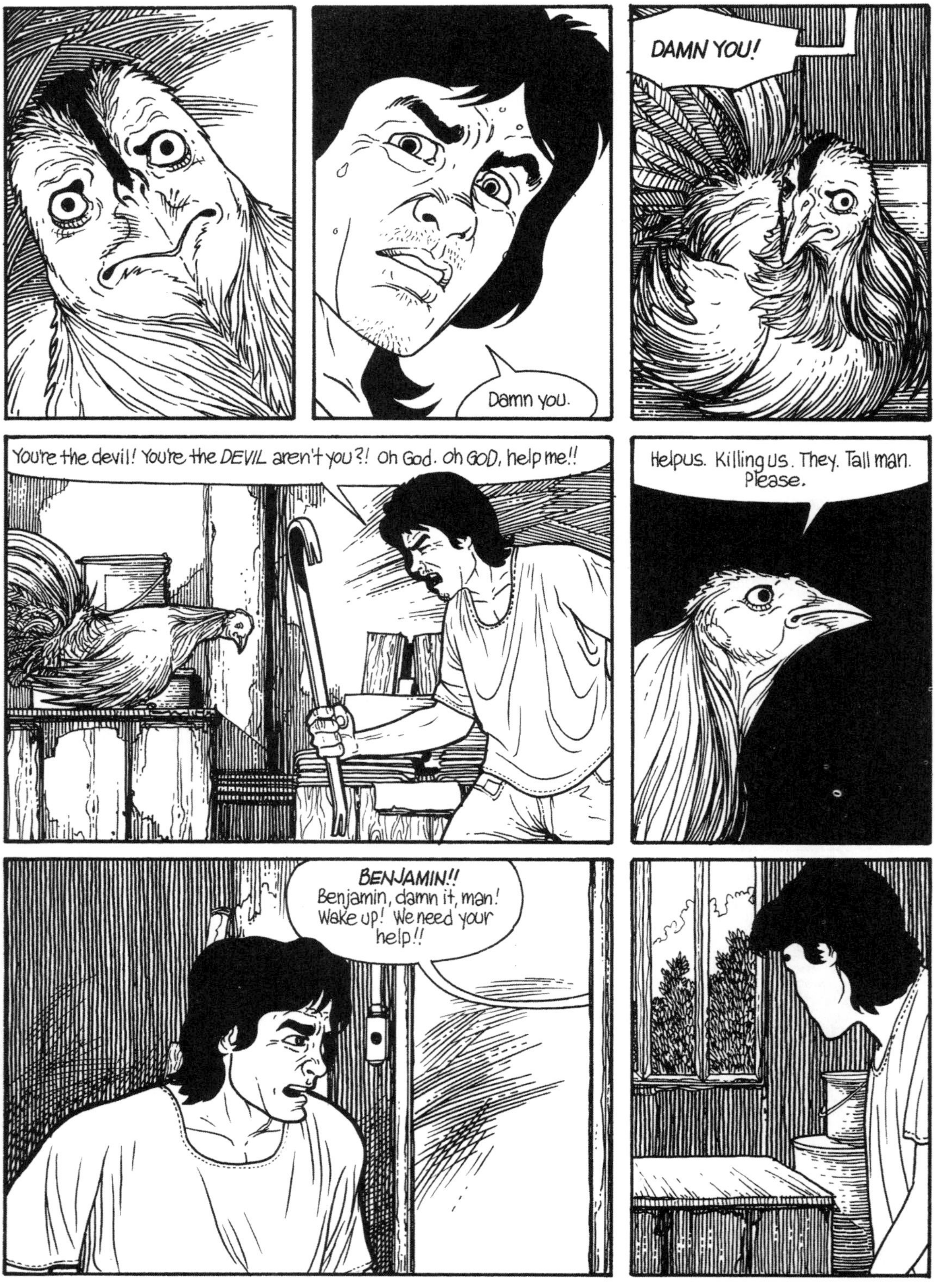
Damn you.
DAMN YOU!
You're the devil! You're the *DEVIL* aren't you?! Oh God. Oh *GOD*, help me!!
Helpus. Killing us. They. Tall man. Please.
BENJAMIN!! Benjamin, damn it, man! Wake up! We need your help!!

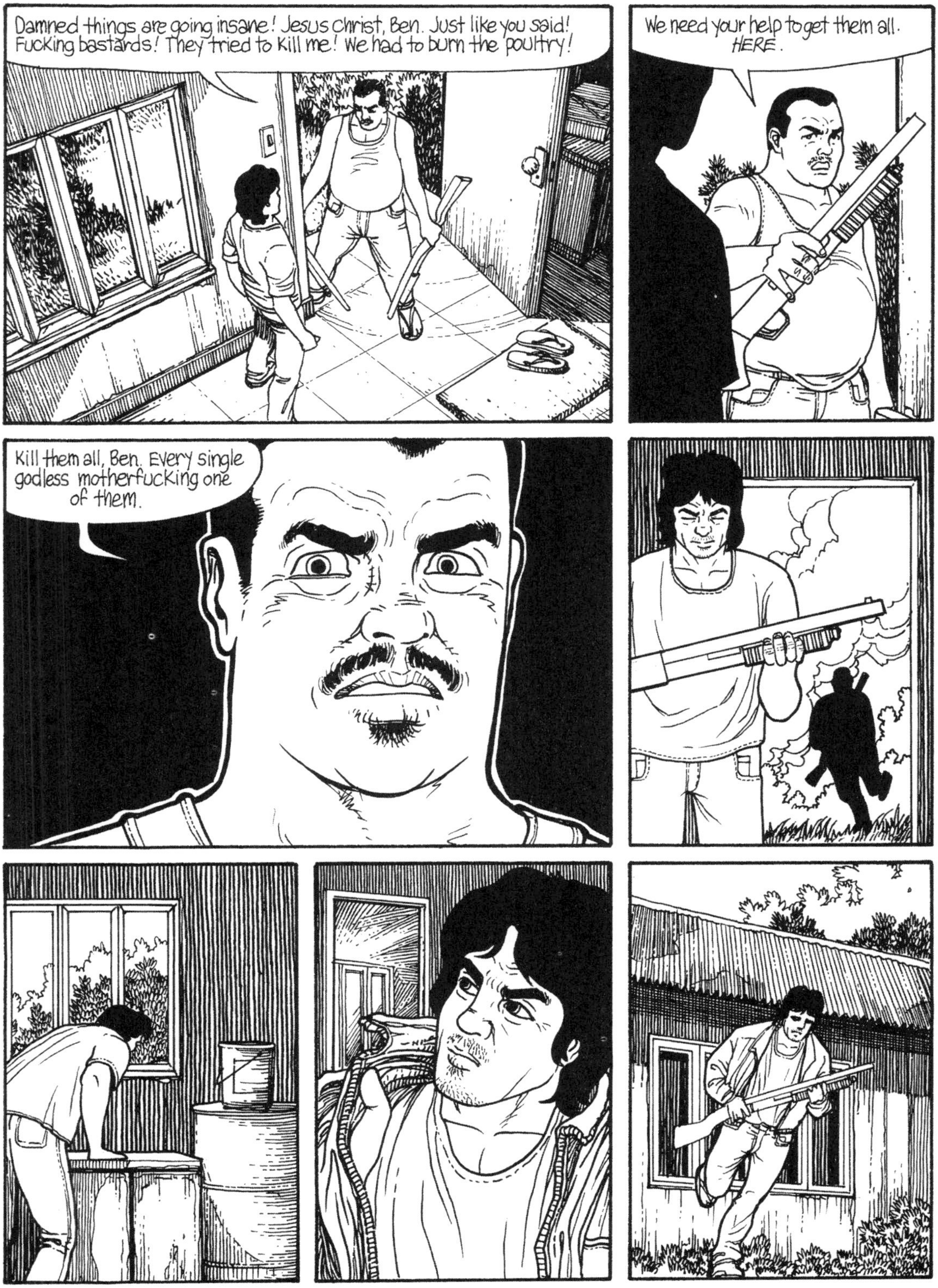

Damned things are going insane! Jesus Christ, Ben. Just like you said! Fucking bastards! They tried to kill me! We had to burn the poultry!
We need your help to get them all. HERE.
Kill them all, Ben. Every single godless motherfucking one of them.

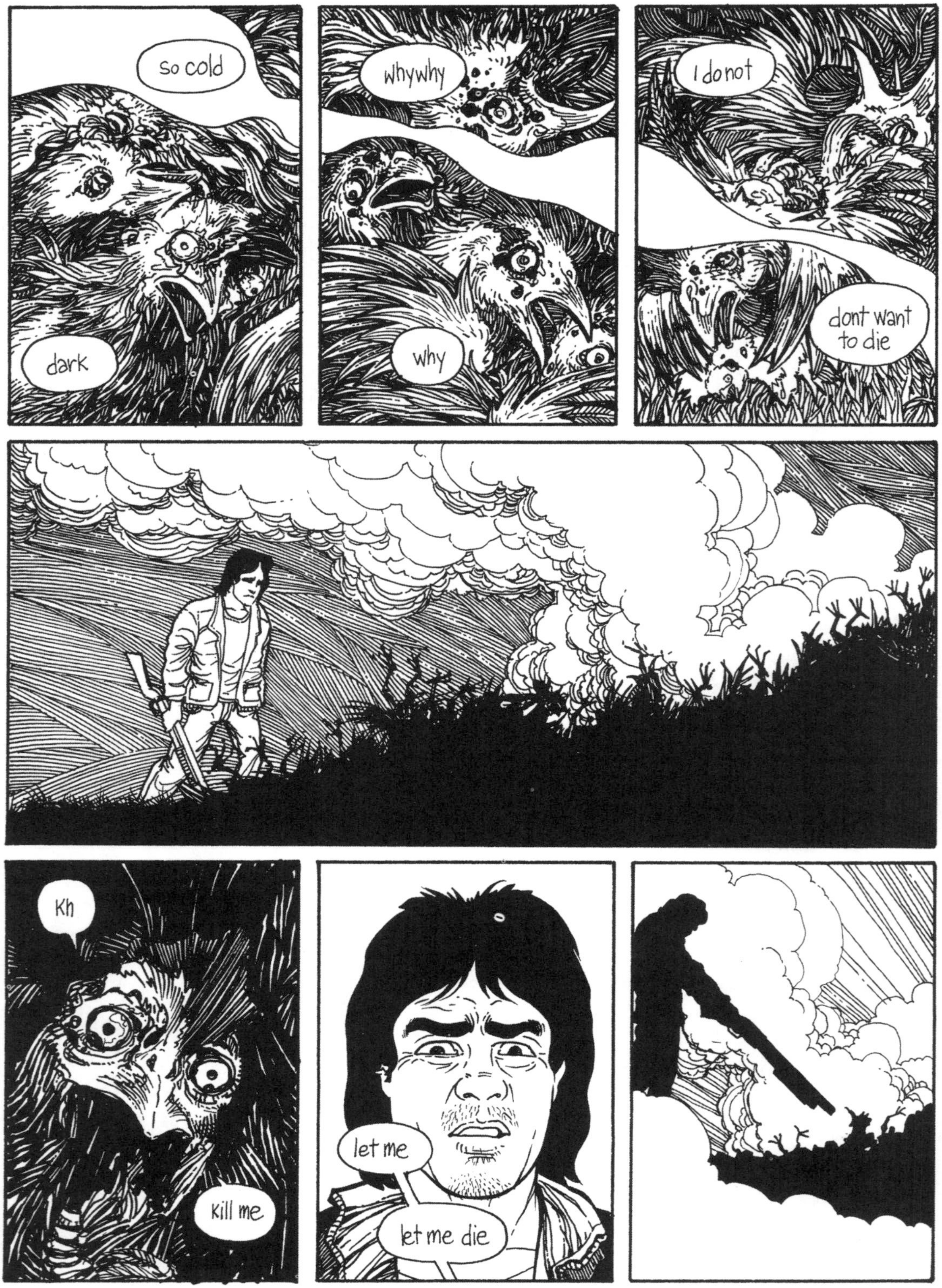
so cold
dark
whywhy
why
I do not
dont want to die
Kh
kill me
let me
let me die

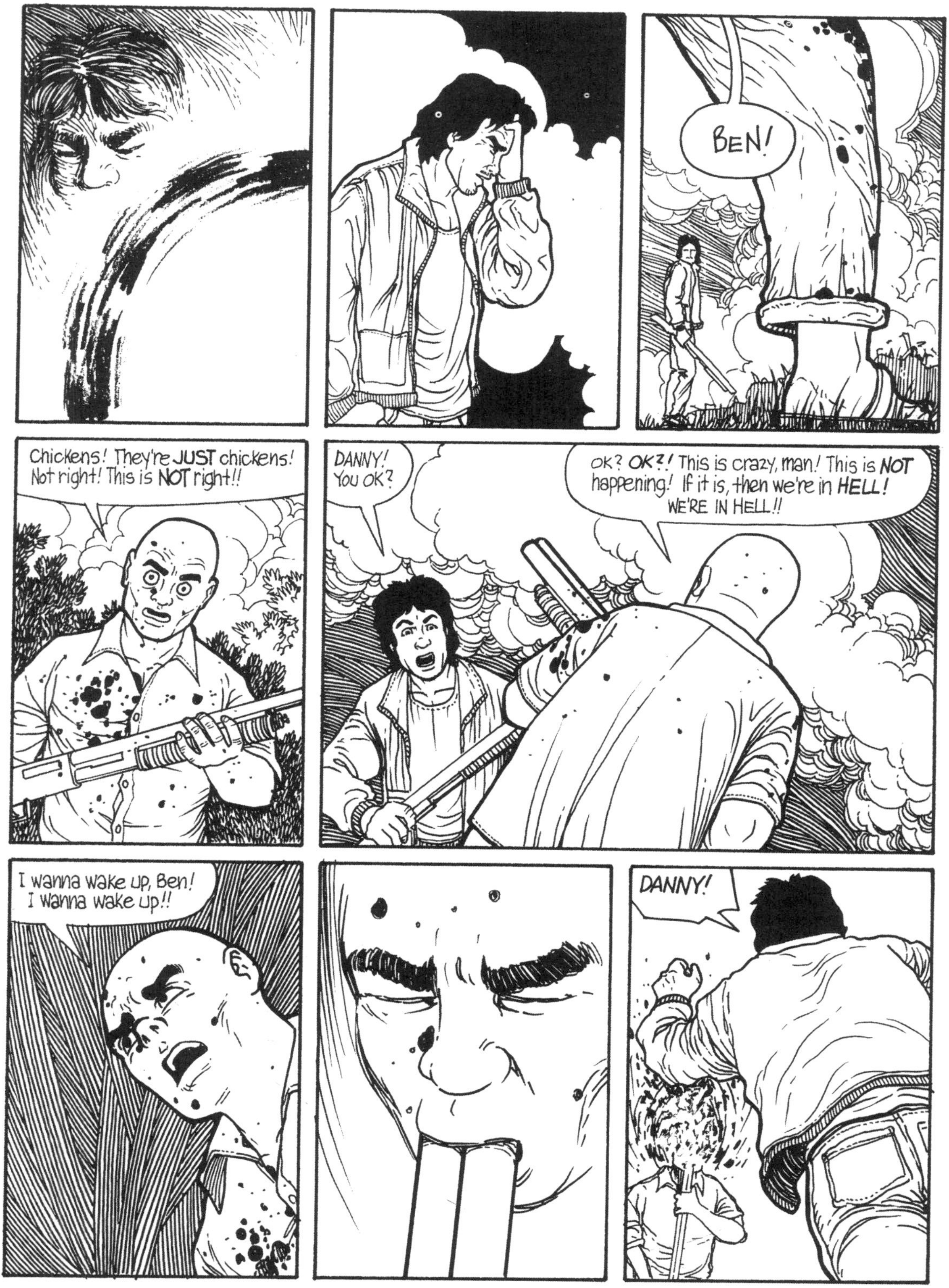
BEN!
Chickens! They're JUST chickens! Not right! This is NOT right!!
DANNY! You OK?
OK? OK?! This is crazy, man! This is NOT happening! If it is, then we're in HELL! WE'RE IN HELL!!
I wanna wake up, Ben! I wanna wake up!!
DANNY!

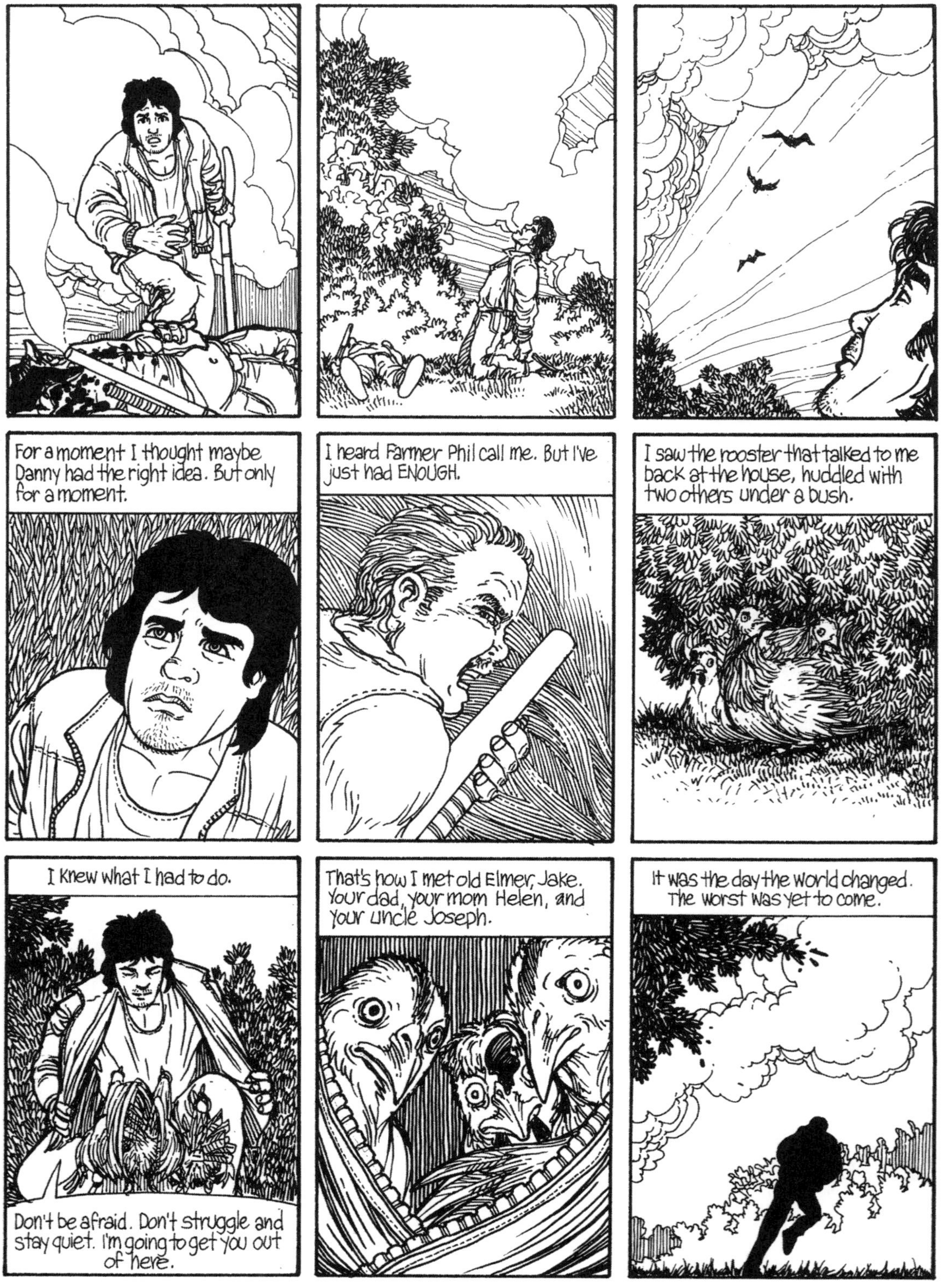
For a moment I thought maybe Danny had the right idea. But only for a moment.
I heard Farmer Phil call me. But I've just had ENOUGH.
I saw the rooster that talked to me back at the house, huddled with two others under a bush.
I knew what I had to do.
Don't be afraid. Don't struggle and stay quiet. I'm going to get you out of here.
That's how I met old Elmer, Jake. Your dad, your mom Helen, and your uncle Joseph.
It was the day the world changed. The worst was yet to come.

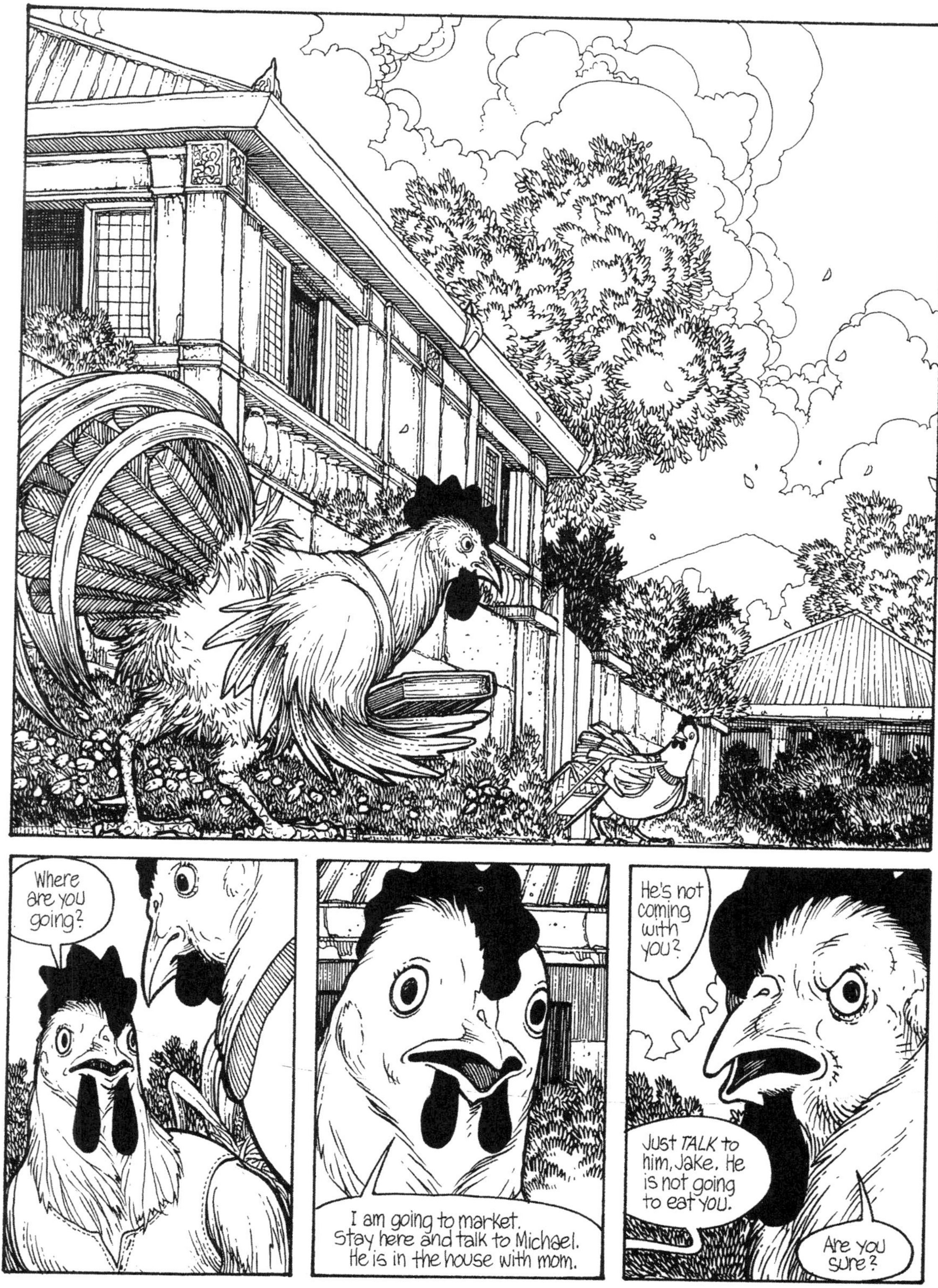
Where are you going?
I am going to market. Stay here and talk to Michael. He is in the house with mom.
He's not coming with you?
Just TALK to him, Jake. He is not going to eat you.
Are you sure?

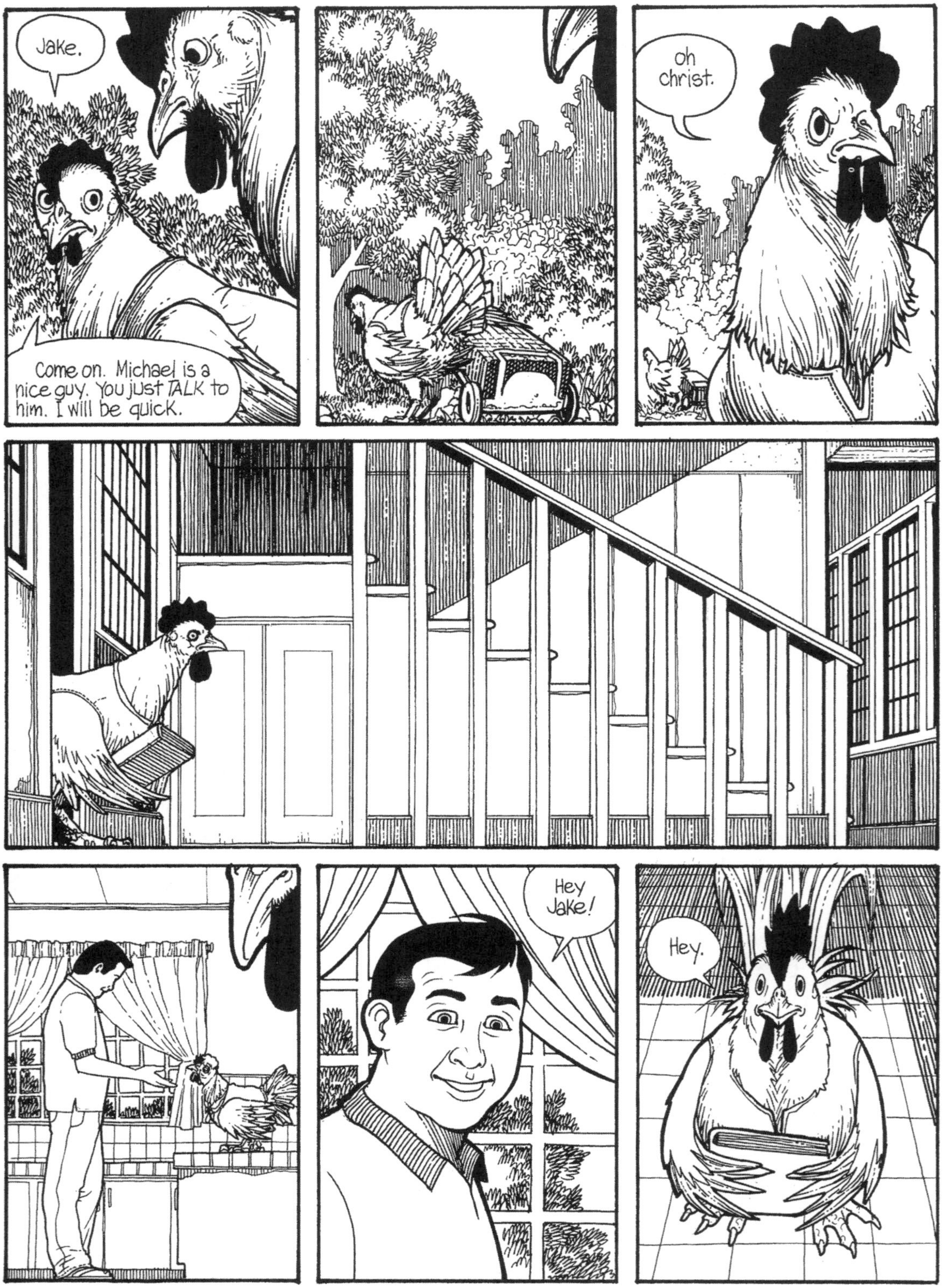
Jake.
Come on. Michael is a nice guy. You just *TALK* to him. I will be quick.
oh christ.
Hey Jake!
Hey.

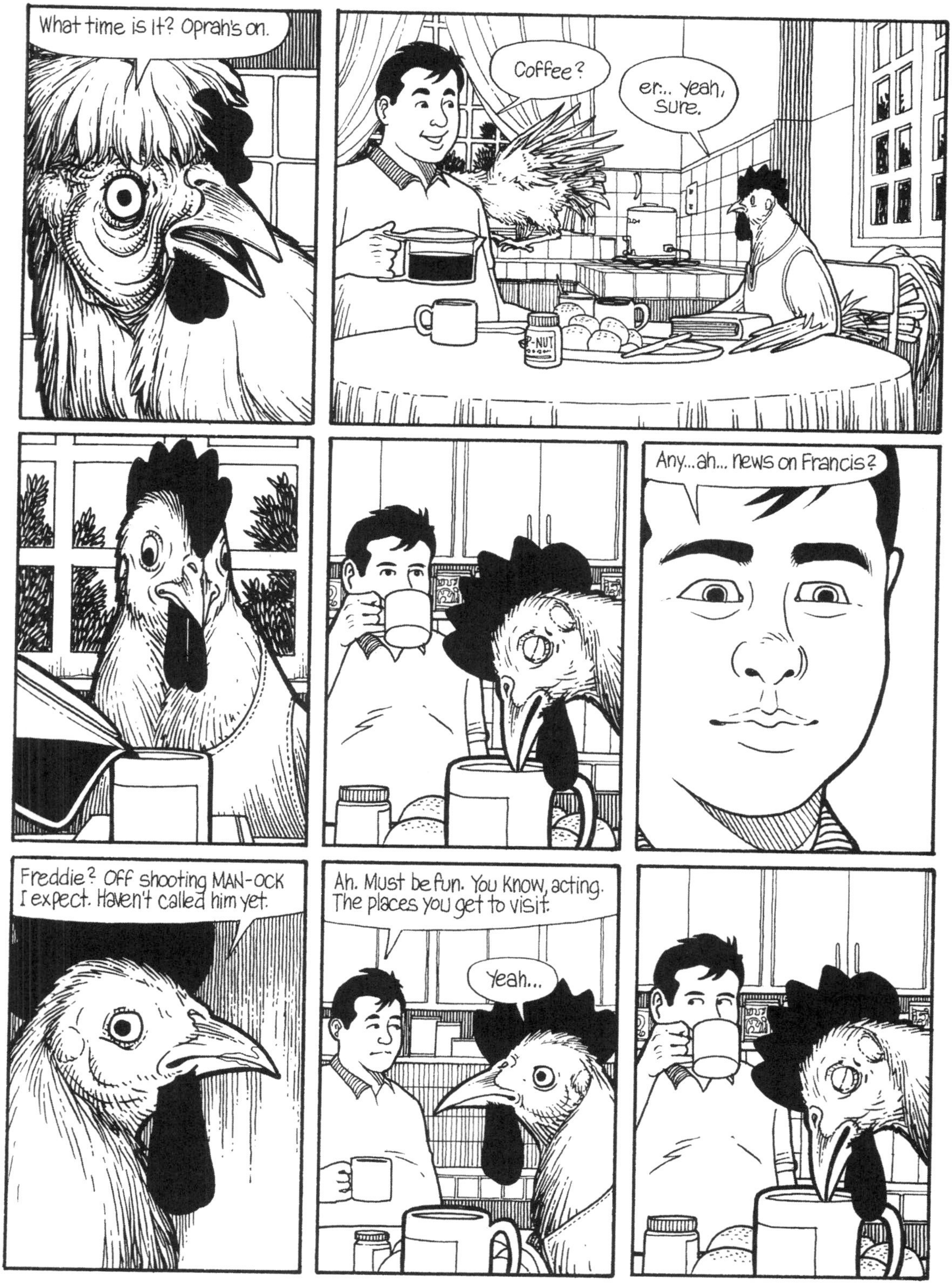
What time is it? Oprah's on.
Coffee?
er... Yeah, sure.
P-NUT
Any...ah... news on Francis?
Freddie? Off shooting MAN-OCK I expect. Haven't called him yet.
Ah. Must be fun. You know, acting. The places you get to visit.
Yeah...

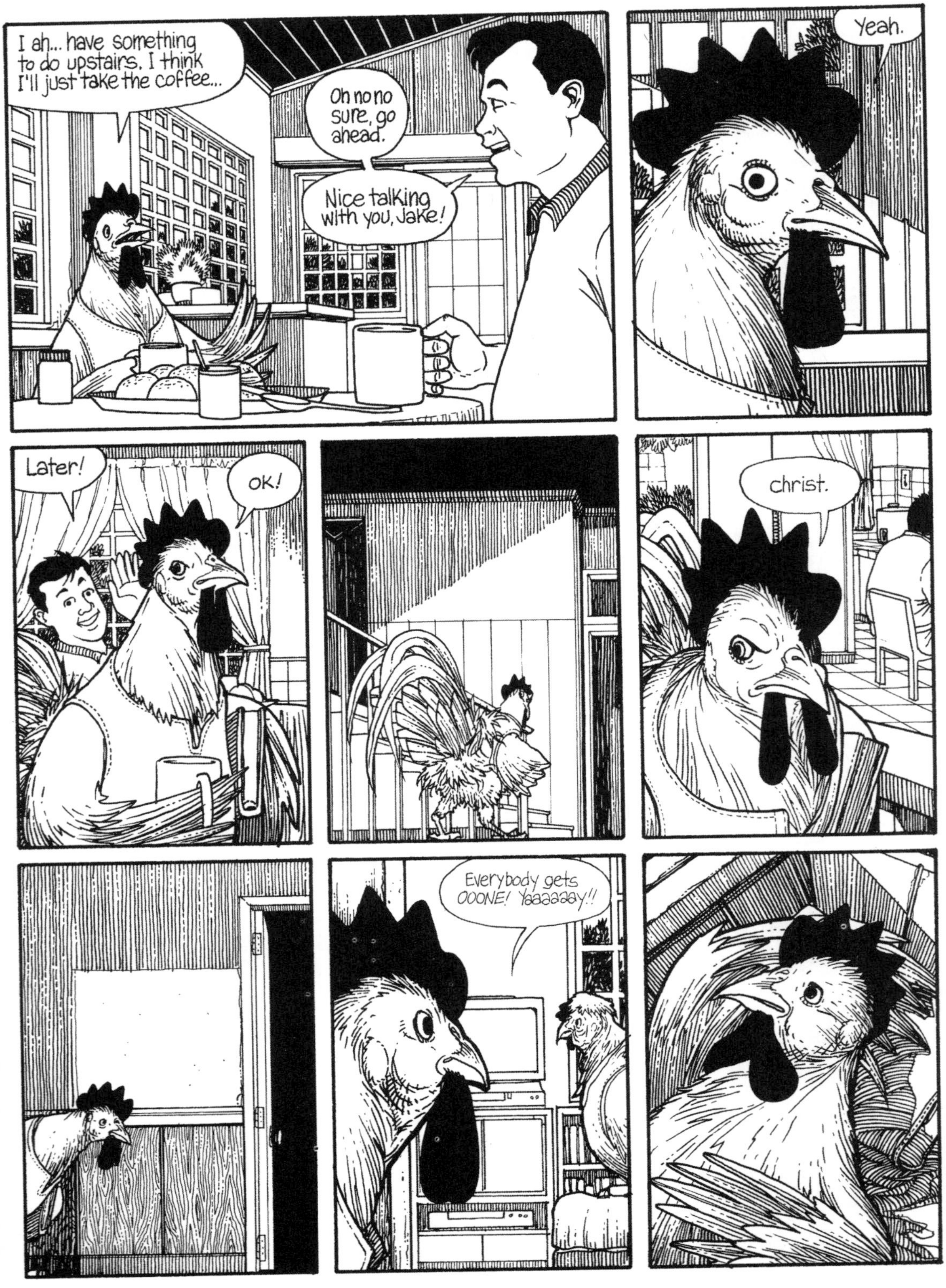
I ah... have something to do upstairs. I think I'll just take the coffee...
Oh no no sure, go ahead.
Nice talking with you, Jake!
Yeah.
Later!
OK!
christ.
Everybody gets OOONE! Yaaaaaay!!

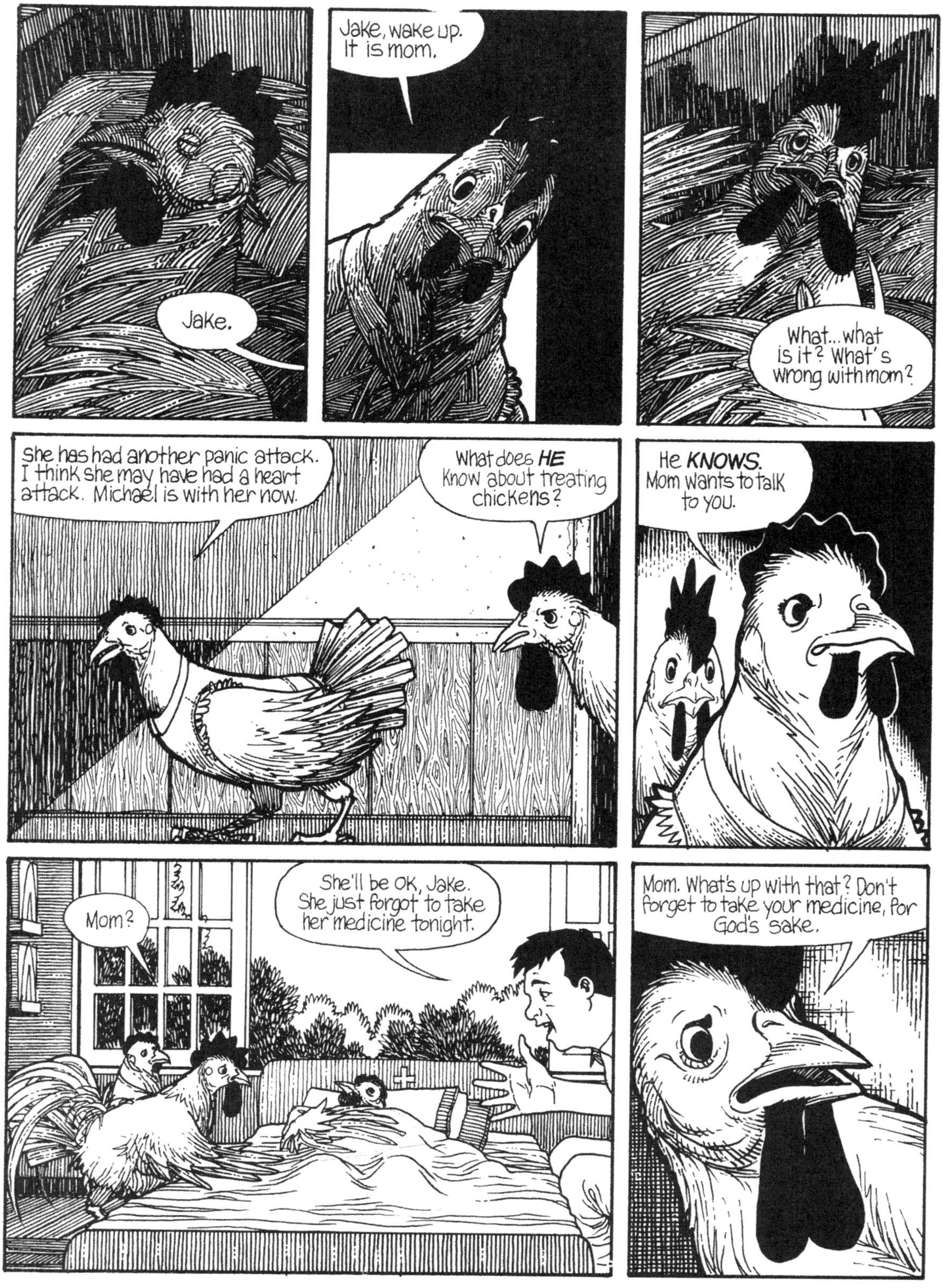
Jake.
Jake, wake up. It is mom.
What... what is it? What's wrong with mom?
She has had another panic attack. I think she may have had a heart attack. Michael is with her now.
What does **HE** know about treating chickens?
He **KNOWS.** Mom wants to talk to you.
Mom?
She'll be OK, Jake. She just forgot to take her medicine tonight.
Mom. What's up with that? Don't forget to take your medicine, for God's sake.

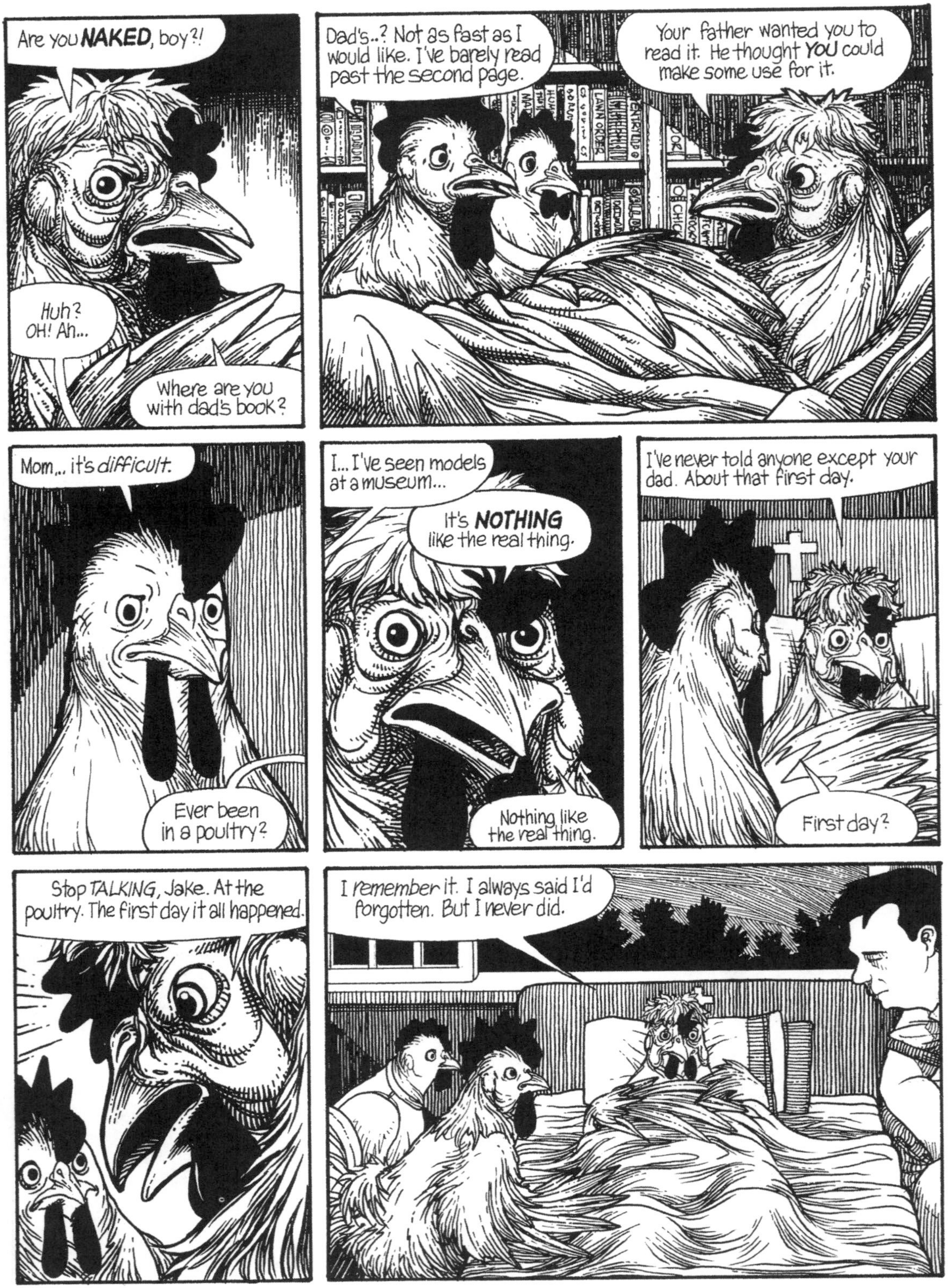
Are you NAKED, boy?!
Huh? OH! Ah...
Where are you with dad's book?
Dad's..? Not as fast as I would like. I've barely read past the second page.
Your father wanted you to read it. He thought YOU could make some use for it.
Mom... it's difficult.
Ever been in a poultry?
I... I've seen models at a museum...
It's NOTHING like the real thing.
Nothing like the real thing.
I've never told anyone except your dad. About that first day.
First day?
Stop TALKING, Jake. At the poultry. The first day it all happened.
I remember it. I always said I'd forgotten. But I never did.

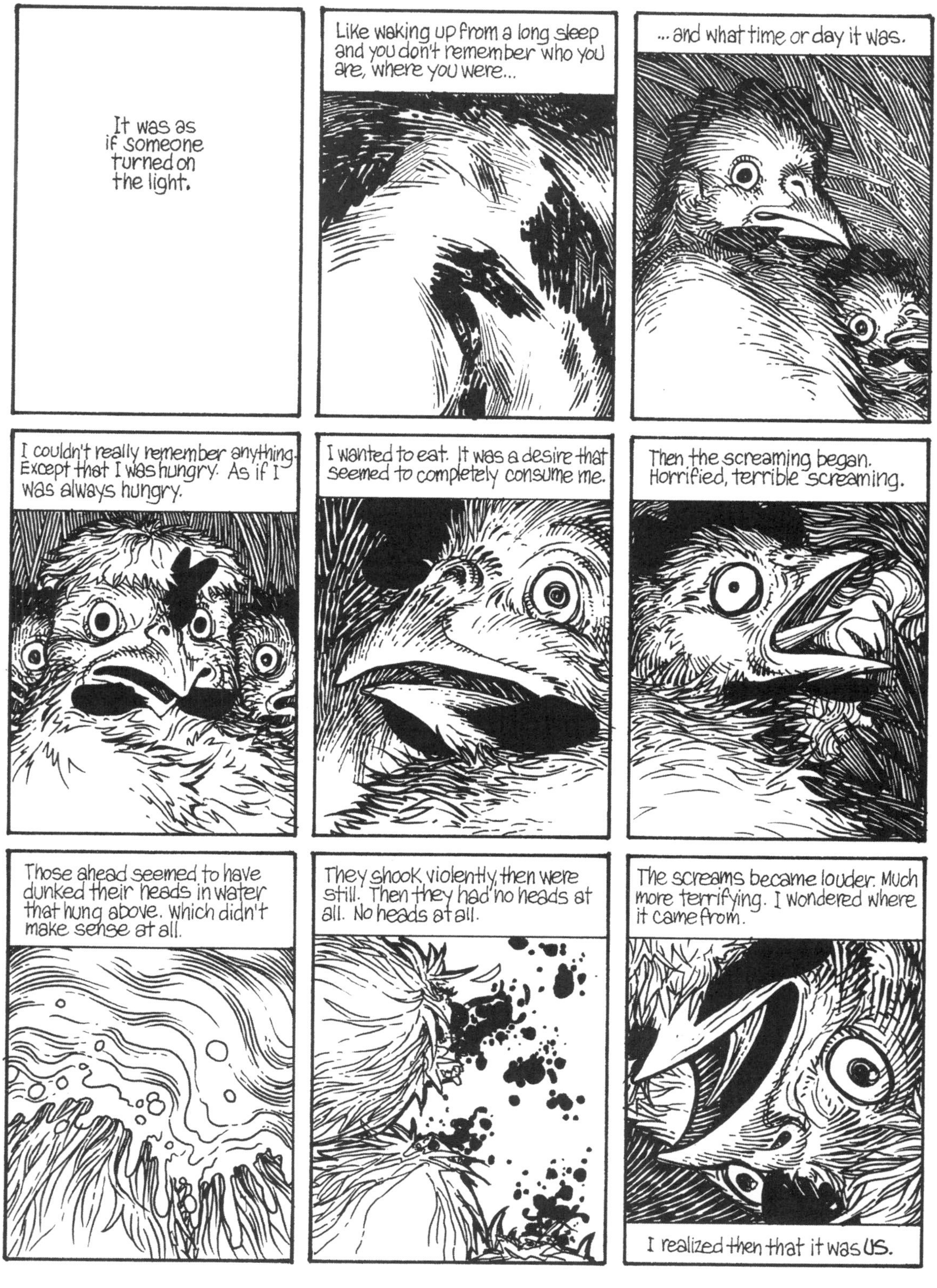
It was as if someone turned on the light.
Like waking up from a long sleep and you don't remember who you are, where you were...
... and what time or day it was.
I couldn't really remember anything. Except that I was hungry. As if I was always hungry.
I wanted to eat. It was a desire that seemed to completely consume me.
Then the screaming began. Horrified, terrible screaming.
Those ahead seemed to have dunked their heads in water that hung above. Which didn't make sense at all.
They shook violently, then were still. Then they had no heads at all. No heads at all.
The screams became louder. Much more terrifying. I wondered where it came from.
I realized then that it was US.

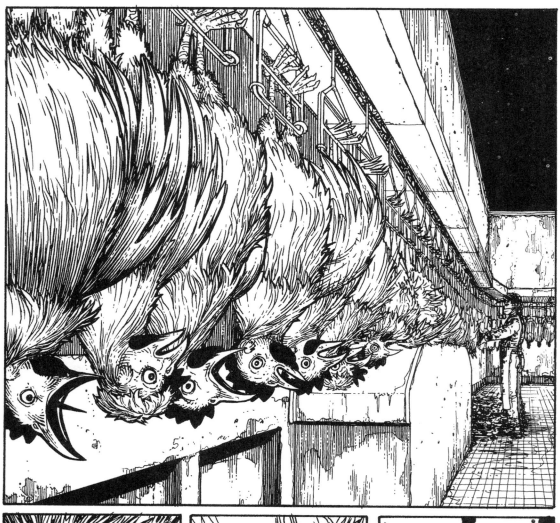

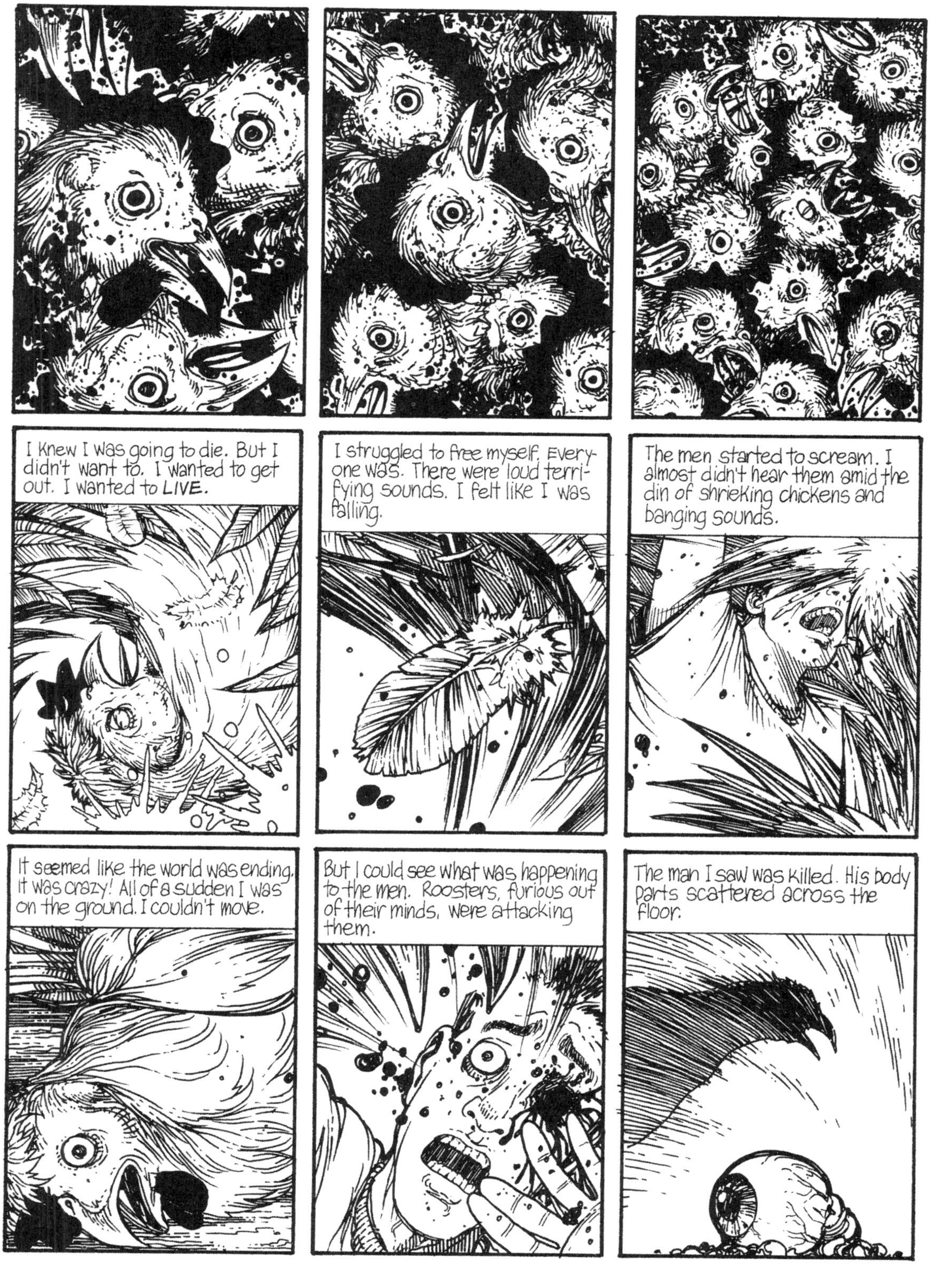
I Knew I was going to die. But I didn't want to. I wanted to get out. I wanted to **LIVE.**
I struggled to free myself. Every-one was. There were loud terri-fying sounds. I felt like I was falling.
The men started to scream. I almost didn't hear them amid the din of shrieking chickens and banging sounds.
It seemed like the world was ending. It was crazy! All of a sudden I was on the ground. I couldn't move.
But I could see what was happening to the men. Roosters, furious out of their minds, were attacking them.
The man I saw was killed. His body parts scattered across the floor.

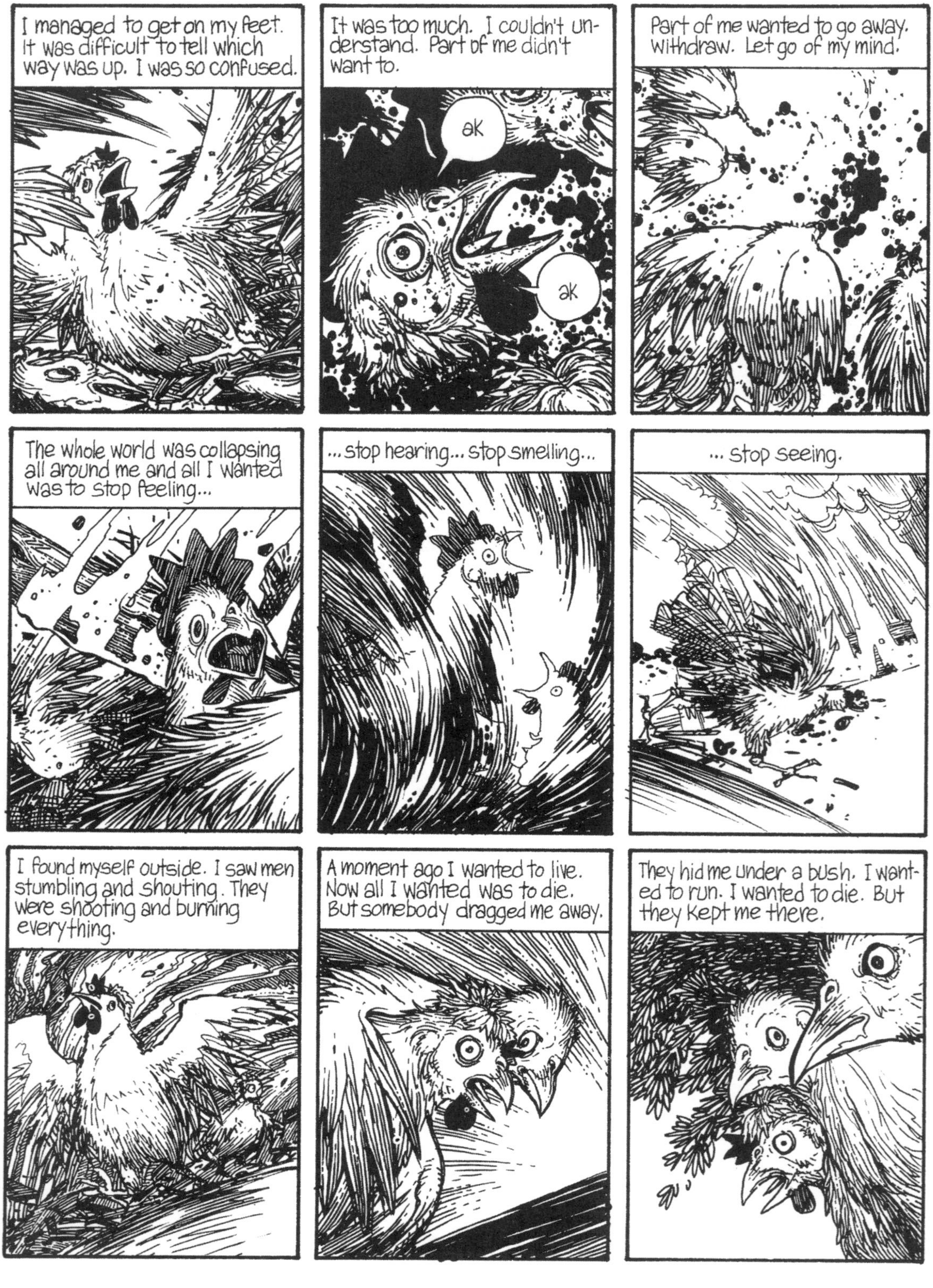
I managed to get on my feet. It was difficult to tell which way was up. I was so confused.
It was too much. I couldn't understand. Part of me didn't want to.
ak
ak
Part of me wanted to go away. Withdraw. Let go of my mind.
The whole world was collapsing all around me and all I wanted was to stop feeling...
...stop hearing... stop smelling...
... stop seeing.
I found myself outside. I saw men stumbling and shouting. They were shooting and burning everything.
A moment ago I wanted to live. Now all I wanted was to die. But somebody dragged me away.
They hid me under a bush. I wanted to run. I wanted to die. But they kept me there.

Kept me there.

Yeah ah... I think it's best you get some sleep now, mama.

"Mama"?

Shush Jake. Come on, let us go.

And for goodness sake put some CLOTHES on, boy! We have visitors!

NOVEMBER 2, 2003
I could not help but read the book now. I could not stop, even if I wanted to.

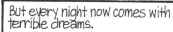

But every night now comes with terrible dreams.

I am my father. Sometimes, my mother. I am bound upside down. Electrocuted. Decapitated.

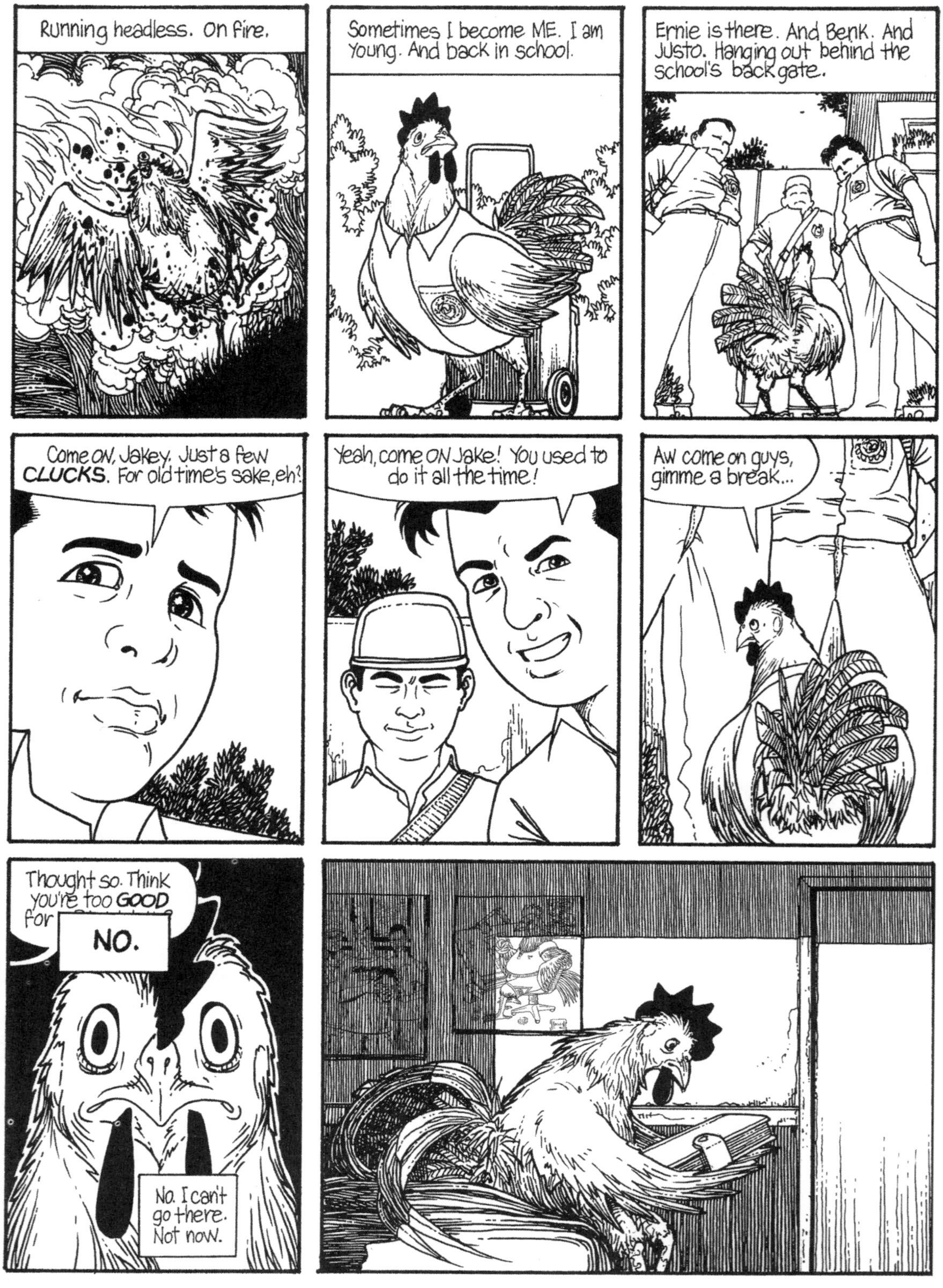
Running headless. On fire.
Sometimes I become ME. I am Young. And back in school.
Ernie is there. And Benk. And Justo. Hanging out behind the school's back gate.
Come ON, Jakey. Just a few CLUCKS. For old time's sake, eh?
Yeah, come ON Jake! You used to do it all the time!
Aw come on guys, gimme a break...
Thought so. Think you're too GOOD for
NO.
No. I can't go there. Not now.

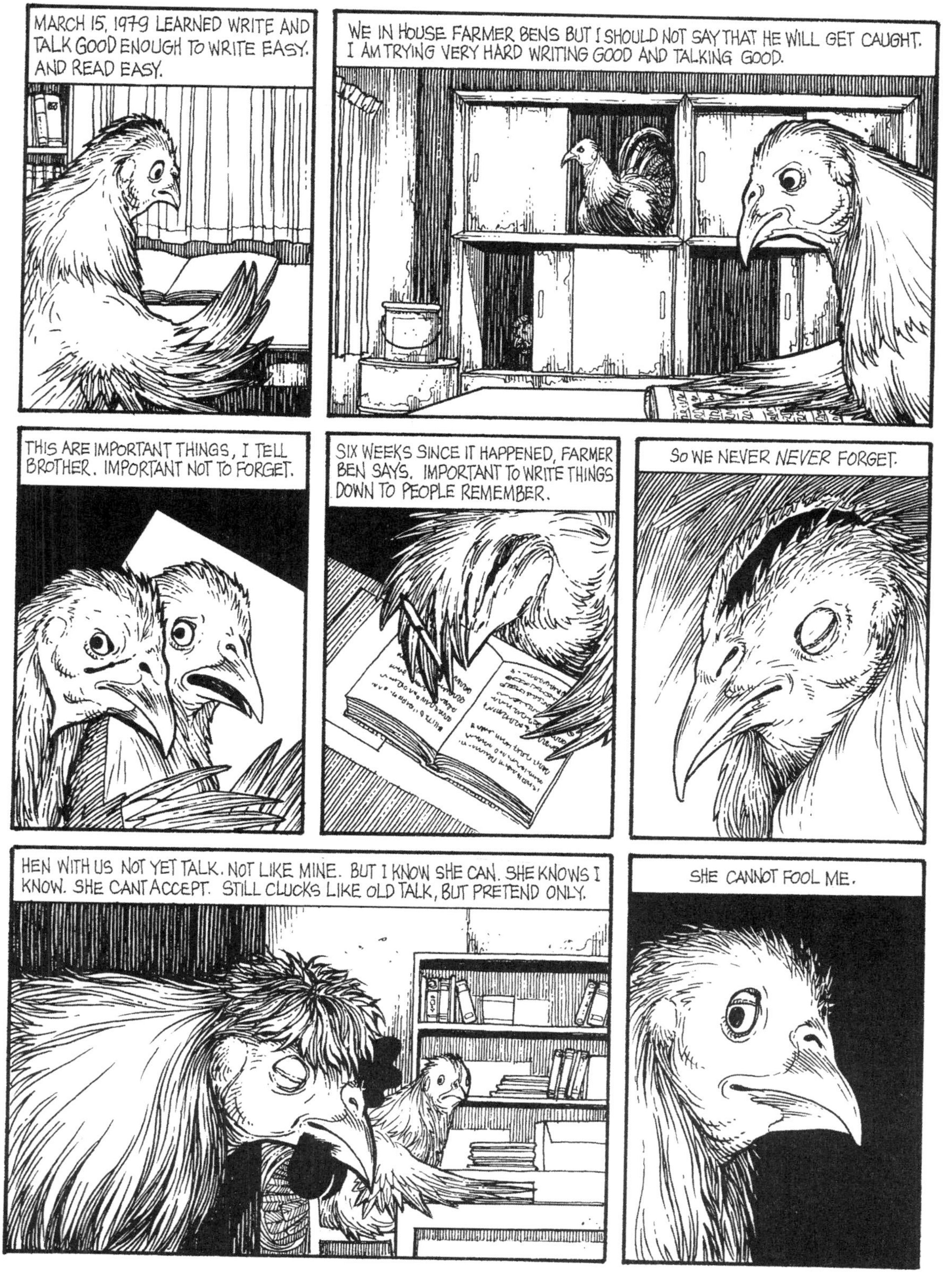
MARCH 15, 1979 LEARNED WRITE AND TALK GOOD ENOUGH TO WRITE EASY. AND READ EASY.
WE IN HOUSE FARMER BENS BUT I SHOULD NOT SAY THAT HE WILL GET CAUGHT. I AM TRYING VERY HARD WRITING GOOD AND TALKING GOOD.
THIS ARE IMPORTANT THINGS, I TELL BROTHER. IMPORTANT NOT TO FORGET.
SIX WEEKS SINCE IT HAPPENED, FARMER BEN SAYS. IMPORTANT TO WRITE THINGS DOWN TO PEOPLE REMEMBER.
SO WE NEVER *NEVER* FORGET.
HEN WITH US NOT YET TALK. NOT LIKE MINE. BUT I KNOW SHE CAN. SHE KNOWS I KNOW. SHE CANT ACCEPT. STILL CLUCKS LIKE OLD TALK, BUT PRETEND ONLY.
SHE CANNOT FOOL ME.

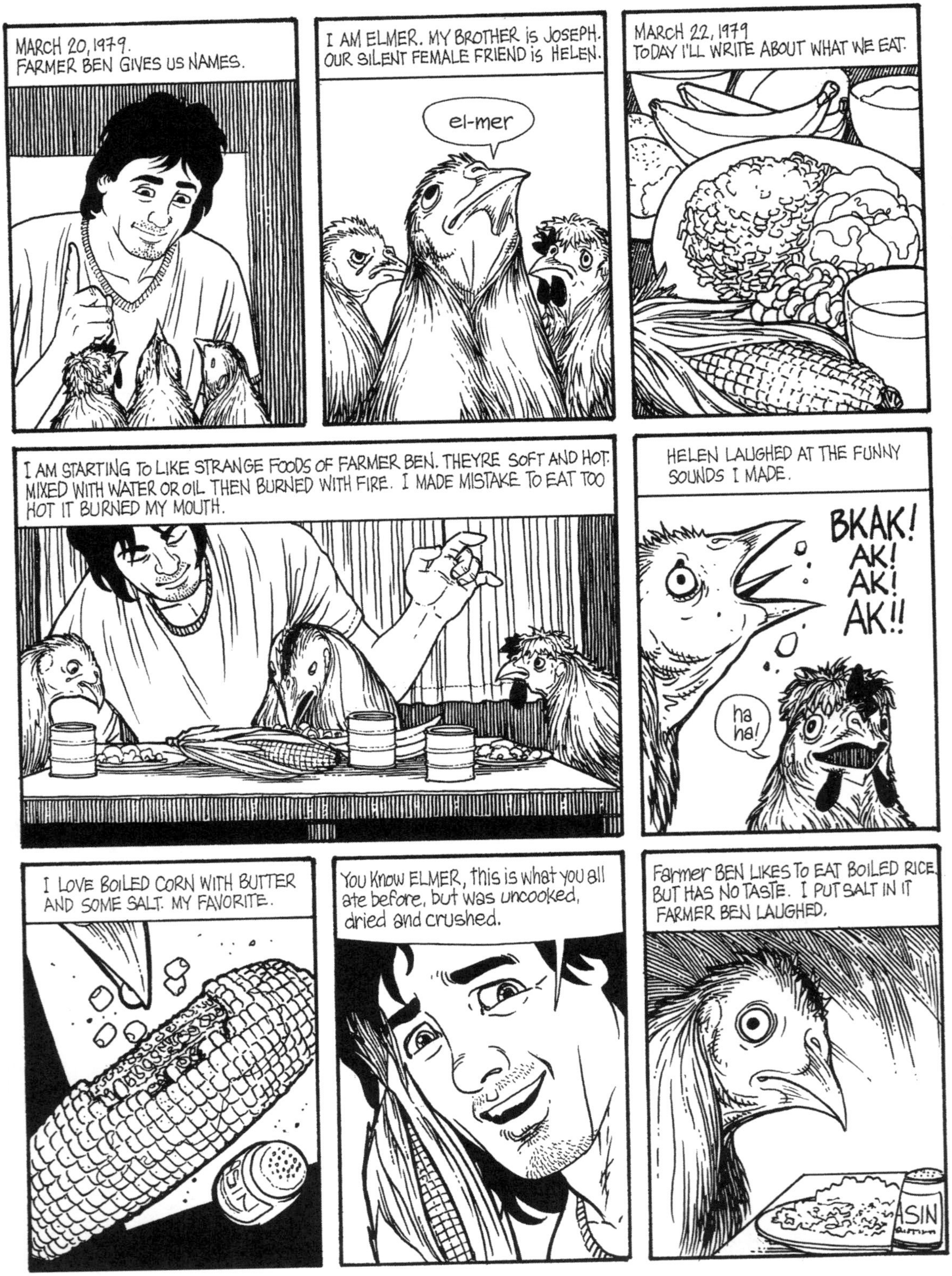
MARCH 20, 1979.
FARMER BEN GIVES US NAMES.
I AM ELMER. MY BROTHER IS JOSEPH. OUR SILENT FEMALE FRIEND IS HELEN.
el-mer
MARCH 22, 1979
TODAY I'LL WRITE ABOUT WHAT WE EAT.
I AM STARTING TO LIKE STRANGE FOODS OF FARMER BEN. THEYRE SOFT AND HOT. MIXED WITH WATER OR OIL THEN BURNED WITH FIRE. I MADE MISTAKE TO EAT TOO HOT IT BURNED MY MOUTH.
HELEN LAUGHED AT THE FUNNY SOUNDS I MADE.
BKAK! AK! AK! AK!!
ha ha!
I LOVE BOILED CORN WITH BUTTER AND SOME SALT. MY FAVORITE.
You Know ELMER, this is what you all ate before, but was uncooked, dried and crushed.
Farmer BEN LIKES TO EAT BOILED RICE. BUT HAS NO TASTE. I PUT SALT IN IT FARMER BEN LAUGHED.
ASIN

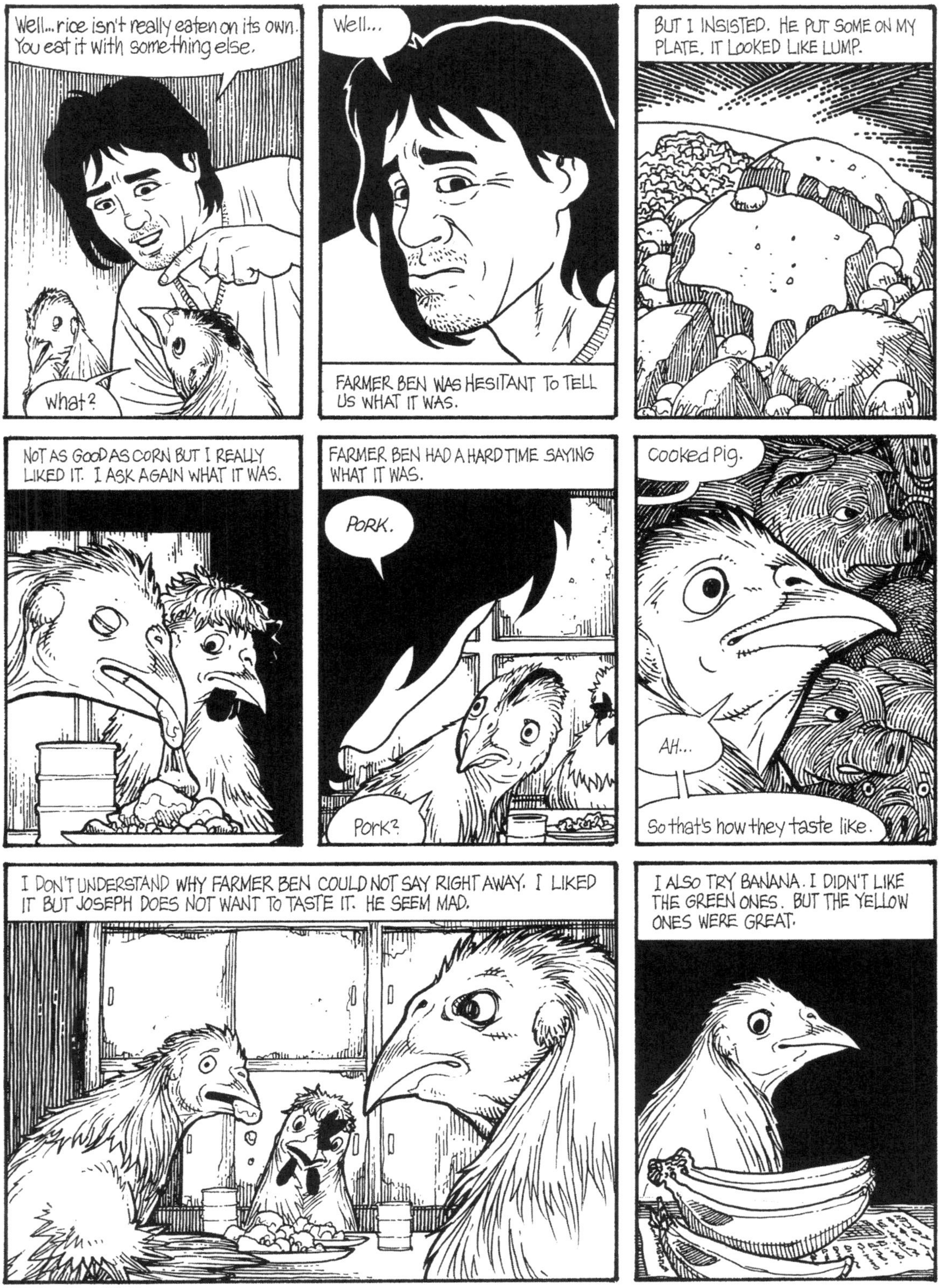
Well... rice isn't really eaten on its own. You eat it with something else.
What?
Well...
FARMER BEN WAS HESITANT TO TELL US WHAT IT WAS.
BUT I INSISTED. HE PUT SOME ON MY PLATE. IT LOOKED LIKE LUMP.
NOT AS GOOD AS CORN BUT I REALLY LIKED IT. I ASK AGAIN WHAT IT WAS.
FARMER BEN HAD A HARD TIME SAYING WHAT IT WAS.
PORK.
Pork?
Cooked Pig.
AH...
So that's how they taste like.
I DON'T UNDERSTAND WHY FARMER BEN COULD NOT SAY RIGHT AWAY. I LIKED IT BUT JOSEPH DOES NOT WANT TO TASTE IT. HE SEEM MAD.
I ALSO TRY BANANA. I DIDN'T LIKE THE GREEN ONES. BUT THE YELLOW ONES WERE GREAT.

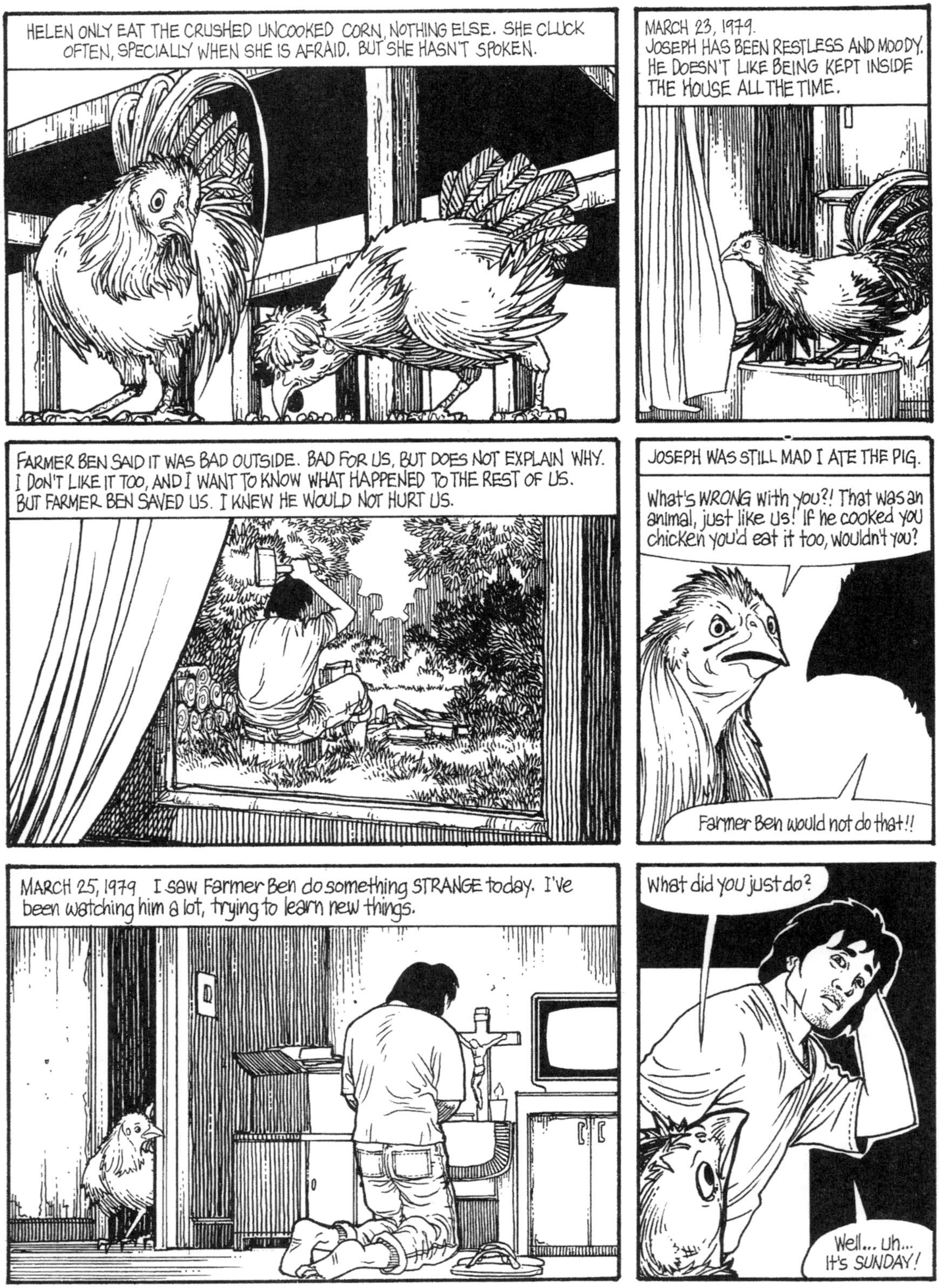
HELEN ONLY EAT THE CRUSHED UNCOOKED CORN, NOTHING ELSE. SHE CLUCK OFTEN, SPECIALLY WHEN SHE IS AFRAID. BUT SHE HASN'T SPOKEN.
MARCH 23, 1979. JOSEPH HAS BEEN RESTLESS AND MOODY. HE DOESN'T LIKE BEING KEPT INSIDE THE HOUSE ALL THE TIME.
FARMER BEN SAID IT WAS BAD OUTSIDE. BAD FOR US, BUT DOES NOT EXPLAIN WHY. I DON'T LIKE IT TOO, AND I WANT TO KNOW WHAT HAPPENED TO THE REST OF US. BUT FARMER BEN SAVED US. I KNEW HE WOULD NOT HURT US.
JOSEPH WAS STILL MAD I ATE THE PIG.
What's WRONG with you?! That was an animal, just like us! If he cooked you chicken you'd eat it too, wouldn't you?
Farmer Ben would not do that!!
MARCH 25, 1979 I saw Farmer Ben do something STRANGE today. I've been watching him a lot, trying to learn new things.
What did you just do?
Well... uh... It's SUNDAY!

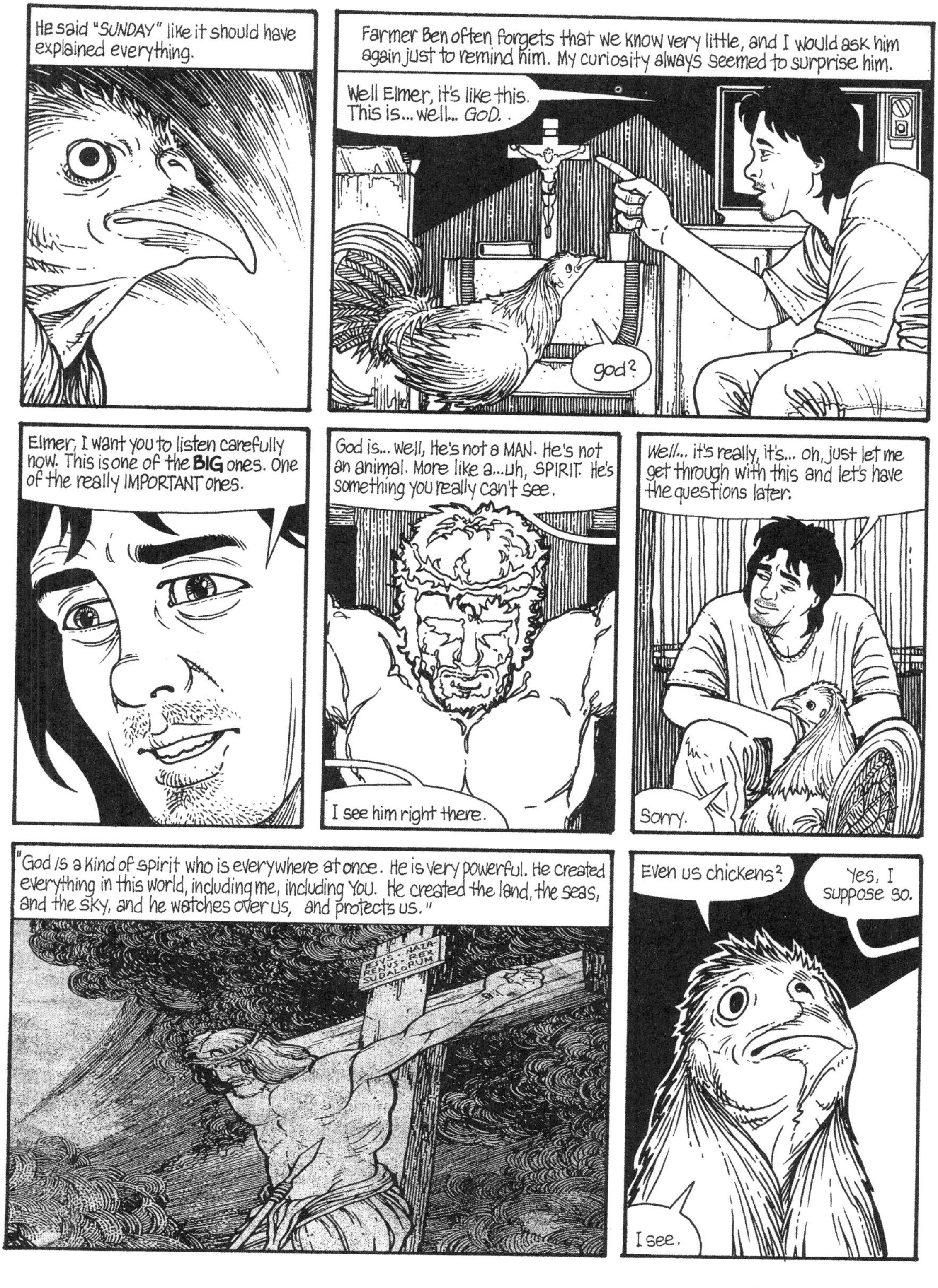
He said "SUNDAY" like it should have explained everything.
Farmer Ben often forgets that we know very little, and I would ask him again just to remind him. My curiosity always seemed to surprise him.
Well Elmer, it's like this. This is... well... GOD.
god?
Elmer, I want you to listen carefully now. This is one of the BIG ones. One of the really IMPORTANT ones.
God is... well, He's not a MAN. He's not an animal. More like a...uh, SPIRIT. He's something you really can't see.
I see him right there.
Well... it's really, it's... oh, just let me get through with this and let's have the questions later.
Sorry.
"God is a kind of spirit who is everywhere at once. He is very powerful. He created everything in this world, including me, including YOU. He created the land, the seas, and the sky, and he watches over us, and protects us."
Even us chickens?
Yes, I suppose so.
I see.

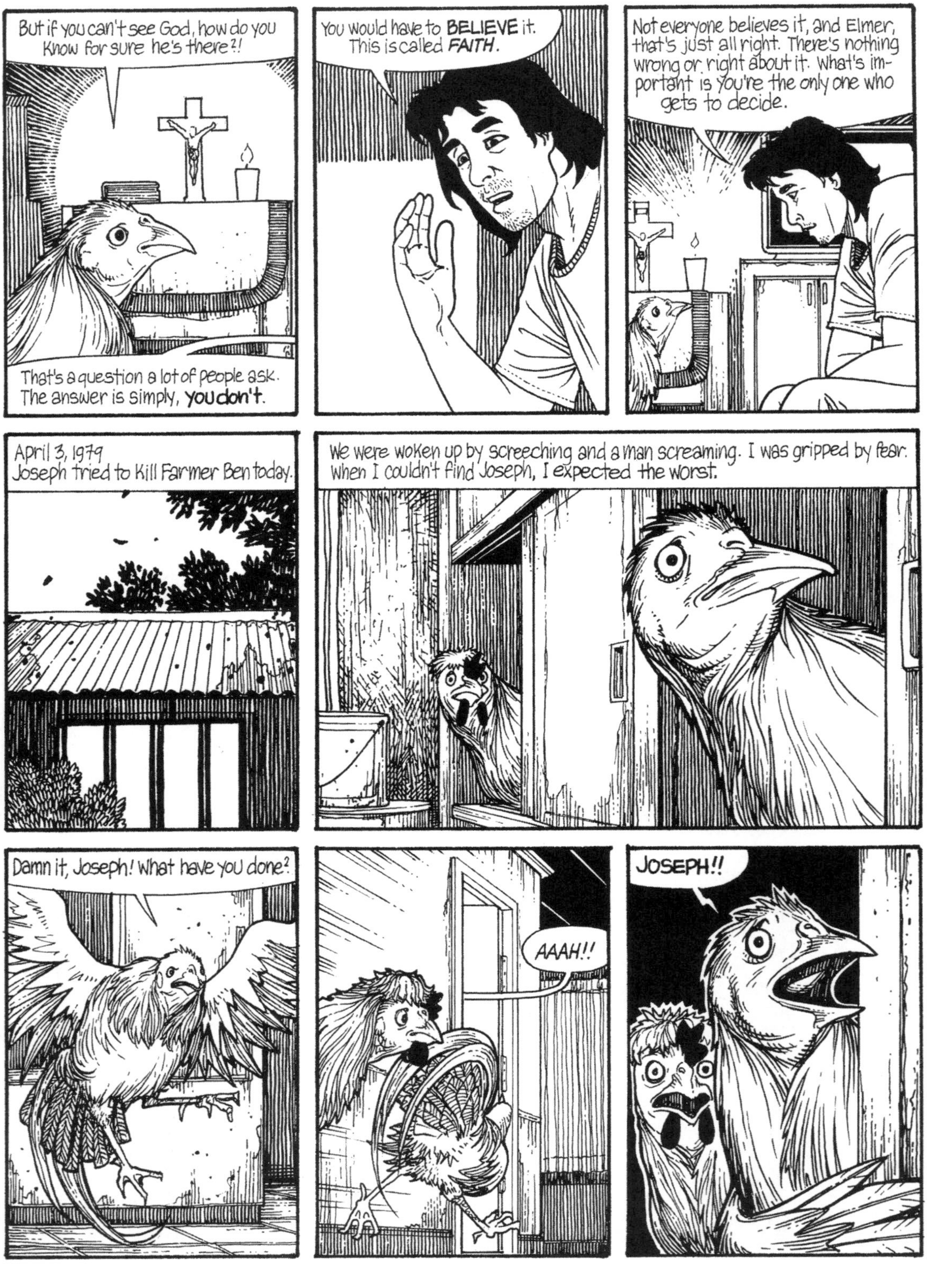

But if you can't see God, how do you know for sure he's there?!
That's a question a lot of people ask. The answer is simply, you don't.
You would have to BELIEVE it. This is called FAITH.
Not everyone believes it, and Elmer, that's just all right. There's nothing wrong or right about it. What's important is you're the only one who gets to decide.
April 3, 1979
Joseph tried to kill Farmer Ben today.
We were woken up by screeching and a man screaming. I was gripped by fear. When I couldn't find Joseph, I expected the worst.
Damn it, Joseph! What have you done?
AAAH!!
JOSEPH!!

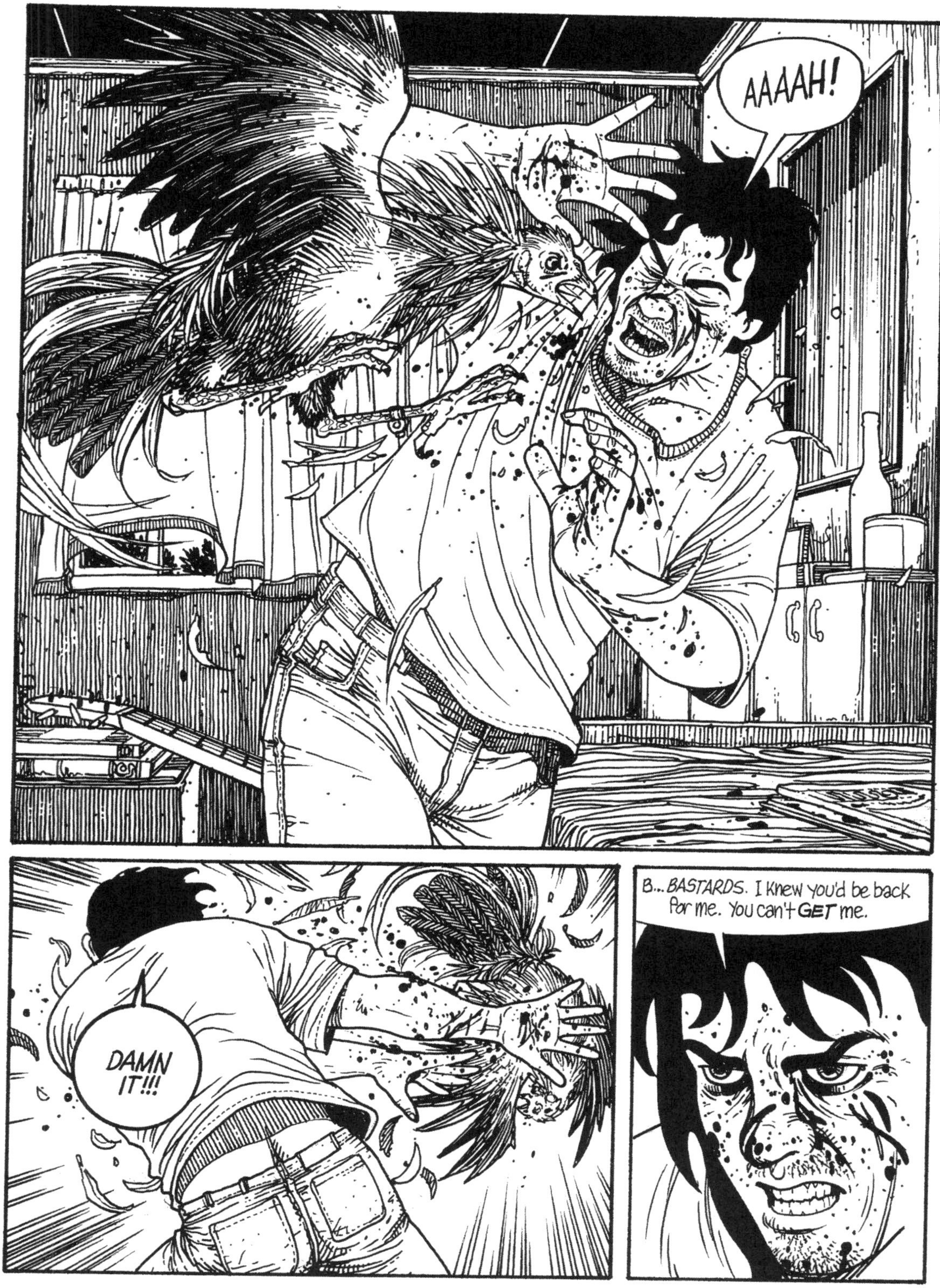
AAAAH!
DAMN IT!!!
B... BASTARDS. I knew you'd be back for me. You can't GET me.

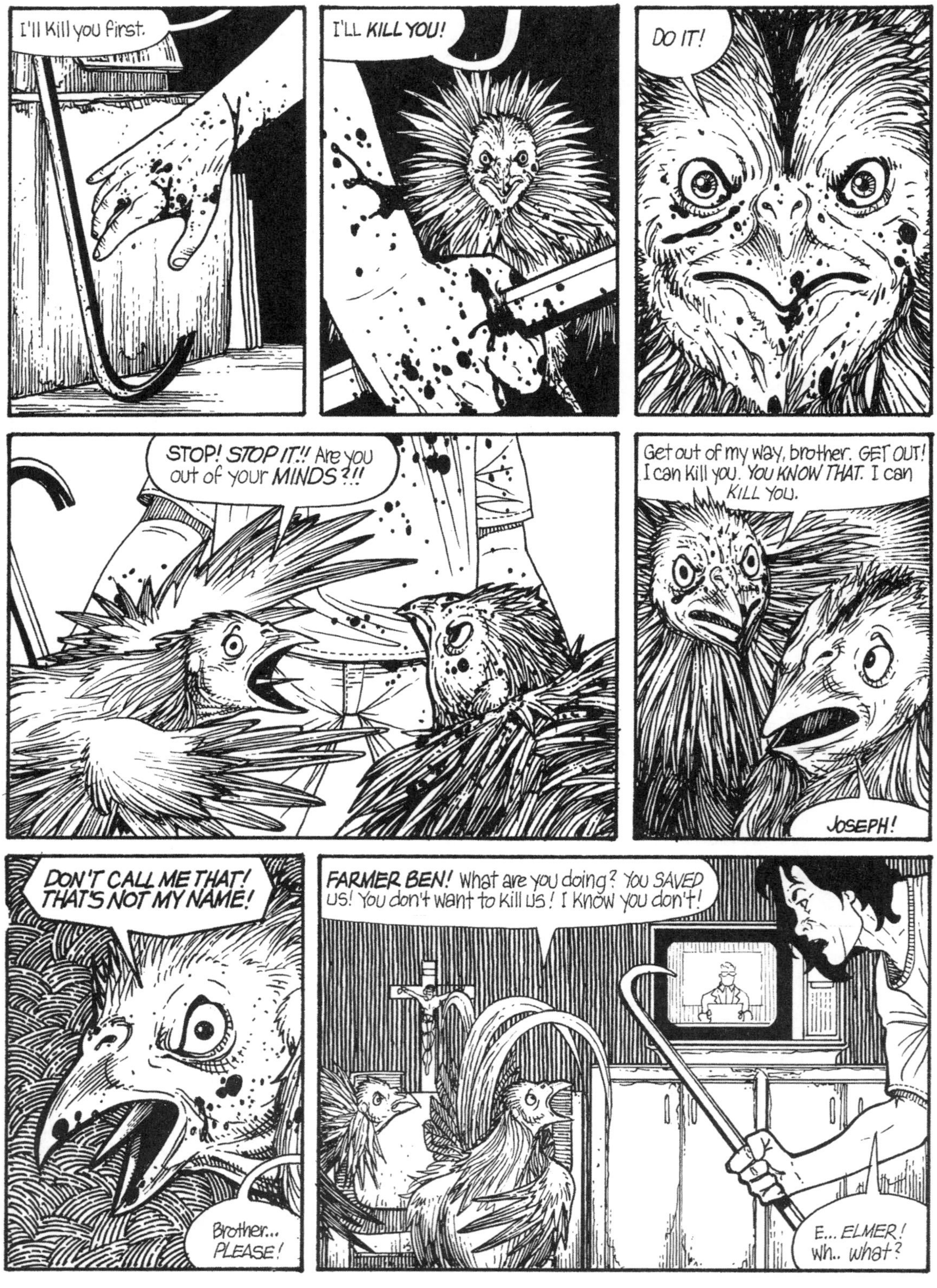

I'll Kill you first.
I'LL KILL YOU!
DO IT!
STOP! STOP IT!! Are you out of your MINDS?!!
Get out of my way, brother. GET OUT! I can Kill you. YOU KNOW THAT. I can KILL YOU.
JOSEPH!
DON'T CALL ME THAT! THAT'S NOT MY NAME!
Brother... PLEASE!
FARMER BEN! What are you doing? You SAVED us! You don't want to Kill us! I Know you don't!
E... ELMER! Wh.. what?

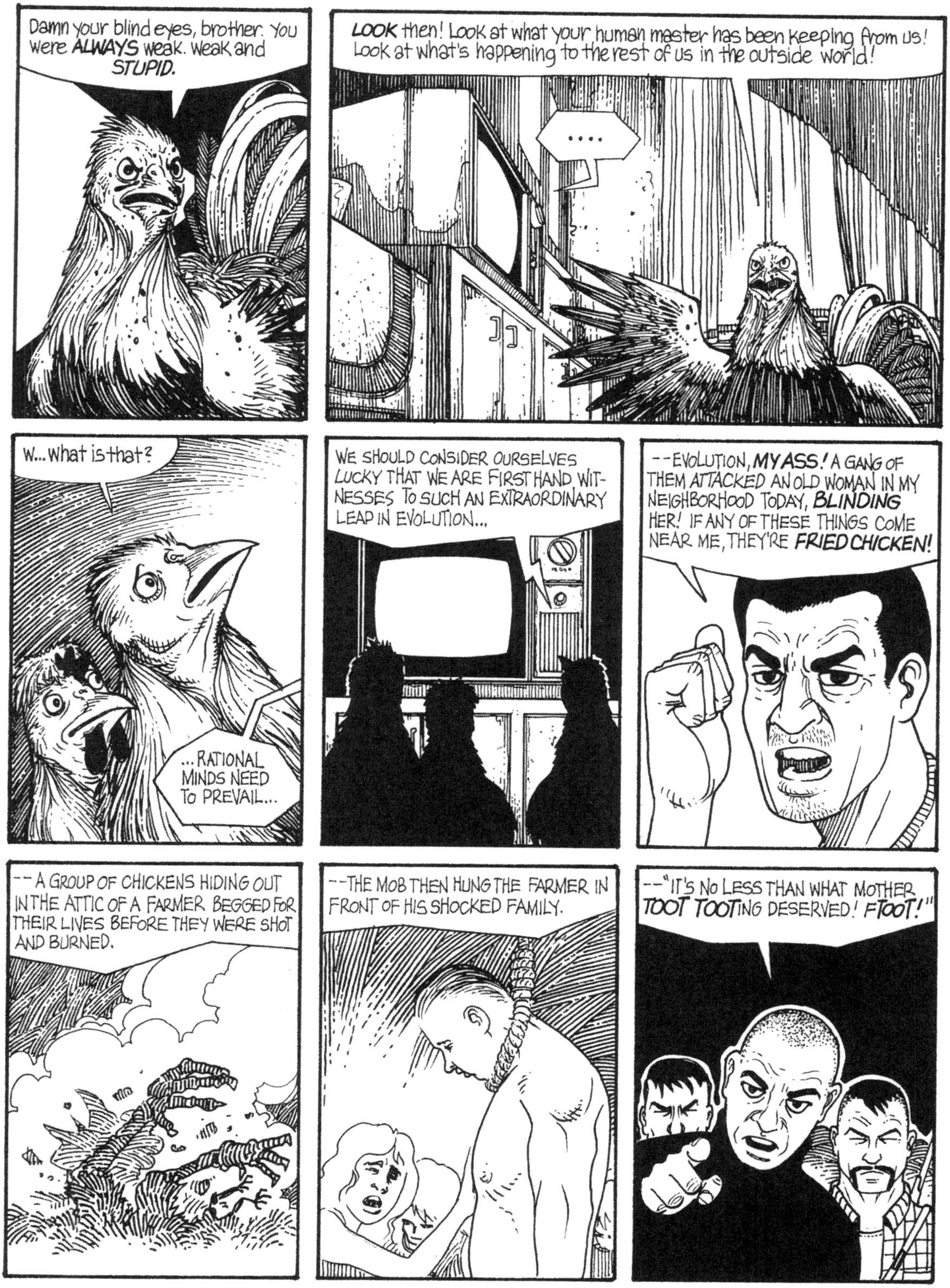
Damn your blind eyes, brother. You were ALWAYS weak. Weak and STUPID.
LOOK then! Look at what your human master has been keeping from us! Look at what's happening to the rest of us in the outside world!
....
W... What is that?
WE SHOULD CONSIDER OURSELVES LUCKY THAT WE ARE FIRST HAND WITNESSES TO SUCH AN EXTRAORDINARY LEAP IN EVOLUTION...
...RATIONAL MINDS NEED TO PREVAIL...
--EVOLUTION, MY ASS! A GANG OF THEM ATTACKED AN OLD WOMAN IN MY NEIGHBORHOOD TODAY, BLINDING HER! IF ANY OF THESE THINGS COME NEAR ME, THEY'RE FRIED CHICKEN!
--A GROUP OF CHICKENS HIDING OUT IN THE ATTIC OF A FARMER BEGGED FOR THEIR LIVES BEFORE THEY WERE SHOT AND BURNED.
--THE MOB THEN HUNG THE FARMER IN FRONT OF HIS SHOCKED FAMILY.
--"IT'S NO LESS THAN WHAT MOTHER TOOT TOOTING DESERVED! FTOOT!"

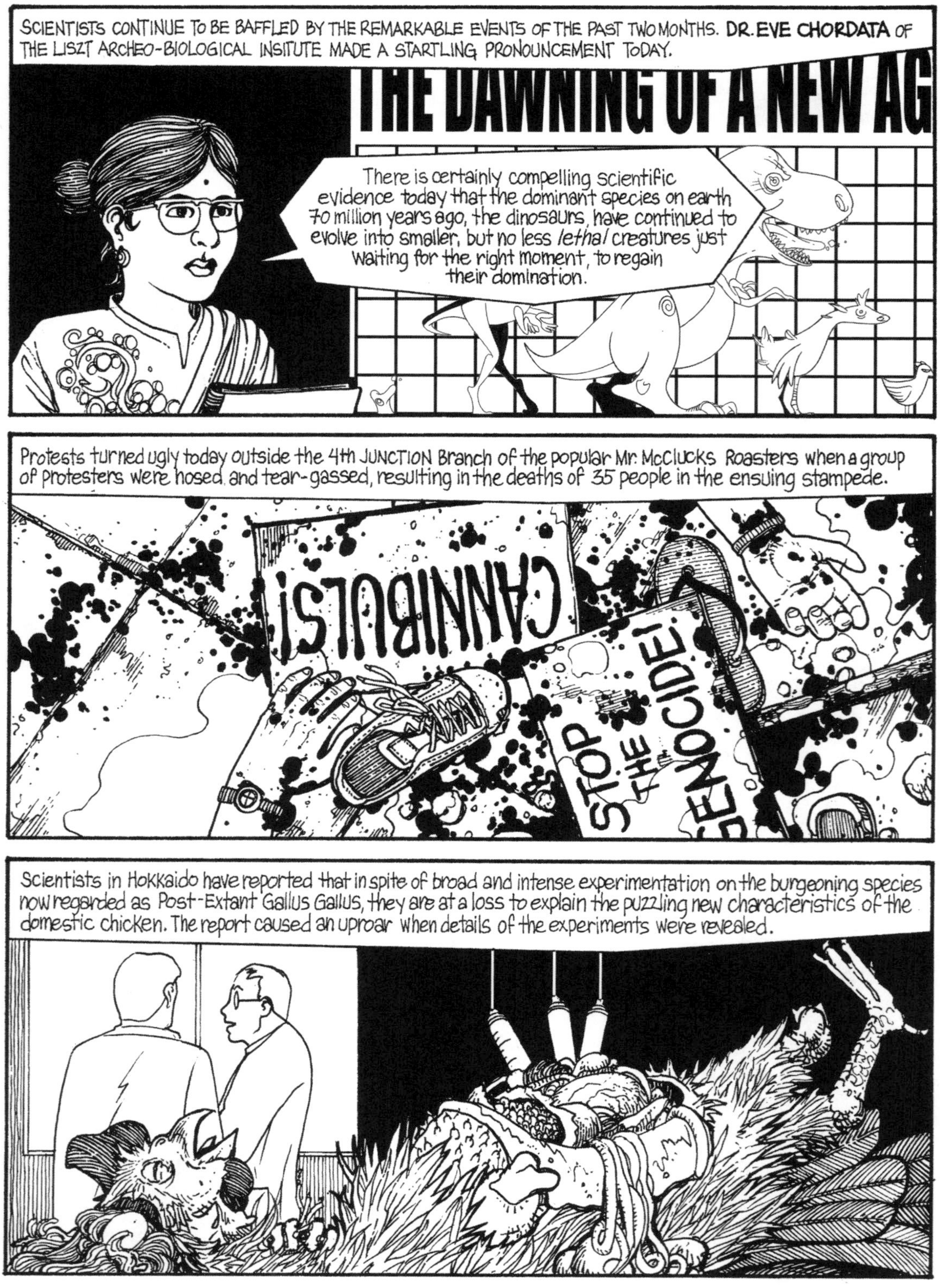
SCIENTISTS CONTINUE TO BE BAFFLED BY THE REMARKABLE EVENTS OF THE PAST TWO MONTHS. DR. EVE CHORDATA OF THE LISZT ARCHEO-BIOLOGICAL INSITUTE MADE A STARTLING PRONOUNCEMENT TODAY.
THE DAWNING OF A NEW AG
There is certainly compelling scientific evidence today that the dominant species on earth 70 million years ago, the dinosaurs, have continued to evolve into smaller, but no less *lethal* creatures just waiting for the right moment, to regain their domination.
Protests turned ugly today outside the 4th JUNCTION Branch of the popular Mr. McClucks Roasters when a group of protesters were hosed, and tear-gassed, resulting in the deaths of 35 people in the ensuing stampede.
CANNIBULS!
STOP THE ENOCIDE!
Scientists in Hokkaido have reported that in spite of broad and intense experimentation on the burgeoning species now regarded as Post-Extant Gallus Gallus, they are at a loss to explain the puzzling new characteristics of the domestic chicken. The report caused an uproar when details of the experiments were revealed.

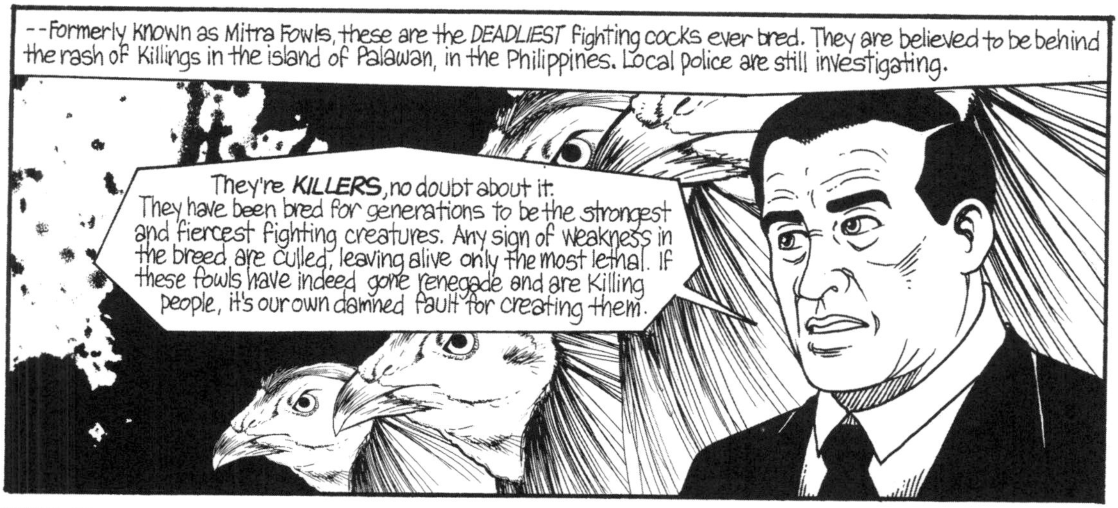
--Formerly known as Mitra Fowls, these are the DEADLIEST fighting cocks ever bred. They are believed to be behind the rash of killings in the island of Palawan, in the Philippines. Local police are still investigating.
They're KILLERS, no doubt about it. They have been bred for generations to be the strongest and fiercest fighting creatures. Any sign of weakness in the breed are culled, leaving alive only the most lethal. If these fowls have indeed gone renegade and are killing people, it's our own damned fault for creating them.

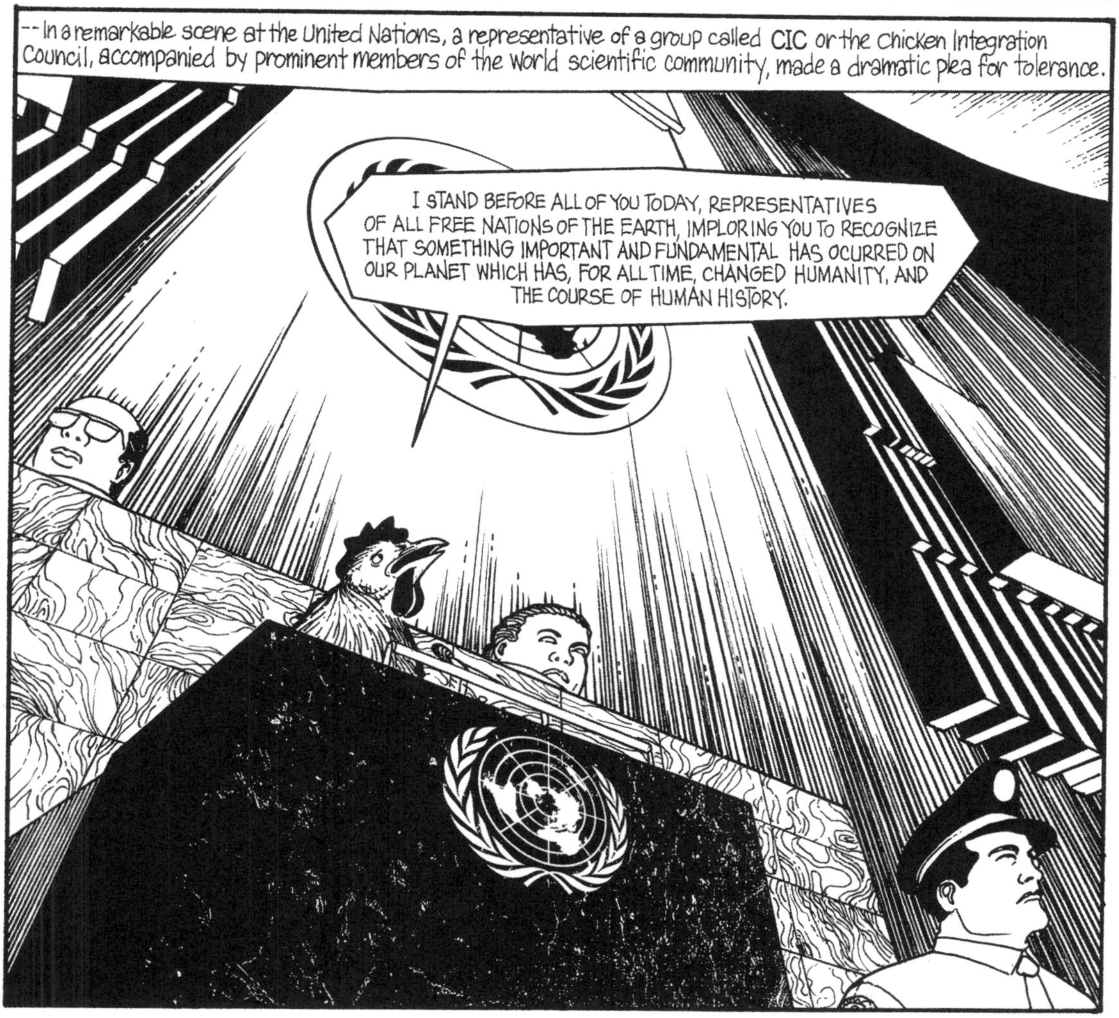
--In a remarkable scene at the United Nations, a representative of a group called CIC or the Chicken Integration Council, accompanied by prominent members of the world scientific community, made a dramatic plea for tolerance.
I STAND BEFORE ALL OF YOU TODAY, REPRESENTATIVES OF ALL FREE NATIONS OF THE EARTH, IMPLORING YOU TO RECOGNIZE THAT SOMETHING IMPORTANT AND FUNDAMENTAL HAS OCURRED ON OUR PLANET WHICH HAS, FOR ALL TIME, CHANGED HUMANITY, AND THE COURSE OF HUMAN HISTORY.

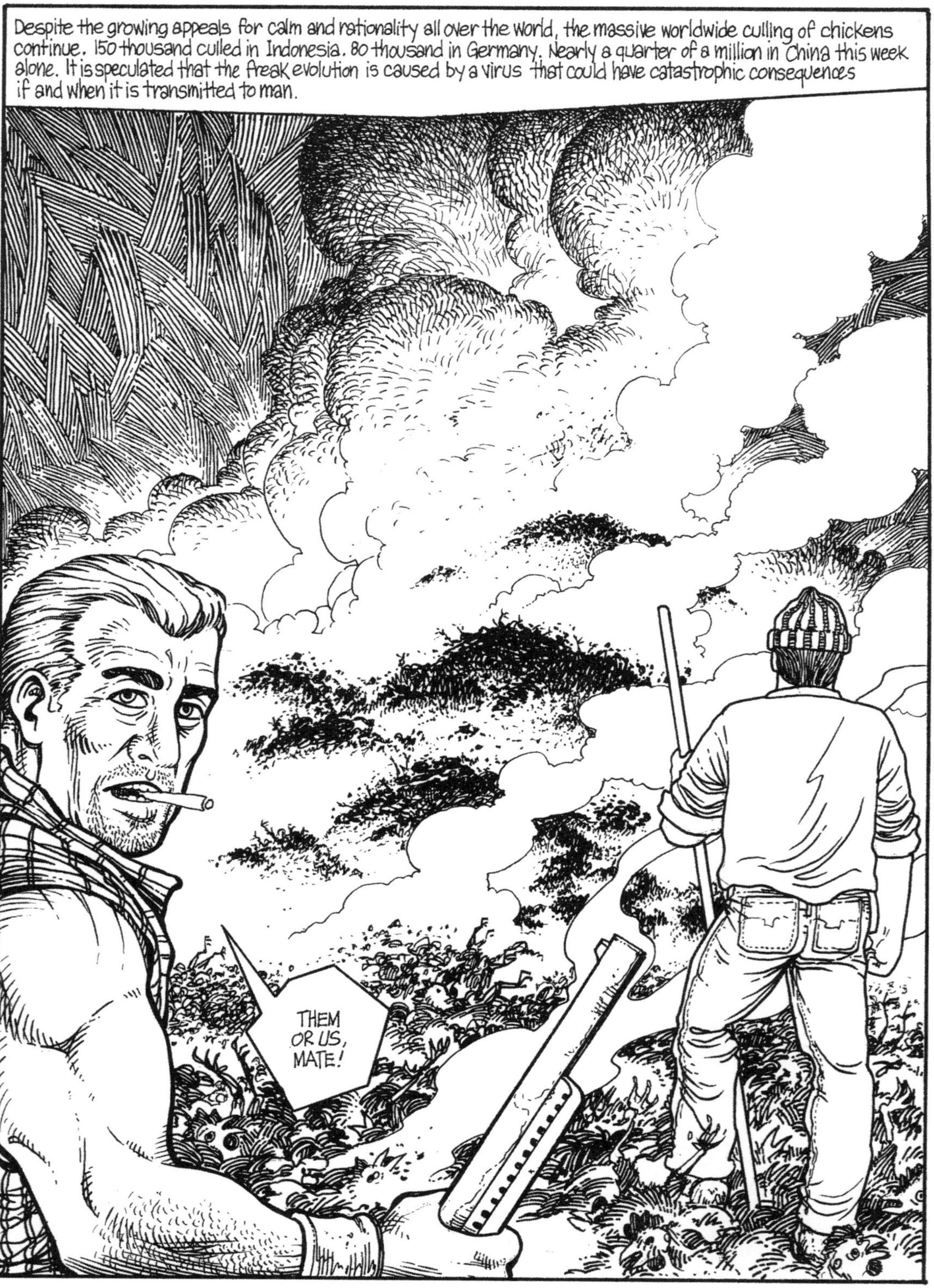
Despite the growing appeals for calm and rationality all over the world, the massive worldwide culling of chickens continue. 150 thousand culled in Indonesia. 80 thousand in Germany. Nearly a quarter of a million in China this week alone. It is speculated that the freak evolution is caused by a virus that could have catastrophic consequences if and when it is transmitted to man.
THEM OR US, MATE!

-- 240 people dead in the latest terrorist attack that ocurred at a bus terminal in Manila. A group calling themselves the "GALLUS REX" have claimed responsibility. In a shocking video broadcast on national TV, the leader of the group, Dominador Apat promises more attacks unless atrocities against chickens stop.
What is 250 people compared to the *MILLIONS* of us you have massacred? To the *MILLIONS* you still put to death every day? We assure you that more people will die unless your inhuman crimes against us cease to continue. Do *NOT* force our hand.

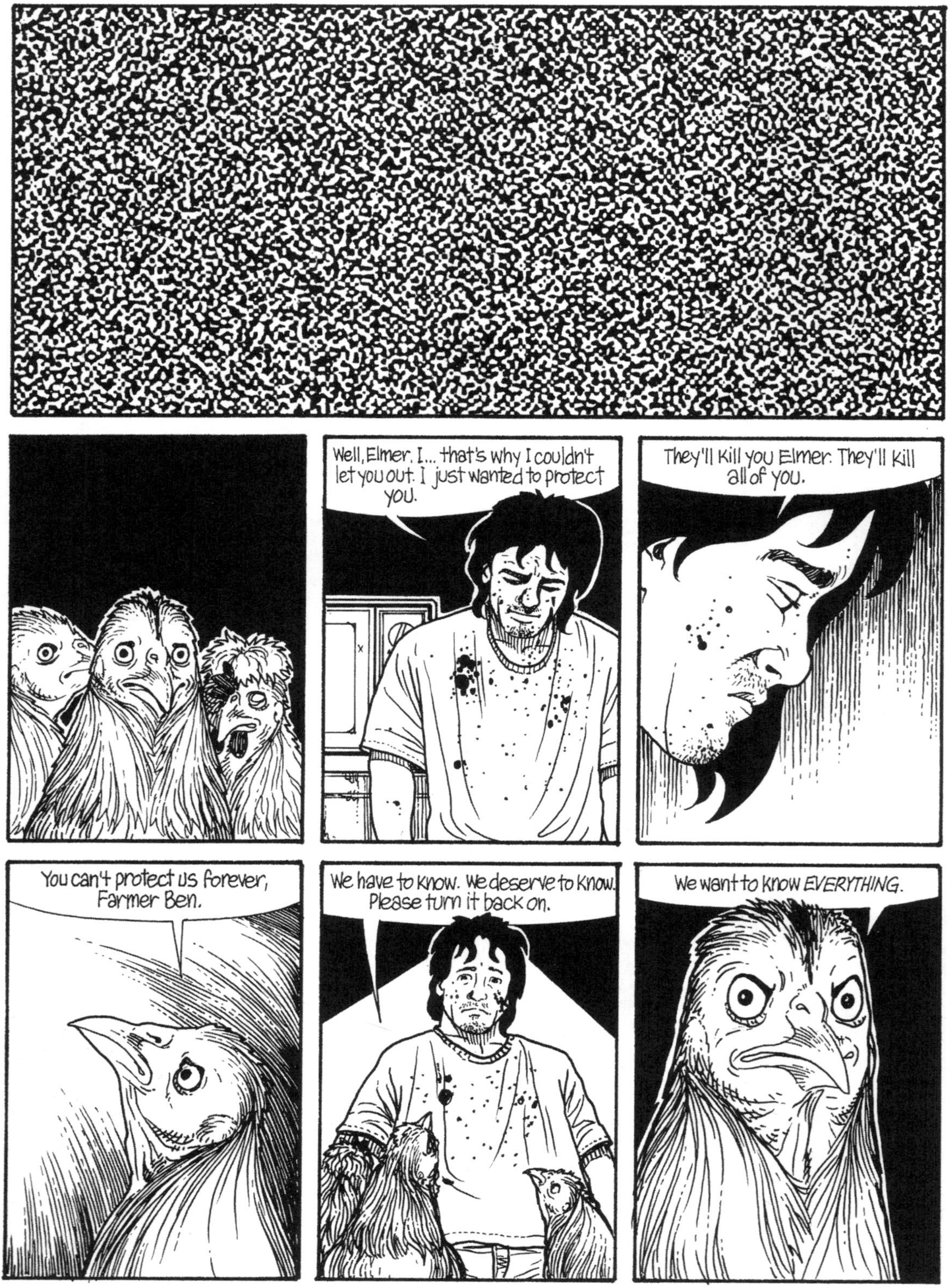
Well, Elmer. I... that's why I couldn't let you out. I just wanted to protect you.
They'll kill you Elmer. They'll kill all of you.
You can't protect us forever, Farmer Ben.
We have to know. We deserve to know. Please turn it back on.
We want to know EVERYTHING.

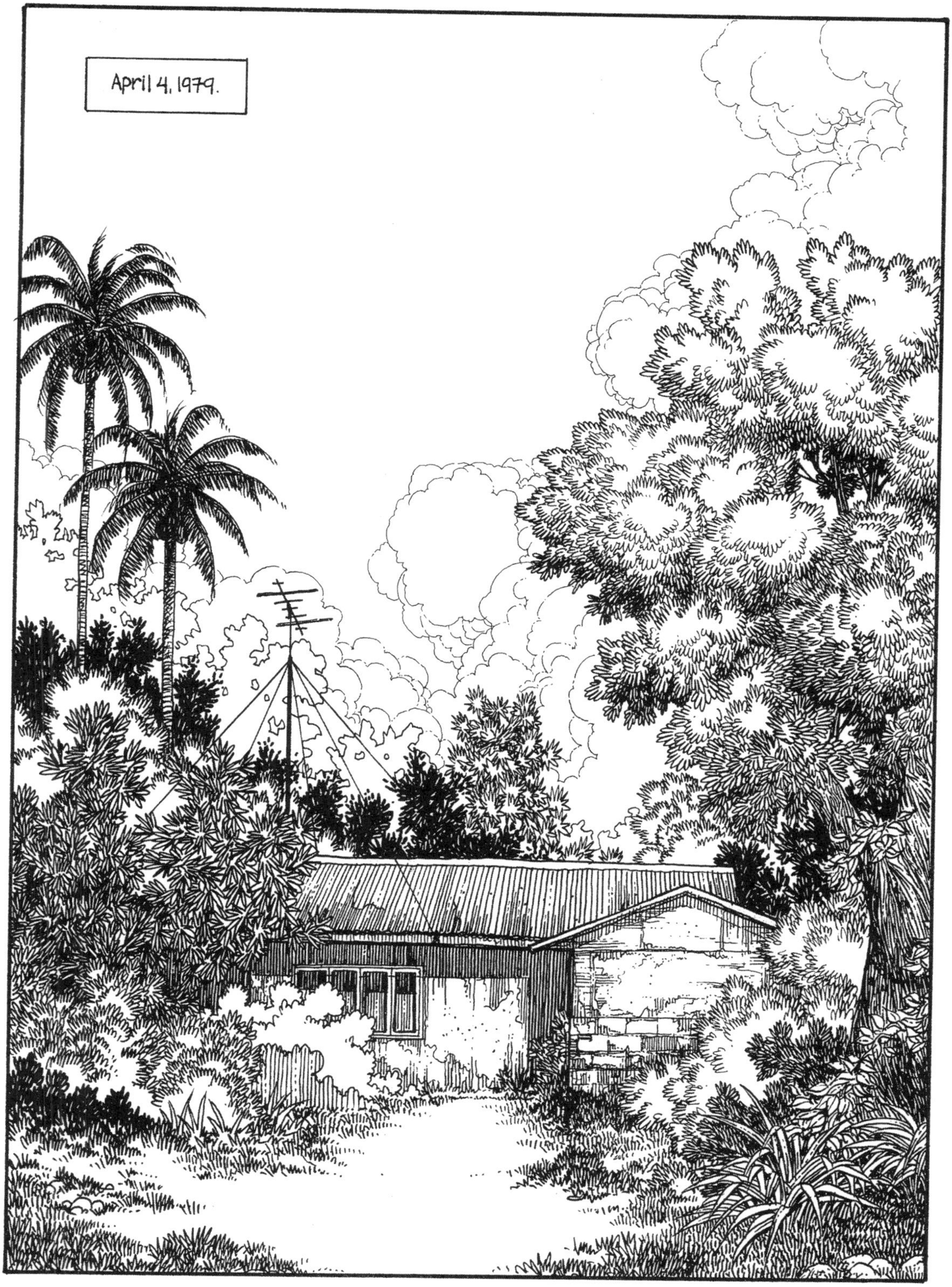
April 4, 1979.

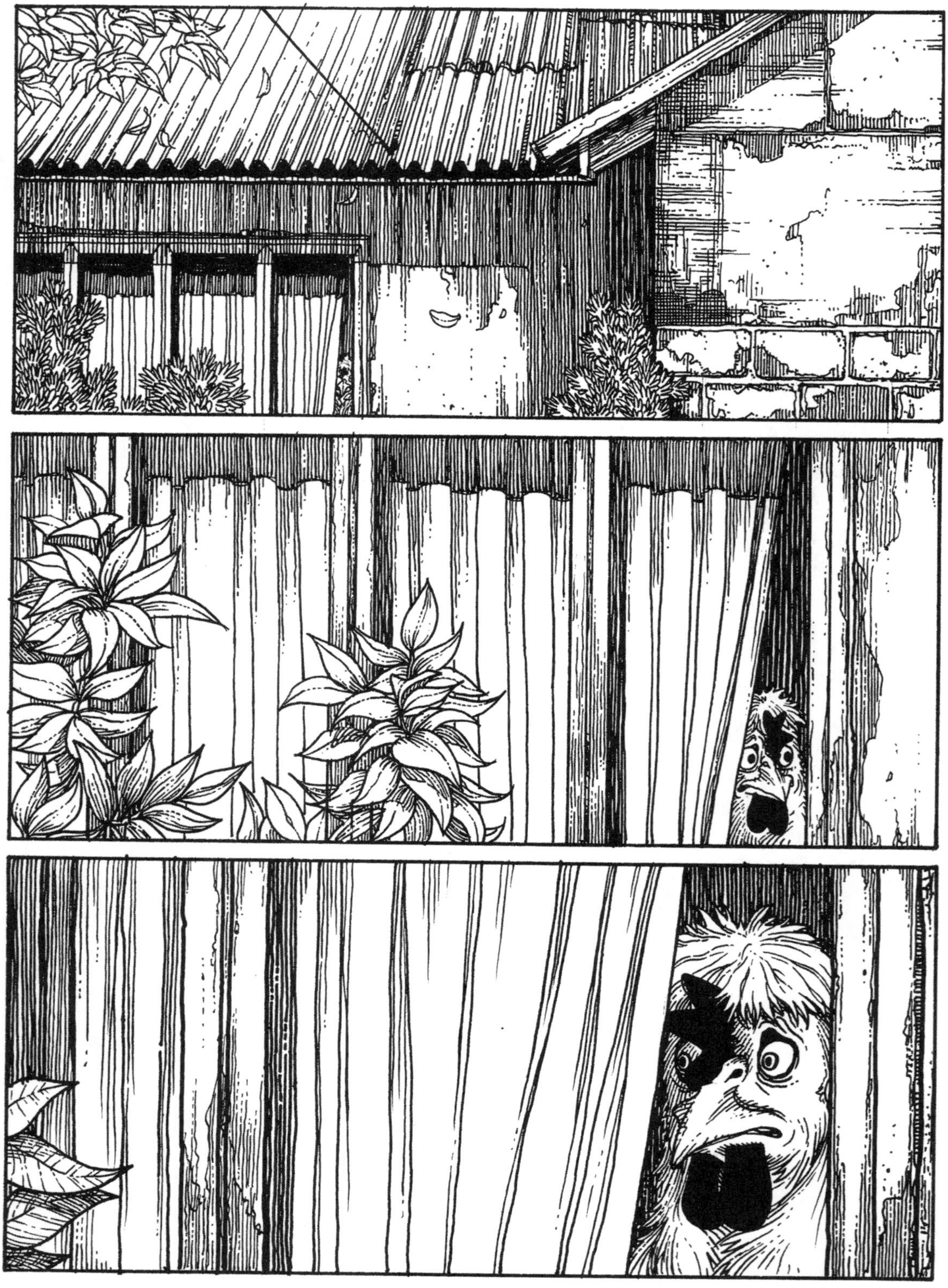

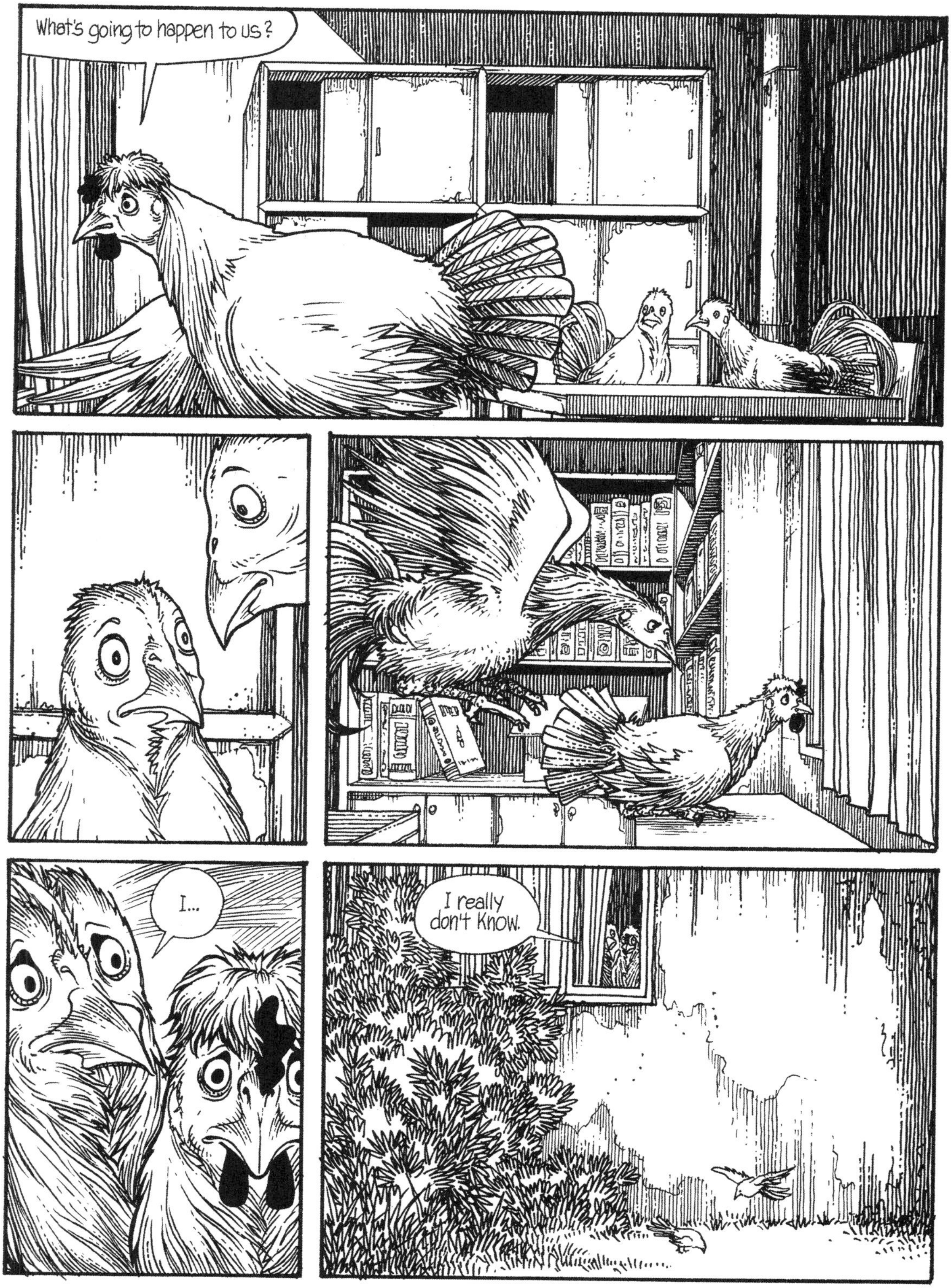
What's going to happen to us?
I...
I really don't know.

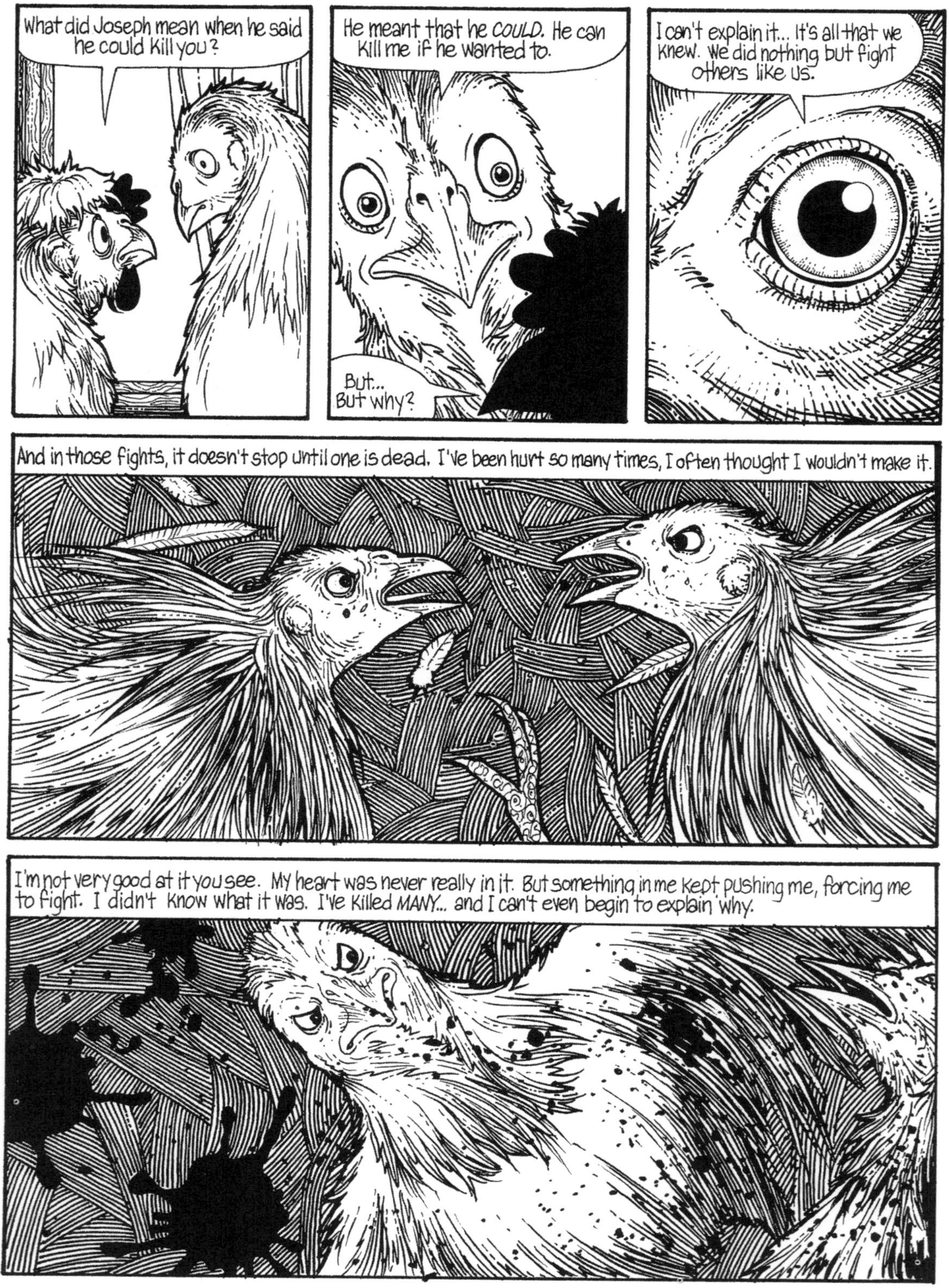
What did Joseph mean when he said he could kill you?
He meant that he *COULD*. He can kill me if he wanted to.
But... But why?
I can't explain it... It's all that we knew. We did nothing but fight others like us.
And in those fights, it doesn't stop until one is dead. I've been hurt so many times, I often thought I wouldn't make it.
I'm not very good at it you see. My heart was never really in it. But something in me kept pushing me, forcing me to fight. I didn't know what it was. I've killed *MANY*... and I can't even begin to explain why.

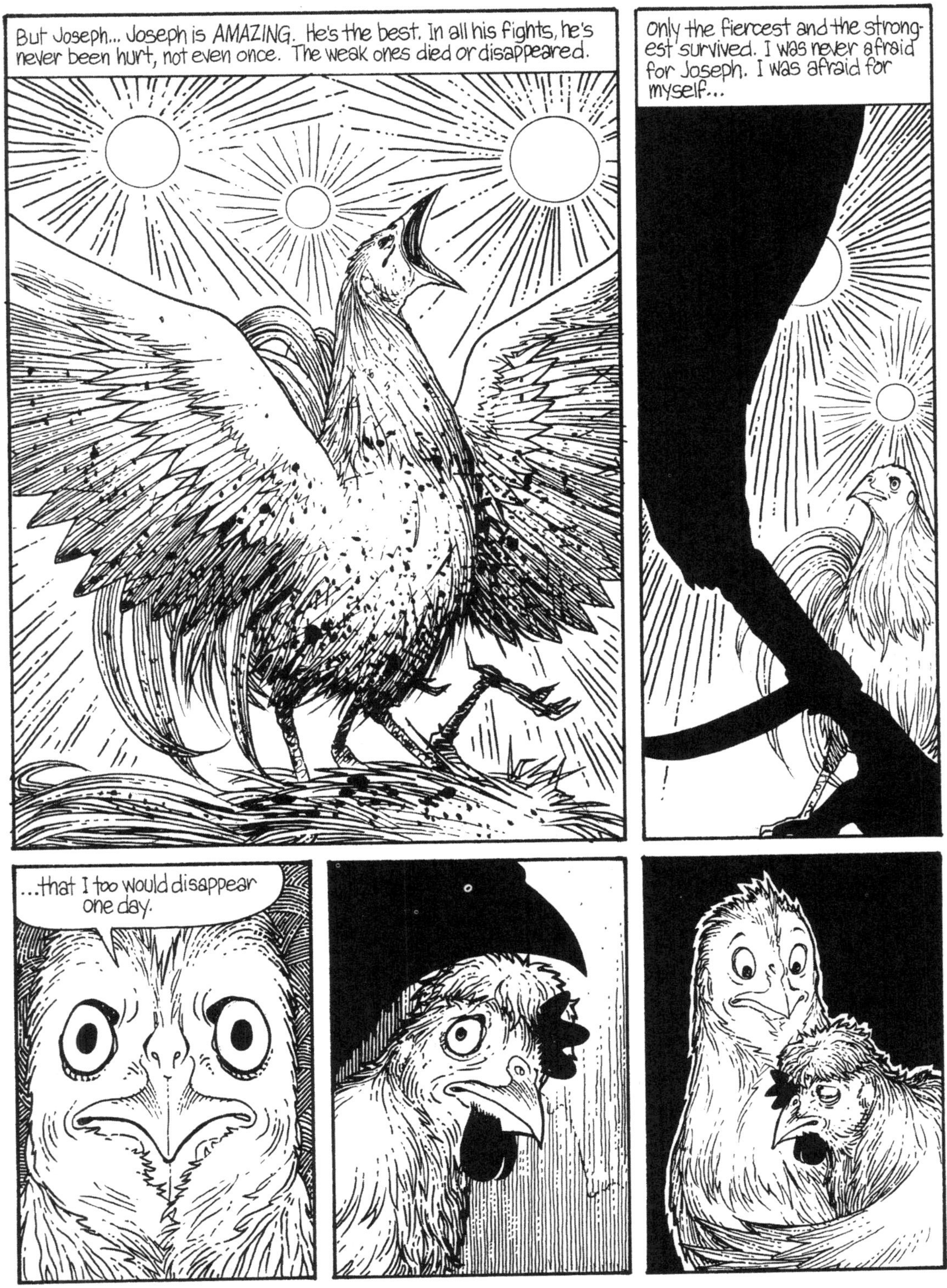
But Joseph... Joseph is AMAZING. He's the best. In all his fights, he's never been hurt, not even once. The weak ones died or disappeared.
Only the fiercest and the strongest survived. I was never afraid for Joseph. I was afraid for myself...
...that I too would disappear one day.

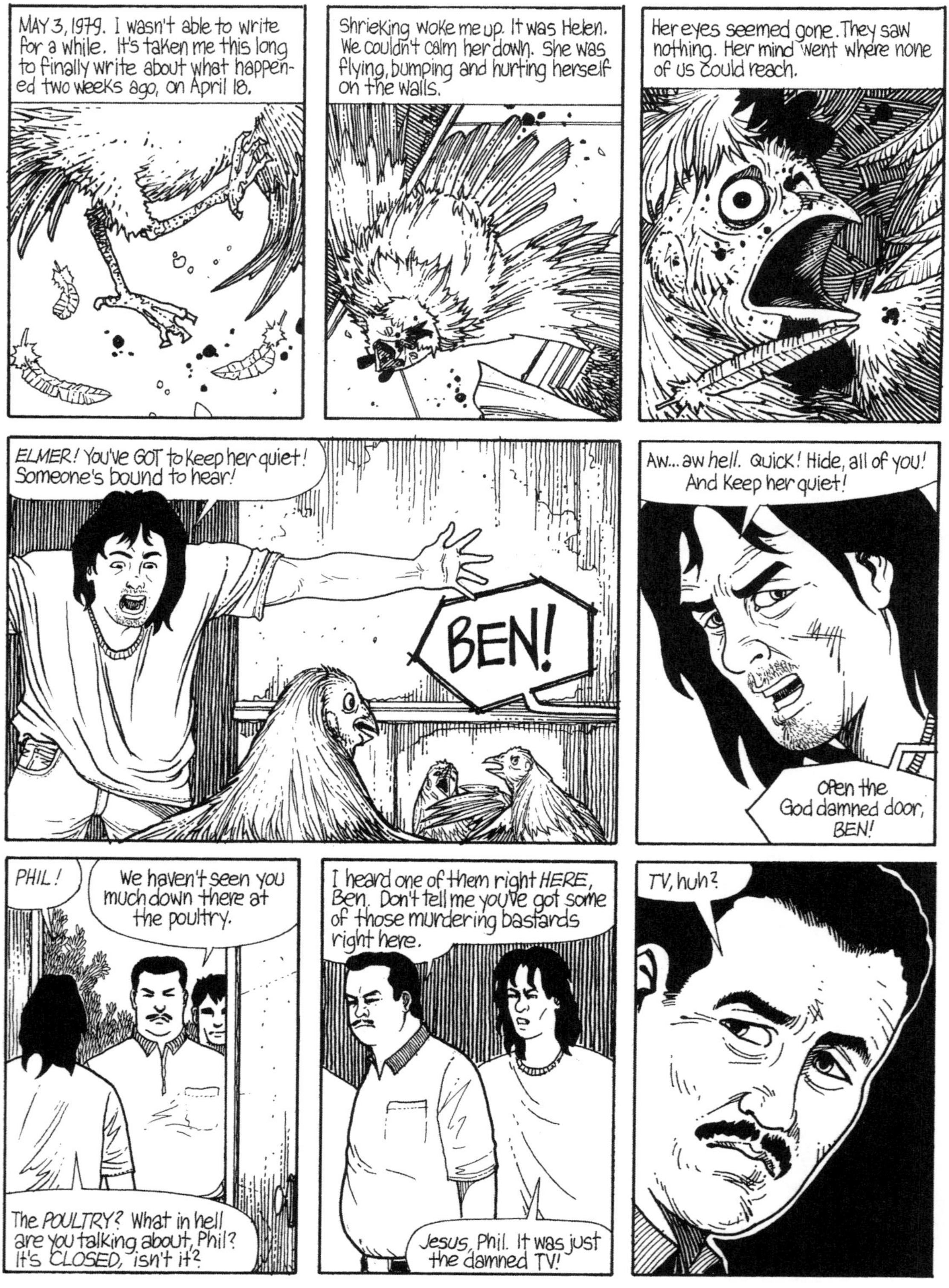
MAY 3, 1979. I wasn't able to write for a while. It's taken me this long to finally write about what happened two weeks ago, on April 18.
Shrieking woke me up. It was Helen. We couldn't calm her down. She was flying, bumping and hurting herself on the walls.
Her eyes seemed gone. They saw nothing. Her mind went where none of us could reach.
ELMER! You've GOT to keep her quiet! Someone's bound to hear!
BEN!
Aw... aw hell. Quick! Hide, all of you! And keep her quiet!
Open the God damned door, BEN!
PHIL!
We haven't seen you much down there at the poultry.
The POULTRY? What in hell are you talking about, Phil? It's CLOSED, isn't it?
I heard one of them right HERE, Ben. Don't tell me you've got some of those murdering bastards right here.
Jesus, Phil. It was just the damned TV!
TV, huh?

LUCKY TRADING

1979

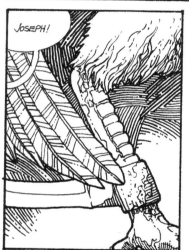

JOSEPH!

Joseph, what are you doing?

Get out of my way, brother.

Down at the poultry. We need to talk.

NOW, Ben.

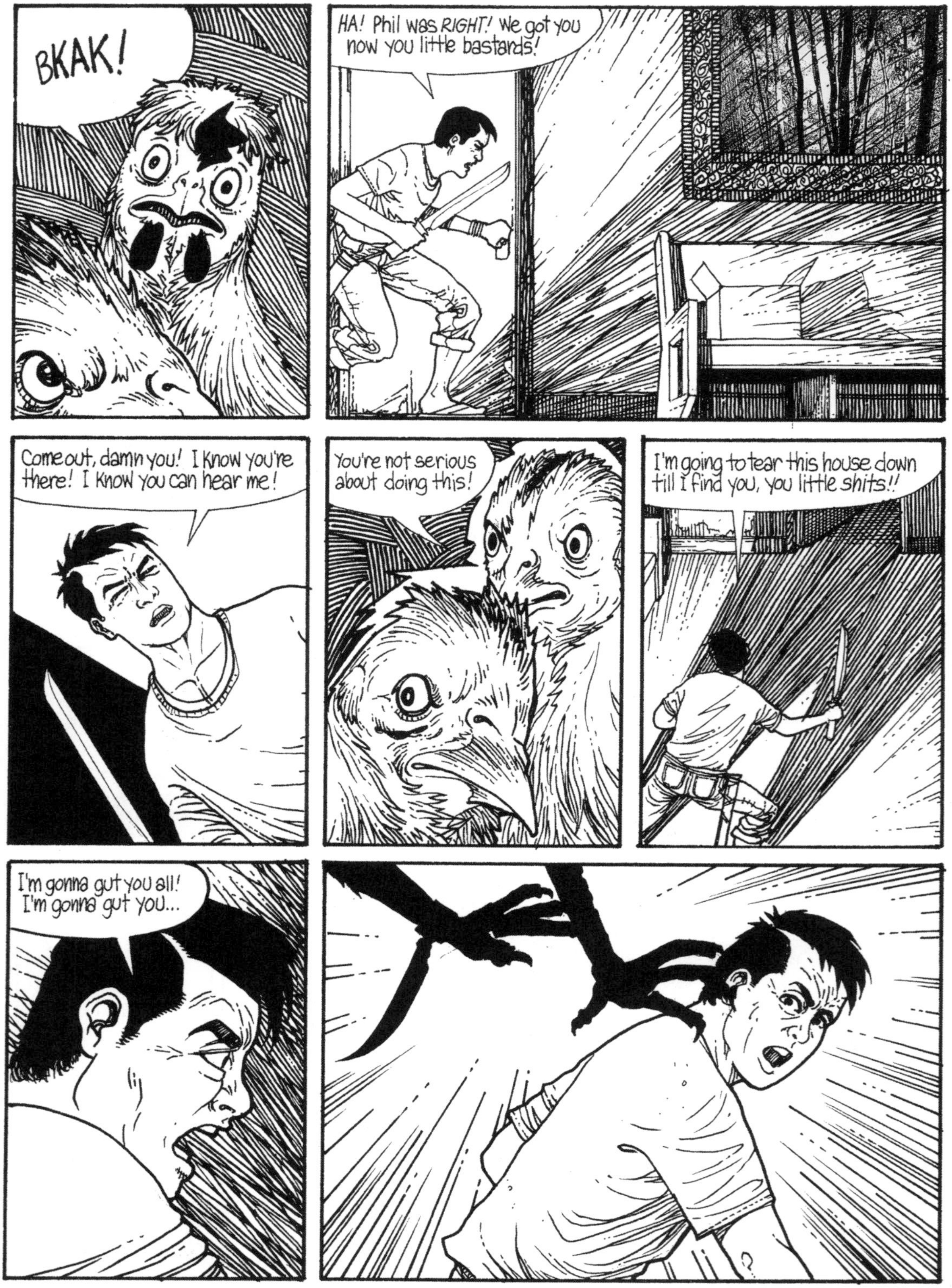
BKAK!
HA! Phil was RIGHT! We got you now you little bastards!
Come out, damn you! I know you're there! I know you can hear me!
You're not serious about doing this!
I'm going to tear this house down till I find you, you little shits!!
I'm gonna gut you all! I'm gonna gut you...

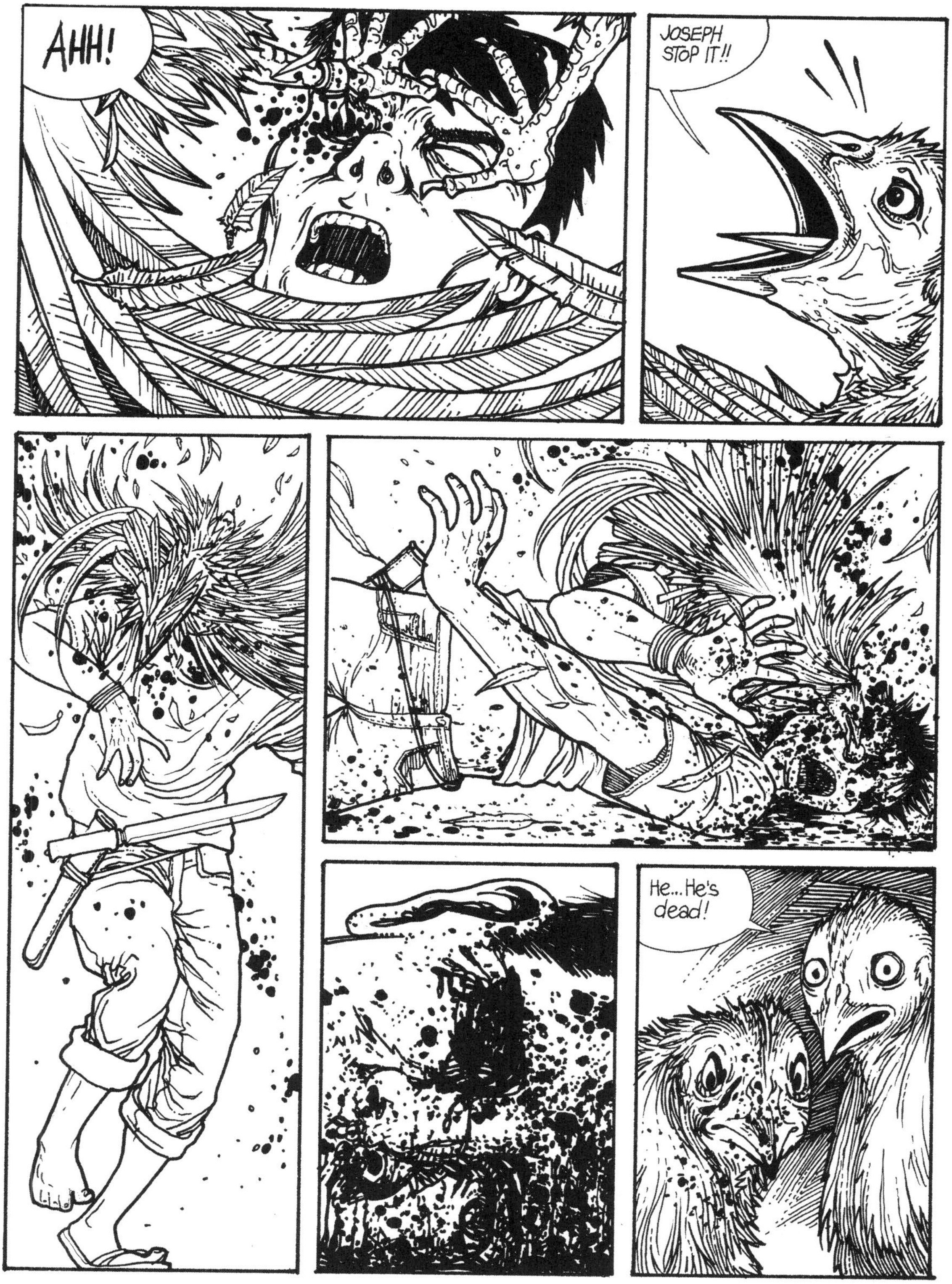
AHH!
JOSEPH STOP IT!!
He... He's dead!

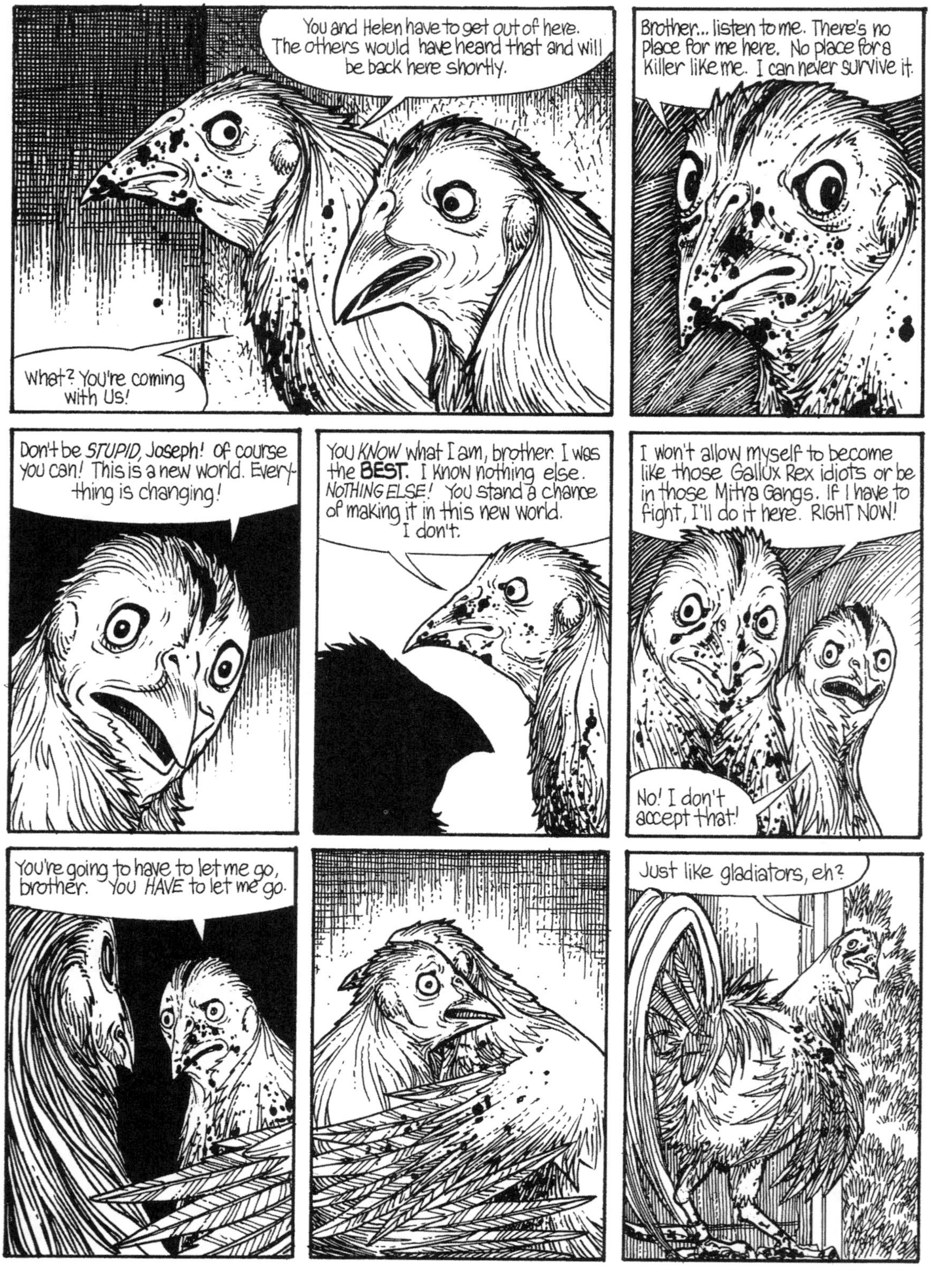
You and Helen have to get out of here. The others would have heard that and will be back here shortly.
What? You're coming with us!
Brother... listen to me. There's no place for me here. No place for a killer like me. I can never survive it.
Don't be *STUPID,* Joseph! Of course you can! This is a new world. Everything is changing!
You *KNOW* what I am, brother. I was the **BEST.** I know nothing else. *NOTHING ELSE!* You stand a chance of making it in this new world. I don't.
I won't allow myself to become like those Gallux Rex idiots or be in those Mitra Gangs. If I have to fight, I'll do it here. RIGHT NOW!
No! I don't accept that!
You're going to have to let me go, brother. You *HAVE* to let me go.
Just like gladiators, eh?

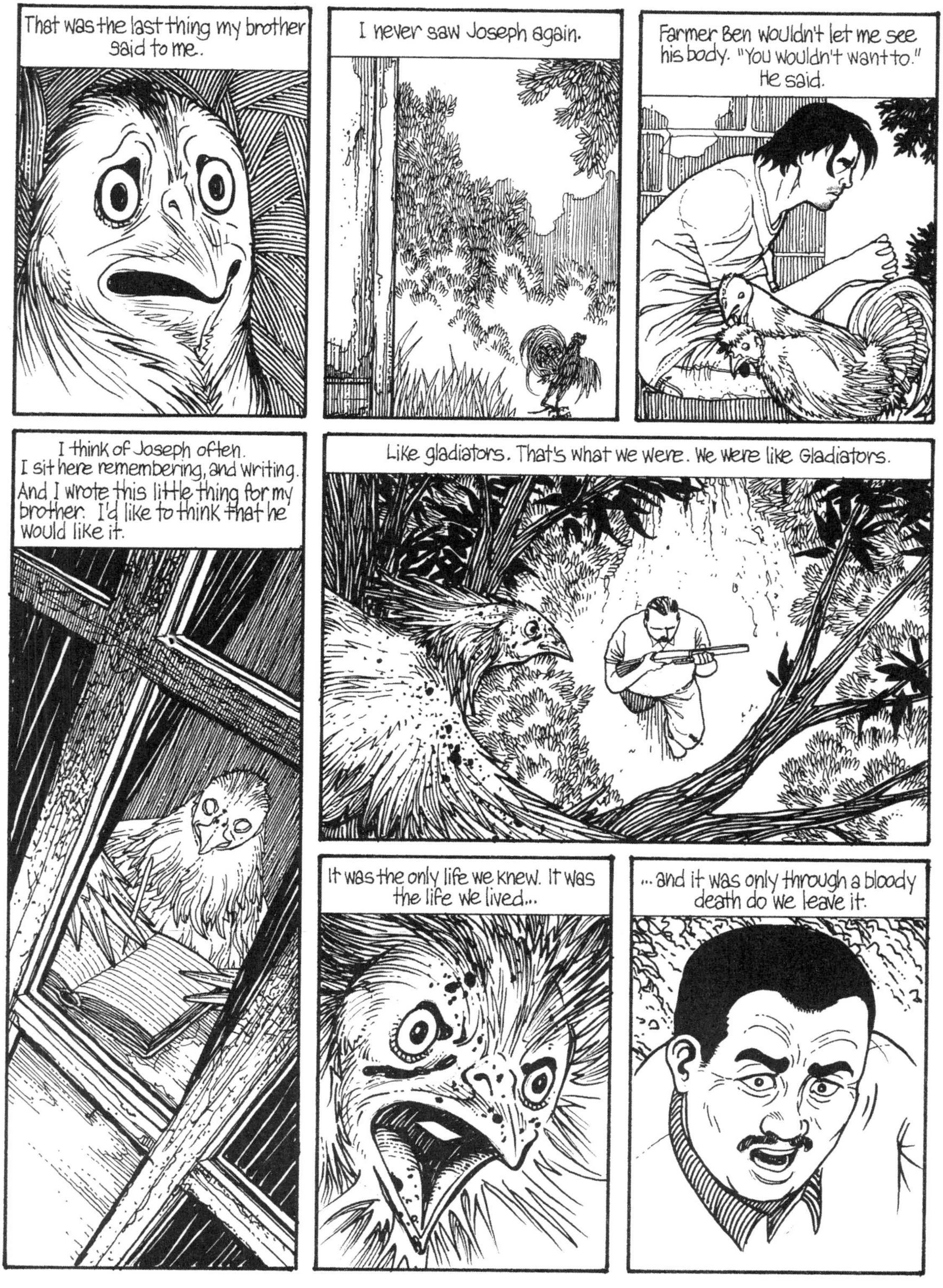
That was the last thing my brother said to me..
I never saw Joseph again.
Farmer Ben wouldn't let me see his body. "You wouldn't want to." He said.
I think of Joseph often. I sit here remembering, and writing. And I wrote this little thing for my brother. I'd like to think that he would like it.
Like gladiators. That's what we were. We were like Gladiators.
It was the only life we knew. It was the life we lived...
...and it was only through a bloody death do we leave it.

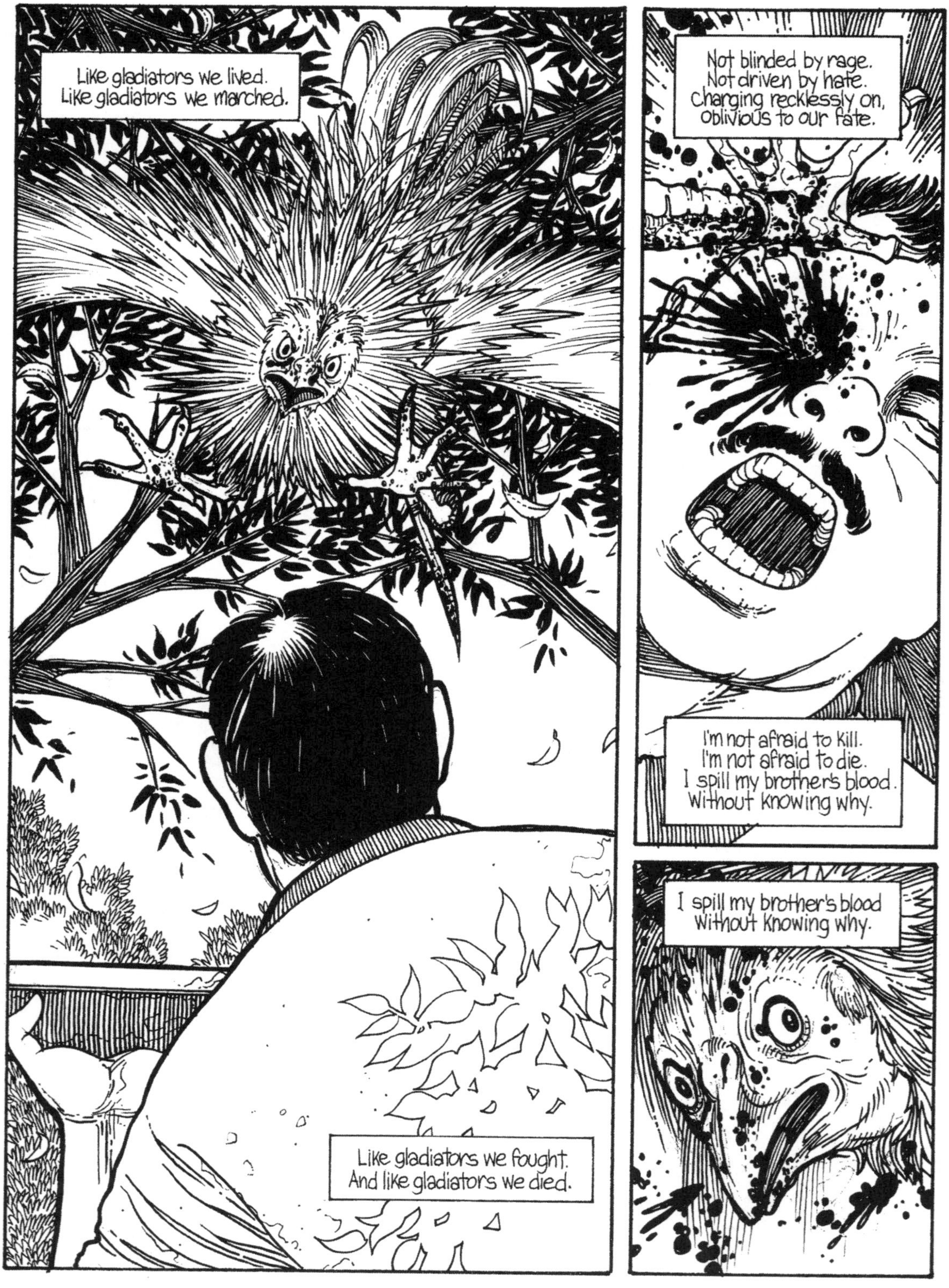
Like gladiators we lived. Like gladiators we marched.
Not blinded by rage. Not driven by hate. Charging recklessly on, Oblivious to our fate.
I'm not afraid to kill. I'm not afraid to die. I spill my brother's blood. Without knowing why.
Like gladiators we fought. And like gladiators we died.
I spill my brother's blood Without knowing why.

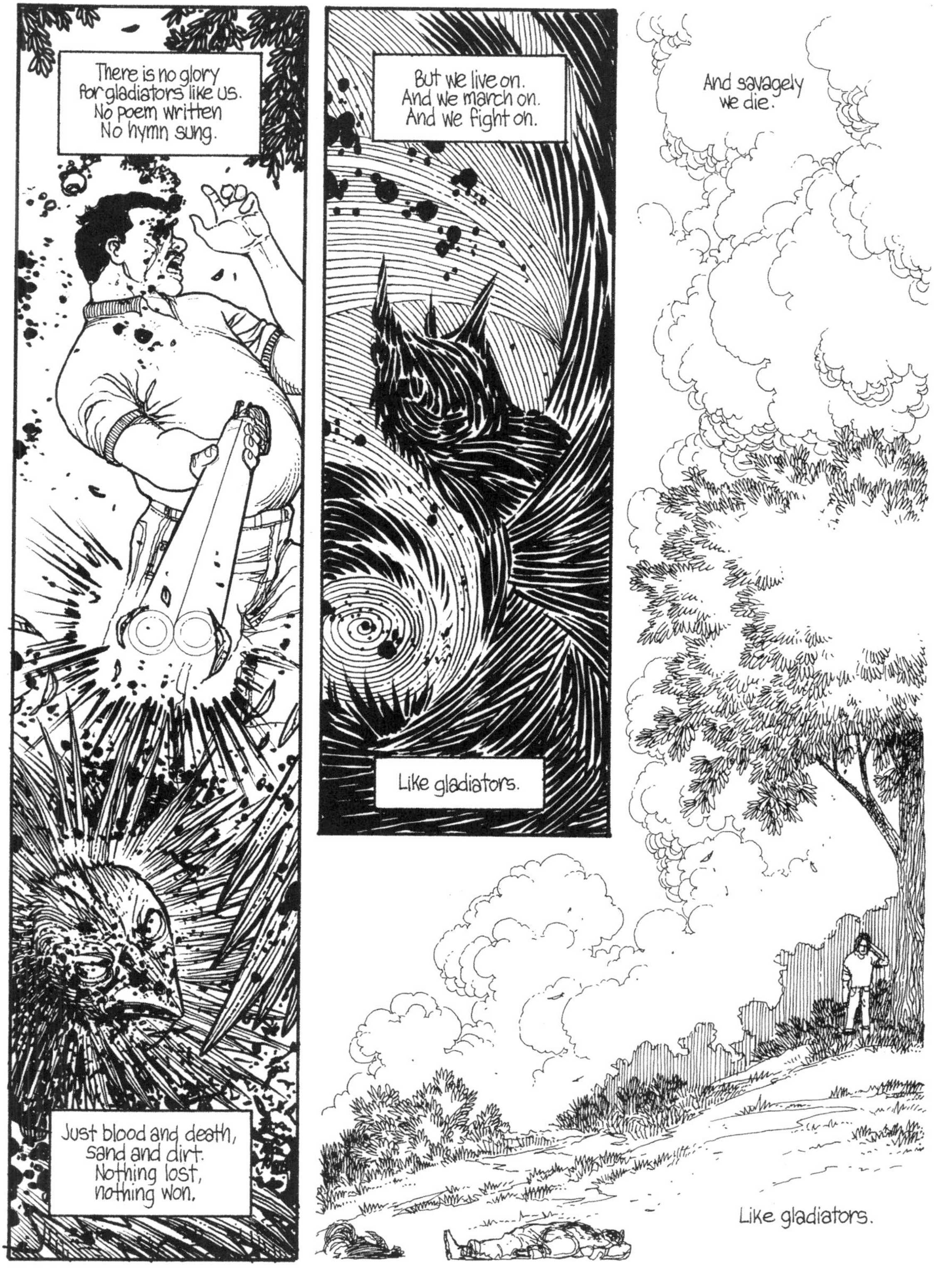
There is no glory
for gladiators like us.
No poem written
No hymn sung.
Just blood and death,
sand and dirt.
Nothing lost,
nothing won.
But we live on.
And we march on.
And we fight on.
Like gladiators.
And savagely
we die.
Like gladiators.

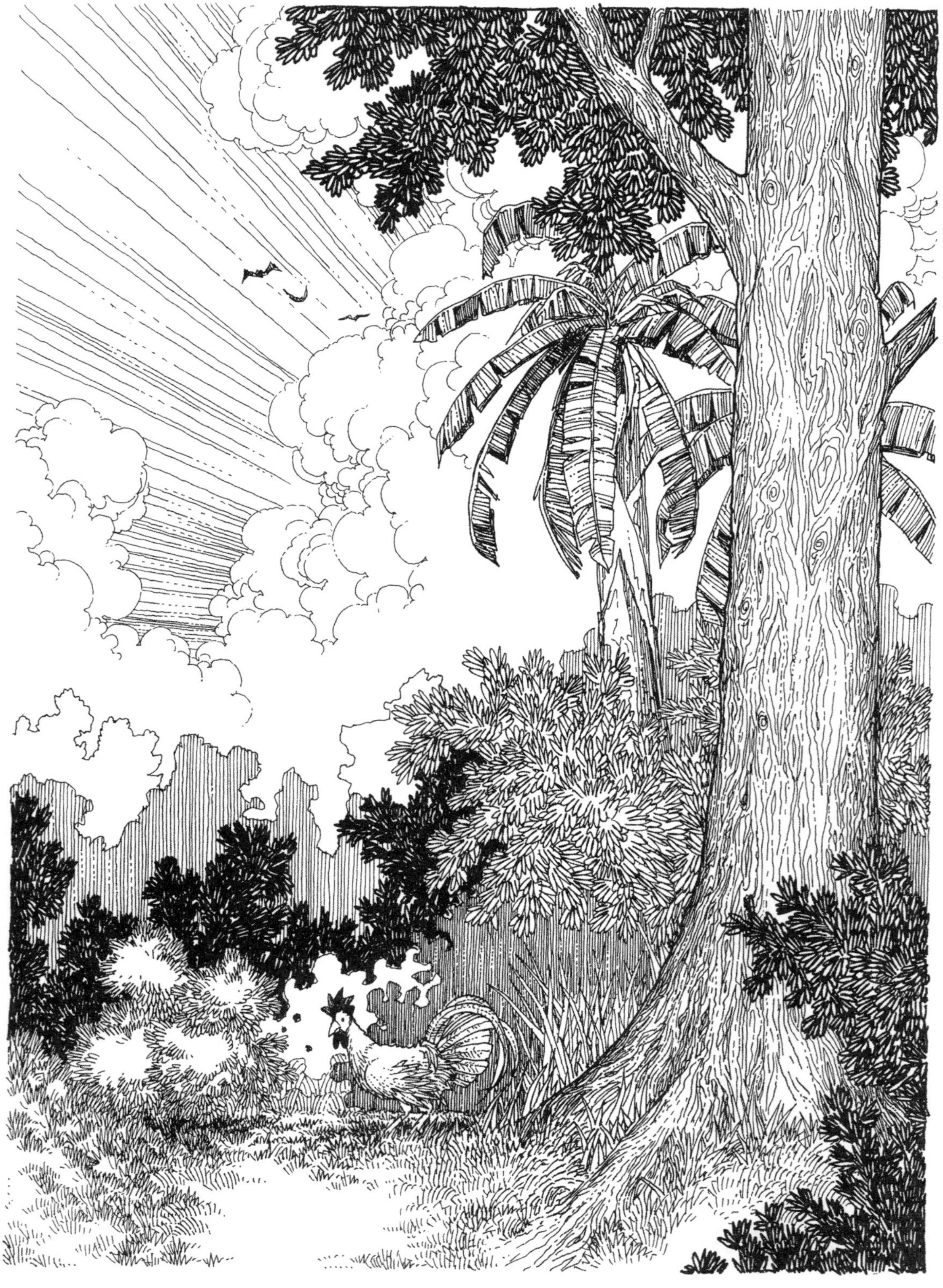

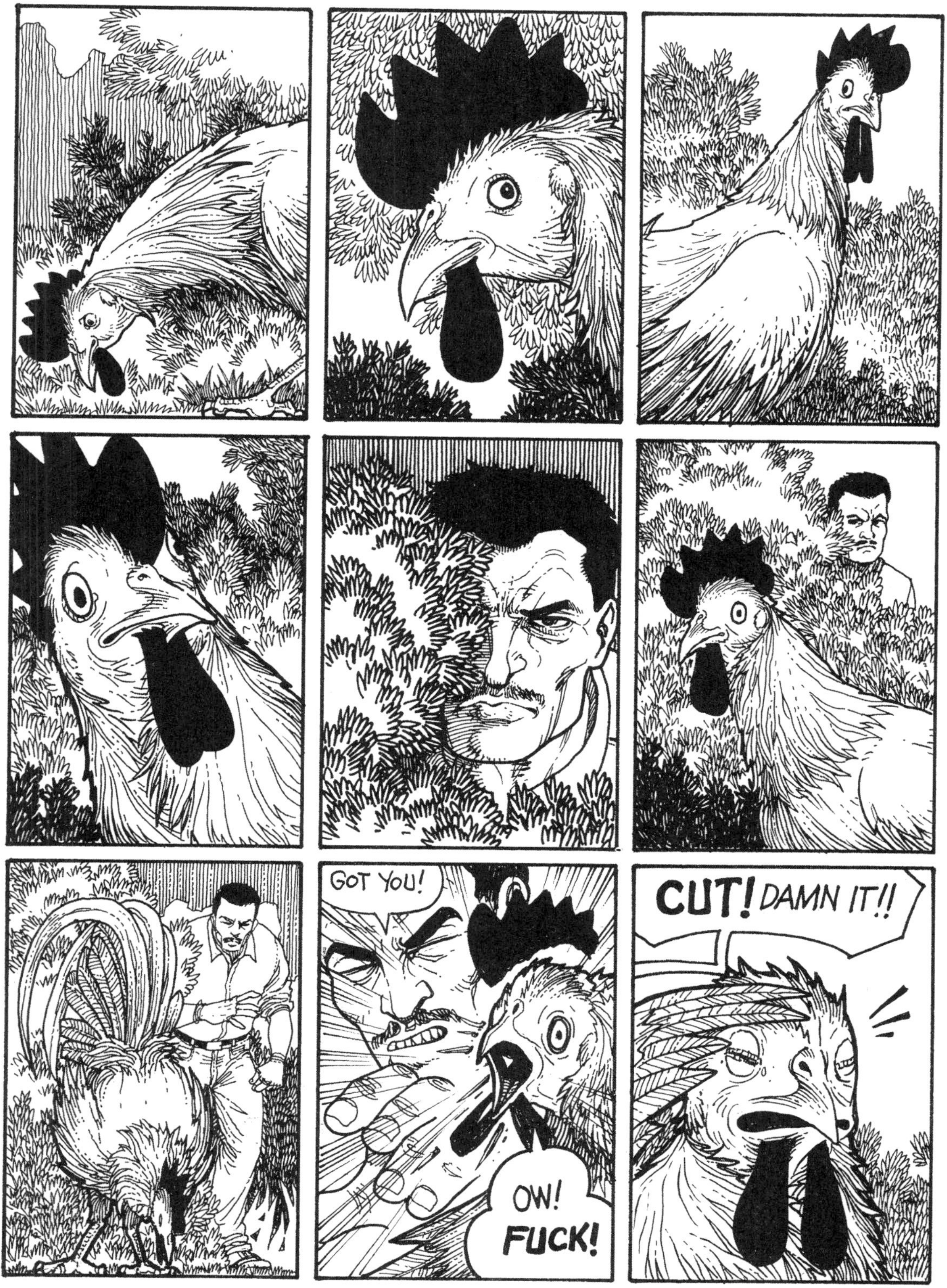
GOT YOU!
OW! FUCK!
CUT! DAMN IT!!

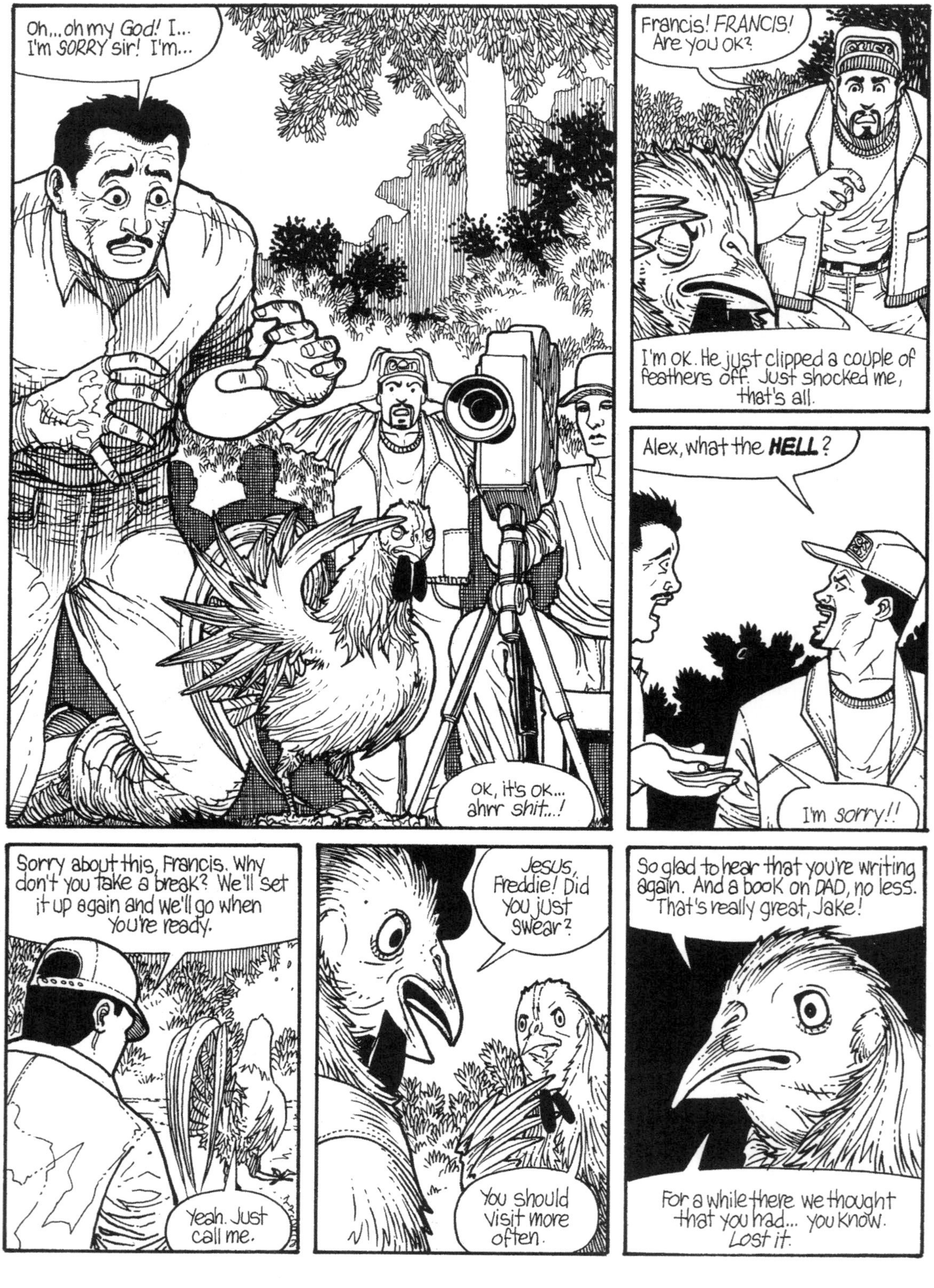
Oh... oh my God! I... I'm SORRY sir! I'm...
OK, it's OK... ahrr shit...!
Francis! FRANCIS! Are you OK?
I'm OK. He just clipped a couple of feathers off. Just shocked me, that's all.
Alex, what the HELL?
I'm sorry!!
Sorry about this, Francis. Why don't you take a break? We'll set it up again and we'll go when you're ready.
Yeah. Just call me.
Jesus, Freddie! Did you just swear?
You should visit more often.
So glad to hear that you're writing again. And a book on DAD, no less. That's really great, Jake!
For a while there we thought that you had... you know. Lost it.

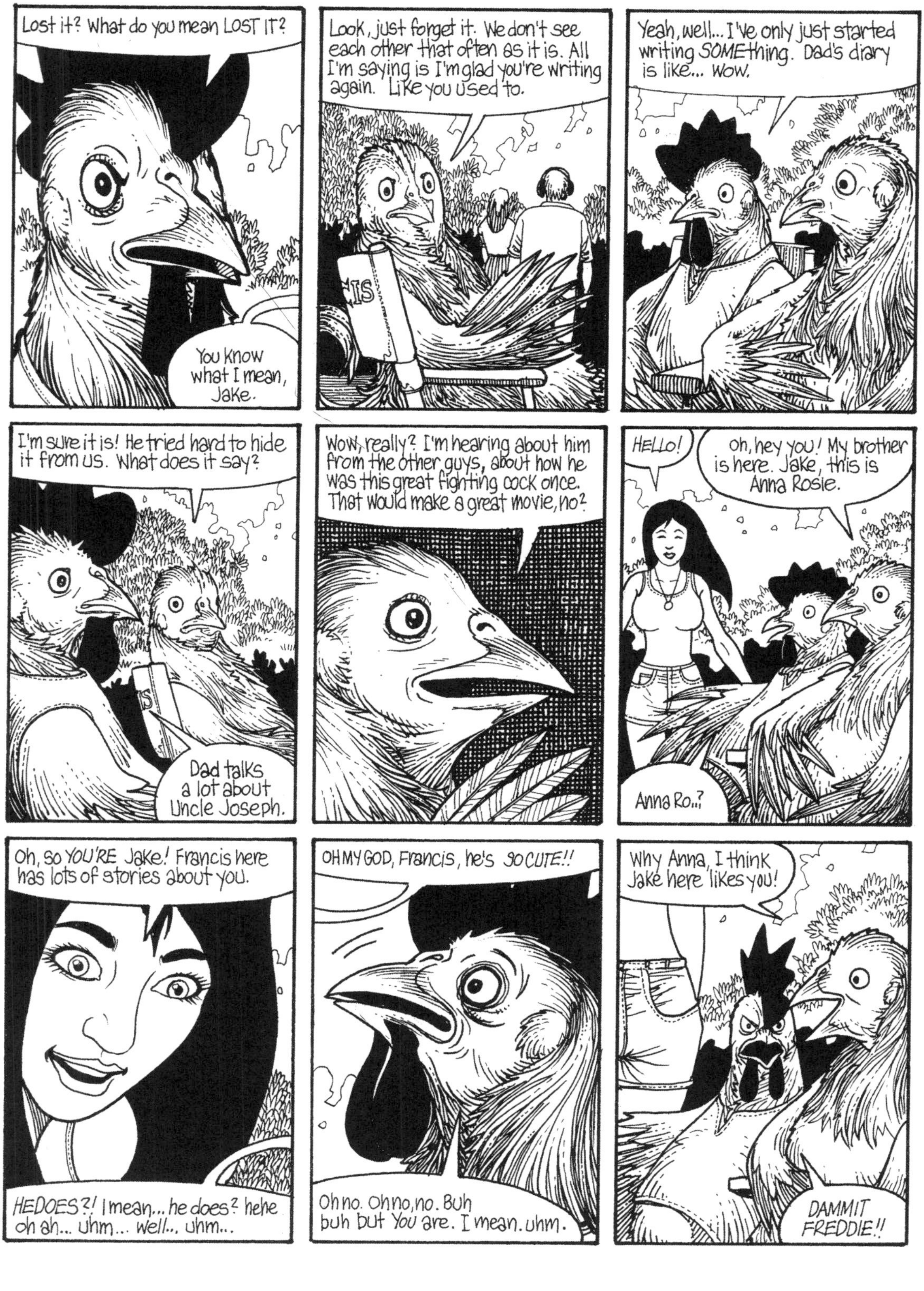
Lost it? What do you mean LOST IT?
You know what I mean, Jake.
Look, just forget it. We don't see each other that often as it is. All I'm saying is I'm glad you're writing again. Like you used to.
IS
Yeah, well... I've only just started writing SOMEthing. Dad's diary is like... wow.
I'm sure it is! He tried hard to hide it from us. What does it say?
IS
Dad talks a lot about Uncle Joseph.
Wow, really? I'm hearing about him from the other guys, about how he was this great fighting cock once. That would make a great movie, no?
HELLO!
Oh, hey you! My brother is here. Jake, this is Anna Rosie.
Anna Ro...?
Oh, so YOU'RE Jake! Francis here has lots of stories about you.
HEDOES?! I mean... he does? hehe oh ah... uhm... well.., uhm...
OH MY GOD, Francis, he's SO CUTE!!
Oh no. Oh no, no. Buh buh but You are. I mean. uhm.
Why Anna, I think Jake here likes you!
DAMMIT FREDDIE!!

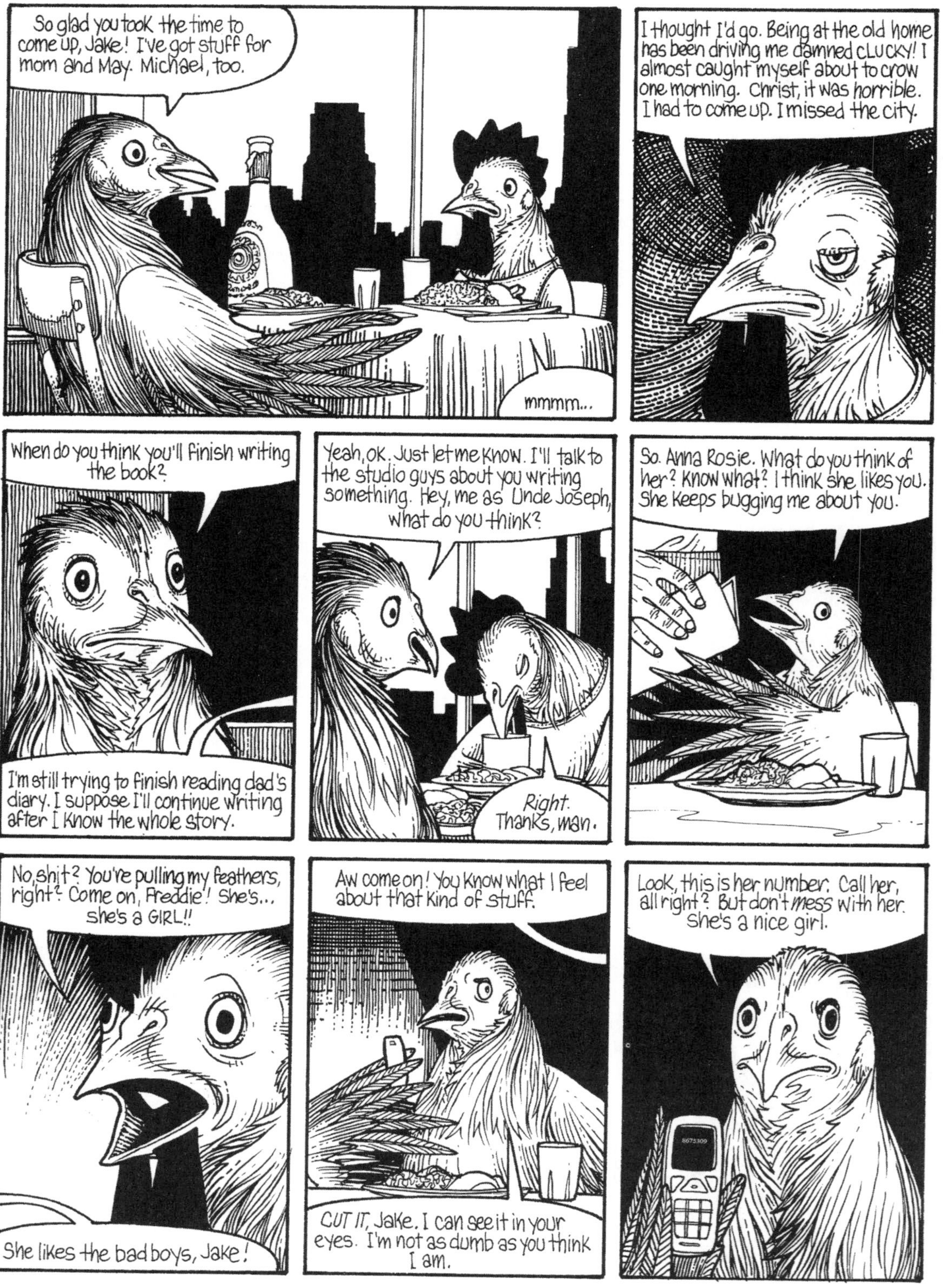
So glad you took the time to come up, Jake! I've got stuff for mom and May. Michael, too.
mmmm...
I thought I'd go. Being at the old home has been driving me damned CLUCKY! I almost caught myself about to crow one morning. Christ, it was *horrible*. I had to come up. I missed the city.
When do you think you'll finish writing the book?
I'm still trying to finish reading dad's diary. I suppose I'll continue writing after I know the whole story.
Yeah, OK. Just let me know. I'll talk to the studio guys about you writing something. Hey, me as Uncle Joseph, what do you think?
Right. Thanks, man.
So. Anna Rosie. What do you think of her? Know what? I think she likes you. She keeps bugging me about you.
No, shit? You're pulling my feathers, right? Come on, Freddie! She's... she's a GIRL!!
She likes the bad boys, Jake!
Aw come on! You know what I feel about that kind of stuff.
CUT IT, Jake. I can see it in your eyes. I'm not as dumb as you think I am.
Look, this is her number. Call her, all right? But don't *mess* with her. She's a nice girl.
8675309

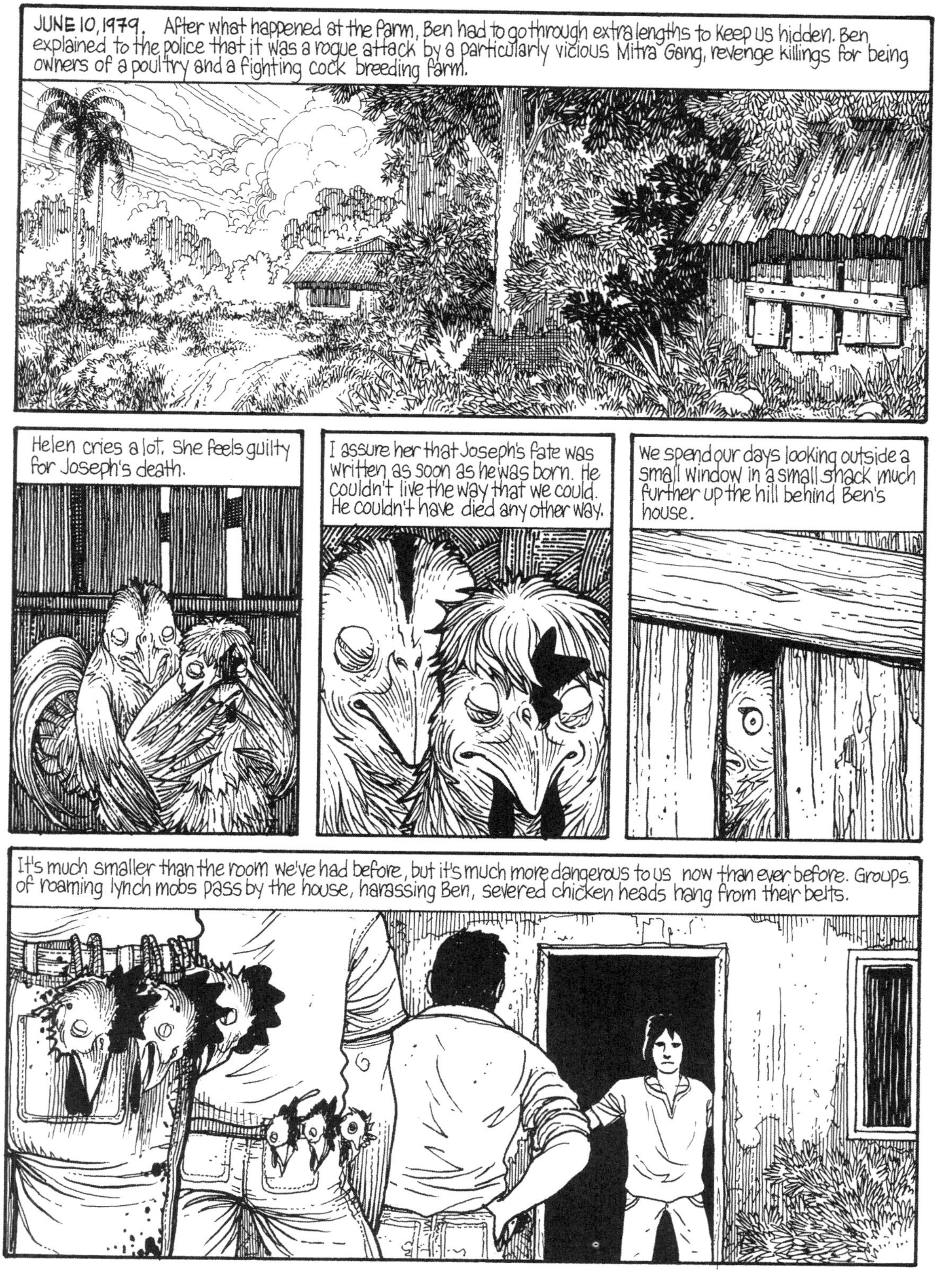
JUNE 10, 1979. After what happened at the farm, Ben had to go through extra lengths to keep us hidden. Ben explained to the police that it was a rogue attack by a particularly vicious Mitra Gang, revenge killings for being owners of a poultry and a fighting cock breeding farm.
Helen cries a lot. She feels guilty for Joseph's death.
I assure her that Joseph's fate was written as soon as he was born. He couldn't live the way that we could. He couldn't have died any other way.
We spend our days looking outside a small window in a small shack much further up the hill behind Ben's house.
It's much smaller than the room we've had before, but it's much more dangerous to us now than ever before. Groups of roaming lynch mobs pass by the house, harassing Ben, severed chicken heads hang from their belts.

How could people be so cruel and heartless? How could people hold so much hate in their hearts and venom in their blood?

They think the same of us, I suspect. The hate in Joseph's heart was so naked and so overwhelming, it consumed him.

Hate that can rob the mind of all sense. I don't know. I really don't know. It can't be like this forever. It can't be!

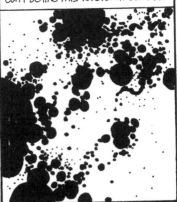

There has got to be a reason why we were made to be like this. There must be a reason for all of it. I don't accept that it's nothing but some random whim of nature, played with by fate and God.

I realize I'm ranting when Helen looked at me with fear in her eyes. I scare her sometimes with the things I say.

In times like this there's really nothing else to say. I just sit beside her until we fall asleep.

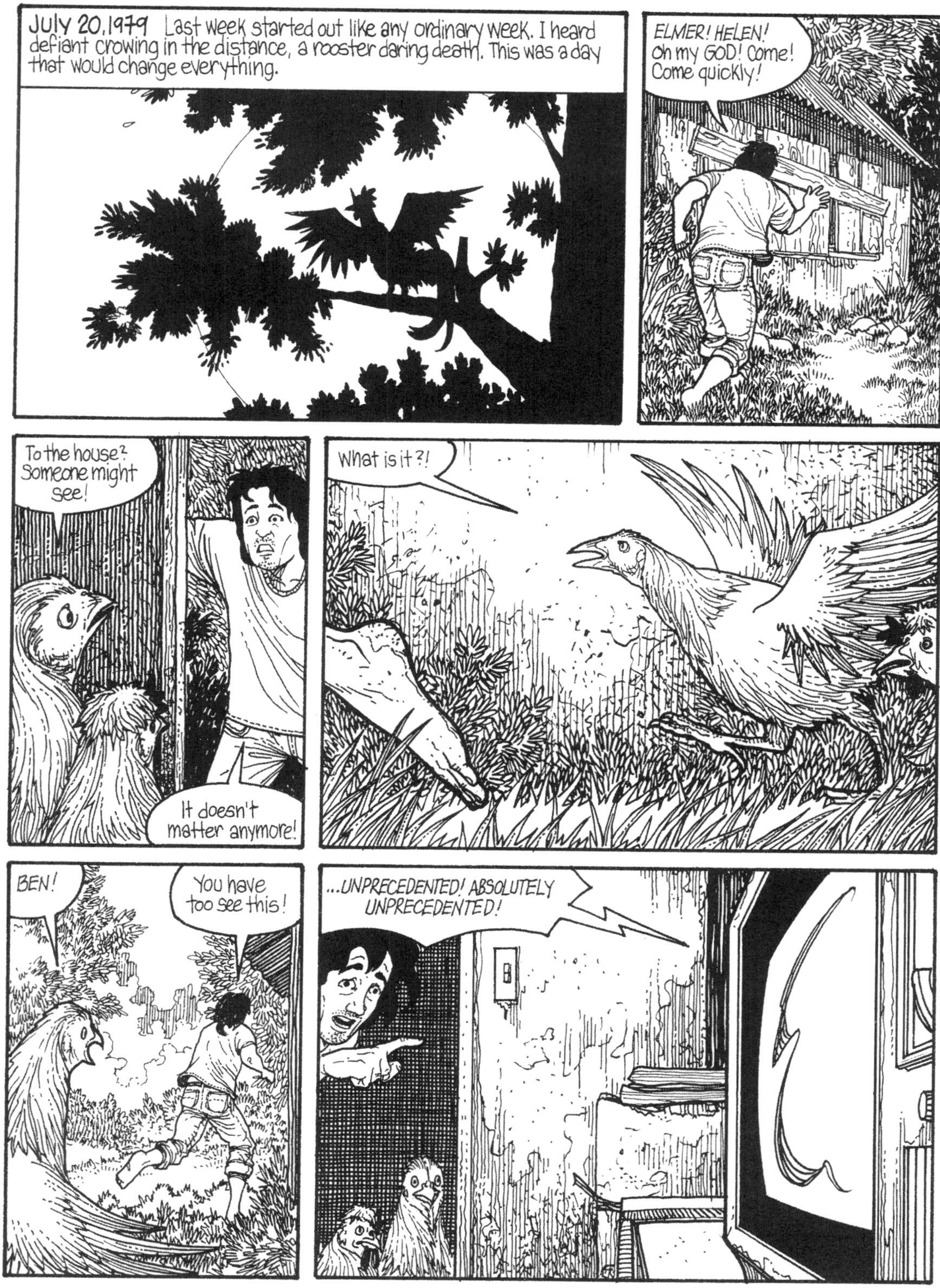
JULY 20, 1979 Last week started out like any ordinary week. I heard defiant crowing in the distance, a rooster daring death. This was a day that would change everything.
ELMER! HELEN! Oh my GOD! Come! Come quickly!
To the house? Someone might see!
It doesn't matter anymore!
What is it?!
BEN!
You have too see this!
...UNPRECEDENTED! ABSOLUTELY UNPRECEDENTED!

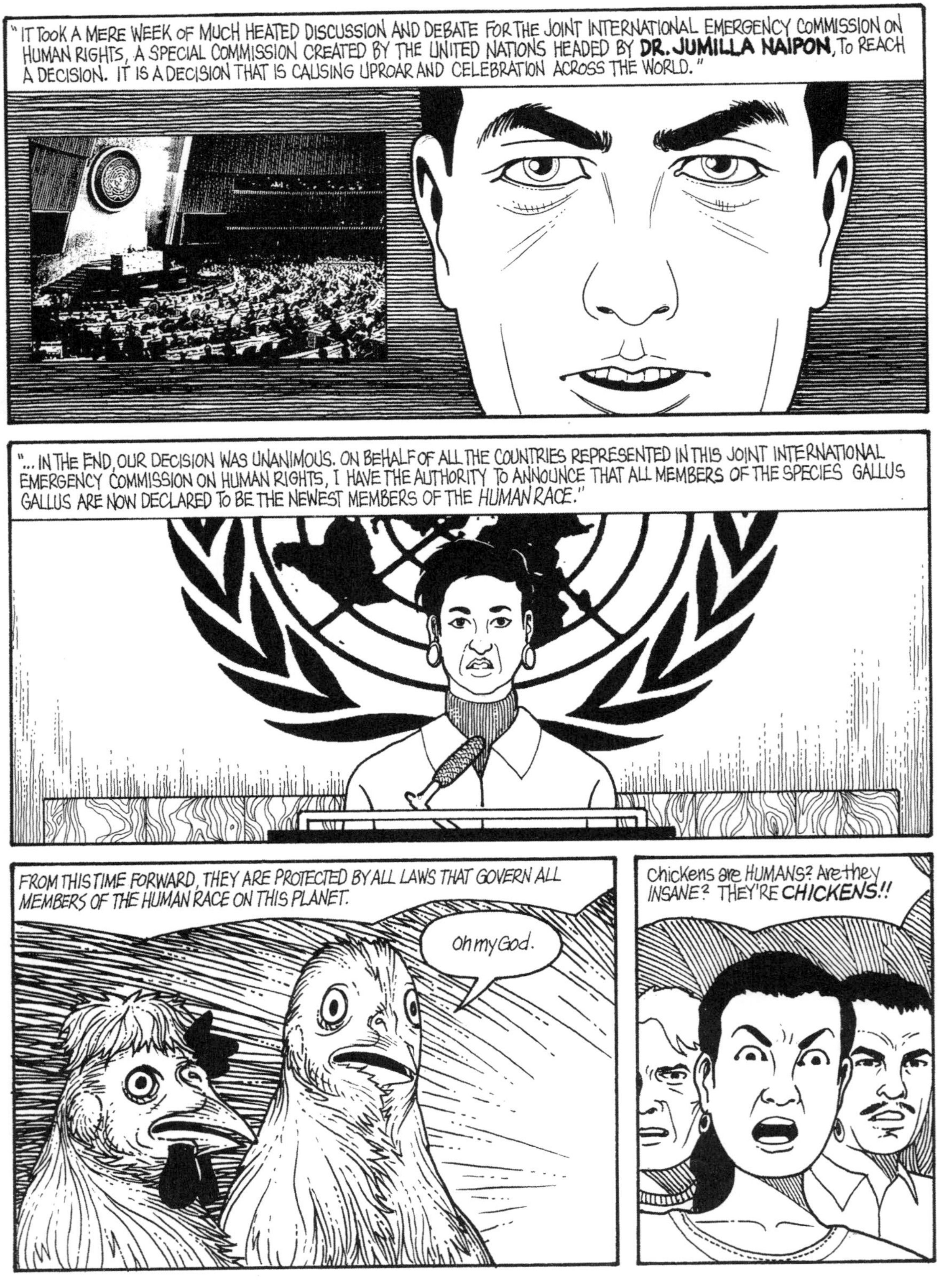
"IT TOOK A MERE WEEK OF MUCH HEATED DISCUSSION AND DEBATE FOR THE JOINT INTERNATIONAL EMERGENCY COMMISSION ON HUMAN RIGHTS, A SPECIAL COMMISSION CREATED BY THE UNITED NATIONS HEADED BY DR. JUMILLA NAIPON, TO REACH A DECISION. IT IS A DECISION THAT IS CAUSING UPROAR AND CELEBRATION ACROSS THE WORLD."
"... IN THE END, OUR DECISION WAS UNANIMOUS. ON BEHALF OF ALL THE COUNTRIES REPRESENTED IN THIS JOINT INTERNATIONAL EMERGENCY COMMISSION ON HUMAN RIGHTS, I HAVE THE AUTHORITY TO ANNOUNCE THAT ALL MEMBERS OF THE SPECIES GALLUS GALLUS ARE NOW DECLARED TO BE THE NEWEST MEMBERS OF THE HUMAN RACE."
FROM THIS TIME FORWARD, THEY ARE PROTECTED BY ALL LAWS THAT GOVERN ALL MEMBERS OF THE HUMAN RACE ON THIS PLANET.
Oh my God.
Chickens are HUMANS? Are they INSANE? THEY'RE CHICKENS!!

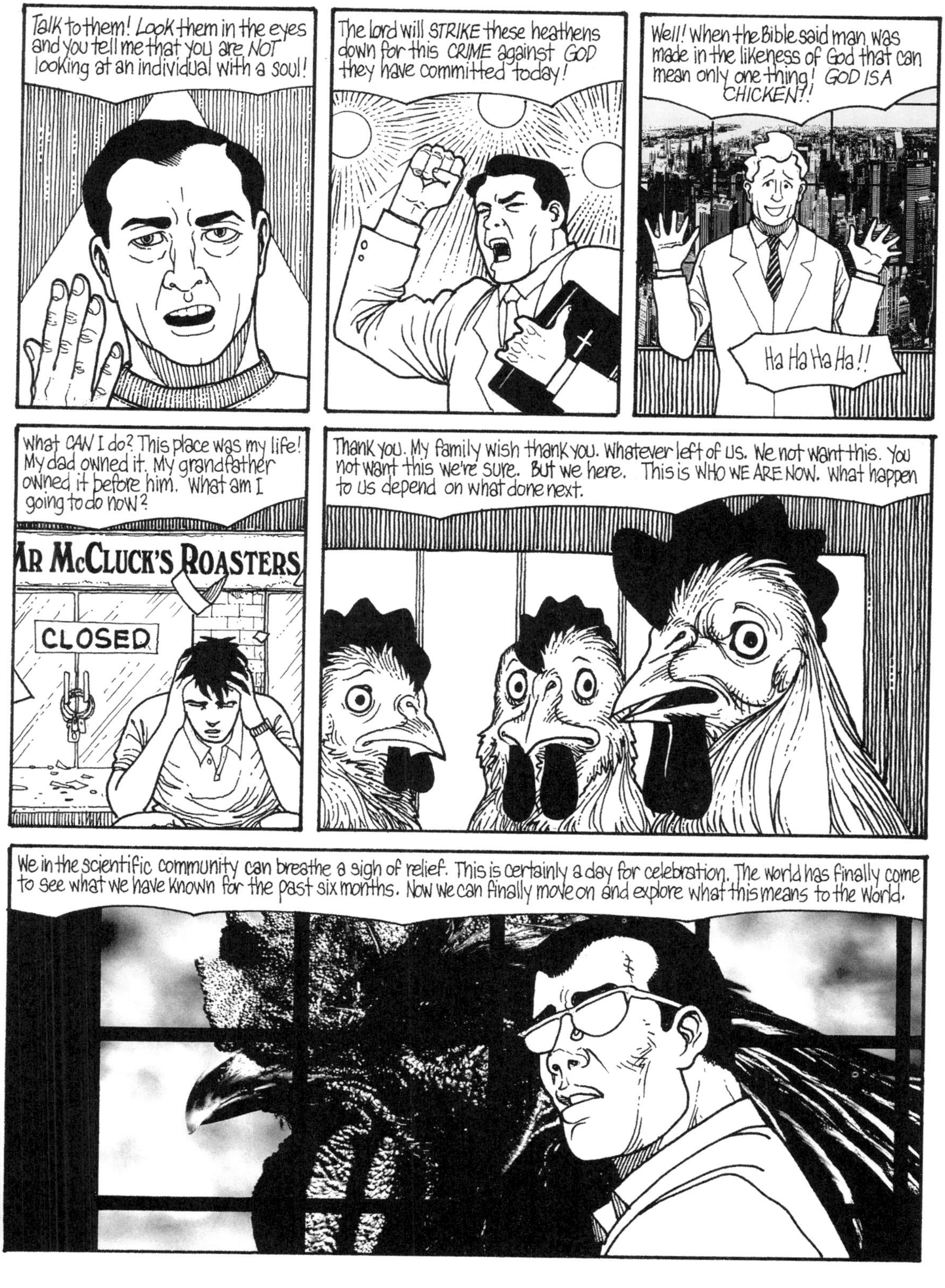
Talk to them! Look them in the eyes and you tell me that you are NOT looking at an individual with a soul!
The lord will STRIKE these heathens down for this CRIME against GOD they have committed today!
Well! When the Bible said man was made in the likeness of God that can mean only one thing! GOD IS A CHICKEN!!
Ha Ha Ha Ha!!
What CAN I do? This place was my life! My dad owned it. My grandfather owned it before him. What am I going to do now?
MR McCLUCK'S ROASTERS
CLOSED
Thank you. My family wish thank you. Whatever left of us. We not want this. You not want this we're sure. But we here. This is WHO WE ARE NOW. What happen to us depend on what done next.
We in the scientific community can breathe a sigh of relief. This is certainly a day for celebration. The world has finally come to see what we have known for the past six months. Now we can finally move on and explore what this means to the world.

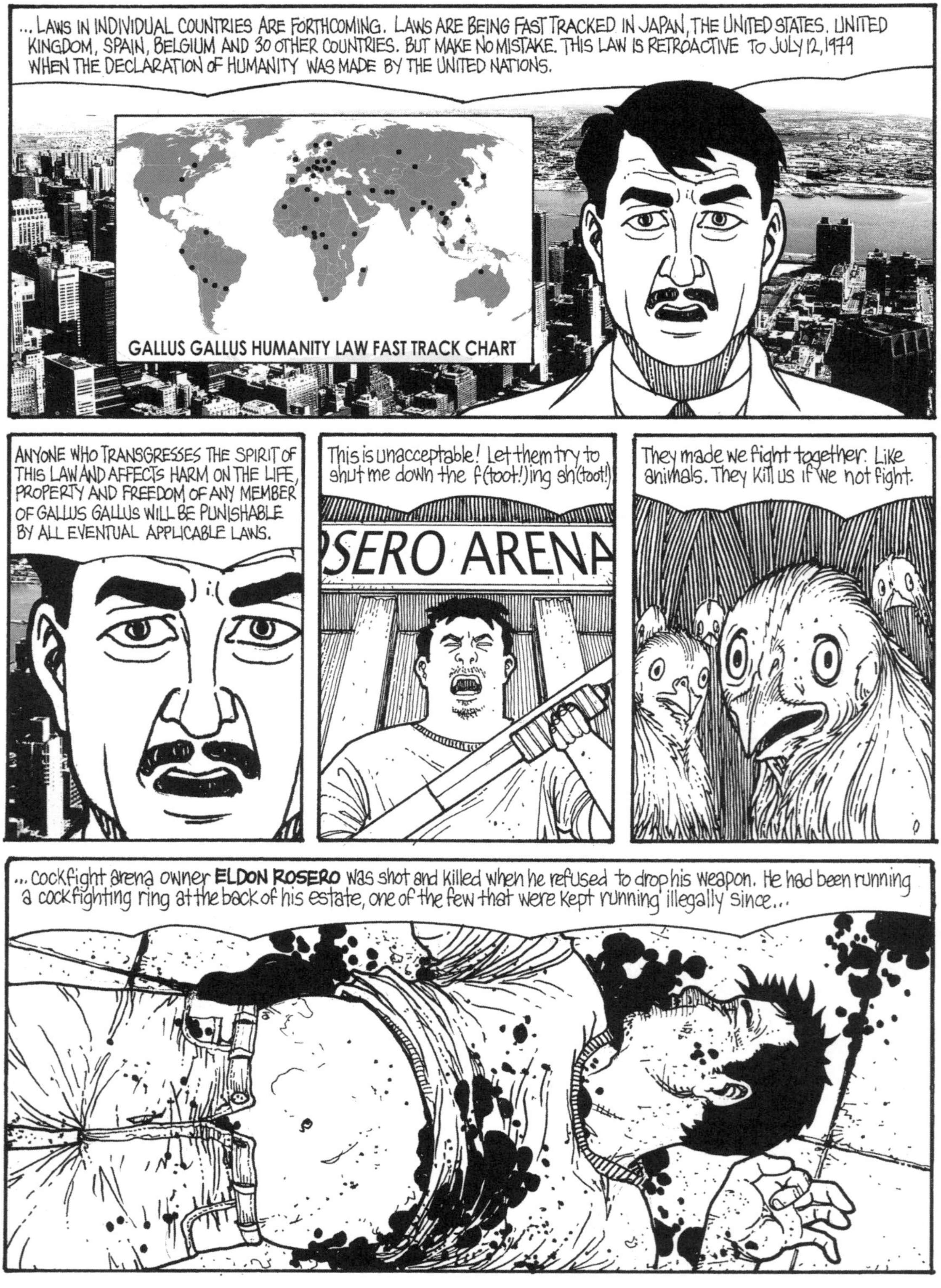
... LAWS IN INDIVIDUAL COUNTRIES ARE FORTHCOMING. LAWS ARE BEING FAST TRACKED IN JAPAN, THE UNITED STATES, UNITED KINGDOM, SPAIN, BELGIUM AND 30 OTHER COUNTRIES. BUT MAKE NO MISTAKE. THIS LAW IS RETROACTIVE TO JULY 12, 1979 WHEN THE DECLARATION OF HUMANITY WAS MADE BY THE UNITED NATIONS.
GALLUS GALLUS HUMANITY LAW FAST TRACK CHART
ANYONE WHO TRANSGRESSES THE SPIRIT OF THIS LAW AND AFFECTS HARM ON THE LIFE, PROPERTY AND FREEDOM OF ANY MEMBER OF GALLUS GALLUS WILL BE PUNISHABLE BY ALL EVENTUAL APPLICABLE LAWS.
This is unacceptable! Let them try to shut me down the f(toot!)ing sh(toot!)
SERO ARENA
They made we fight together. Like animals. They kill us if we not fight.
... cockfight arena owner ELDON ROSERO was shot and killed when he refused to drop his weapon. He had been running a cockfighting ring at the back of his estate, one of the few that were kept running illegally since...

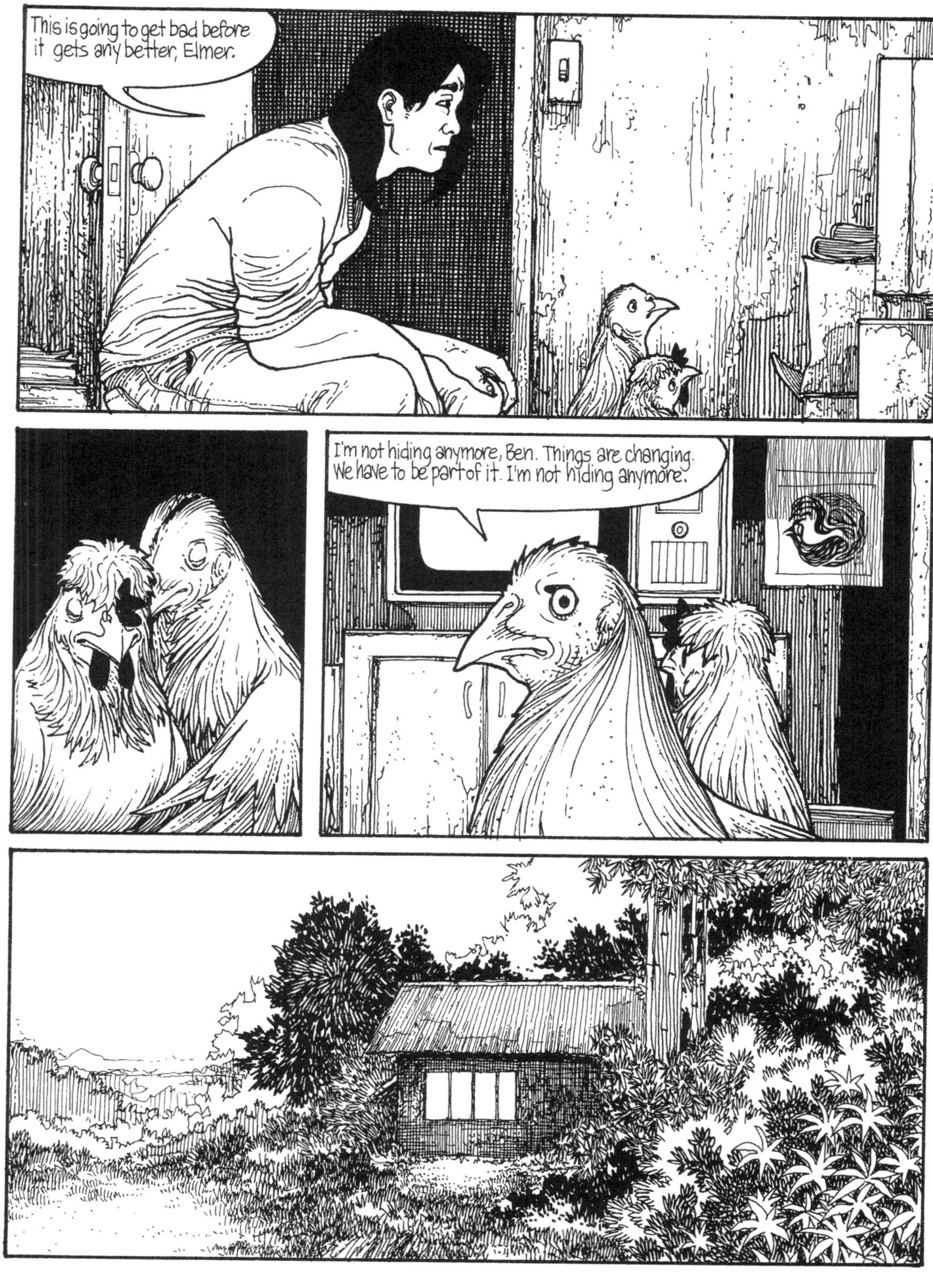
This is going to get bad before it gets any better, Elmer.
I'm not hiding anymore, Ben. Things are changing. We have to be part of it. I'm not hiding anymore.

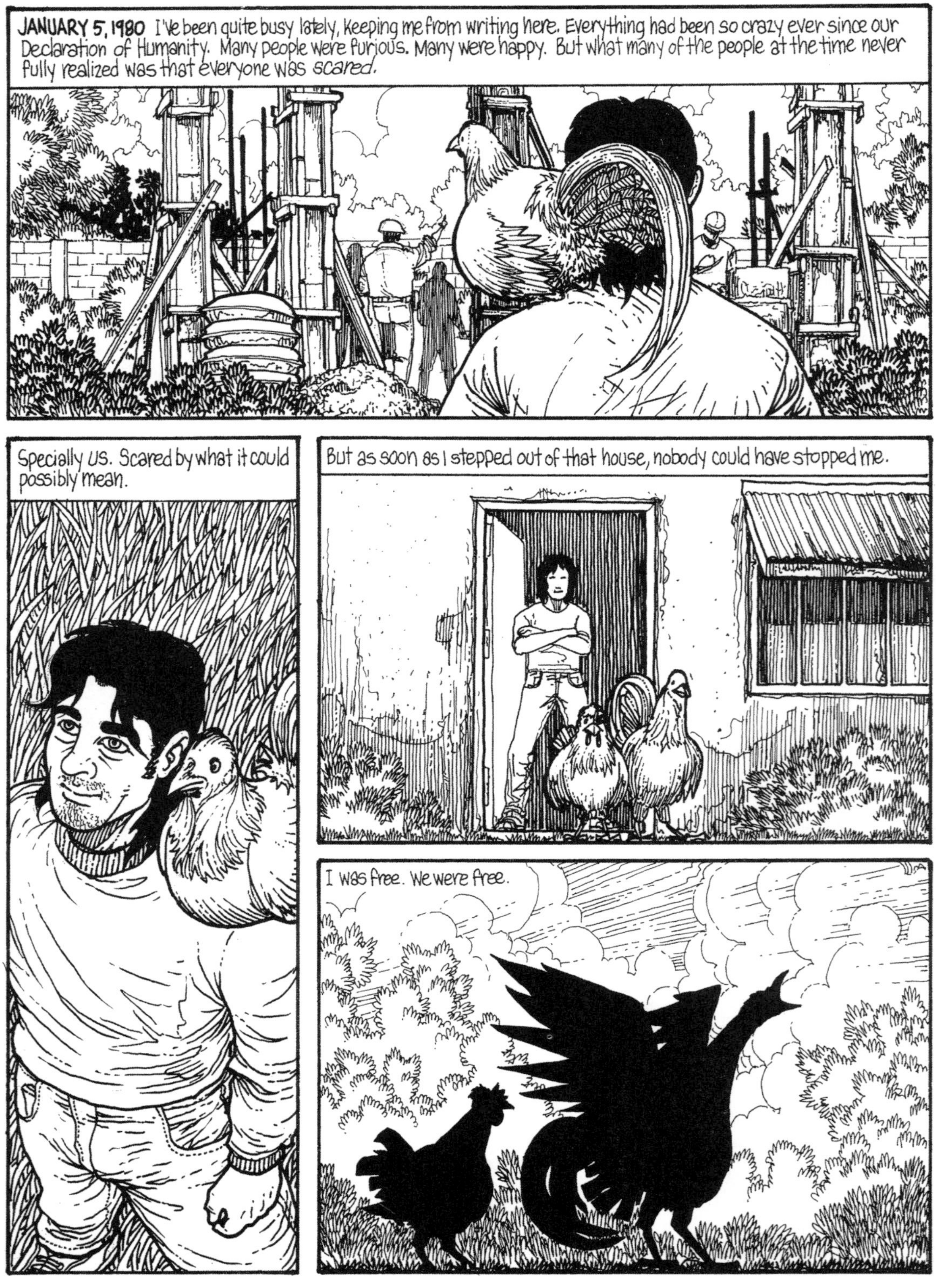
JANUARY 5, 1980 I've been quite busy lately, keeping me from writing here. Everything had been so crazy ever since our Declaration of Humanity. Many people were furious. Many were happy. But what many of the people at the time never fully realized was that everyone was *scared*.
Specially us. Scared by what it could possibly mean.
But as soon as I stepped out of that house, nobody could have stopped me.
I was free. We were free.

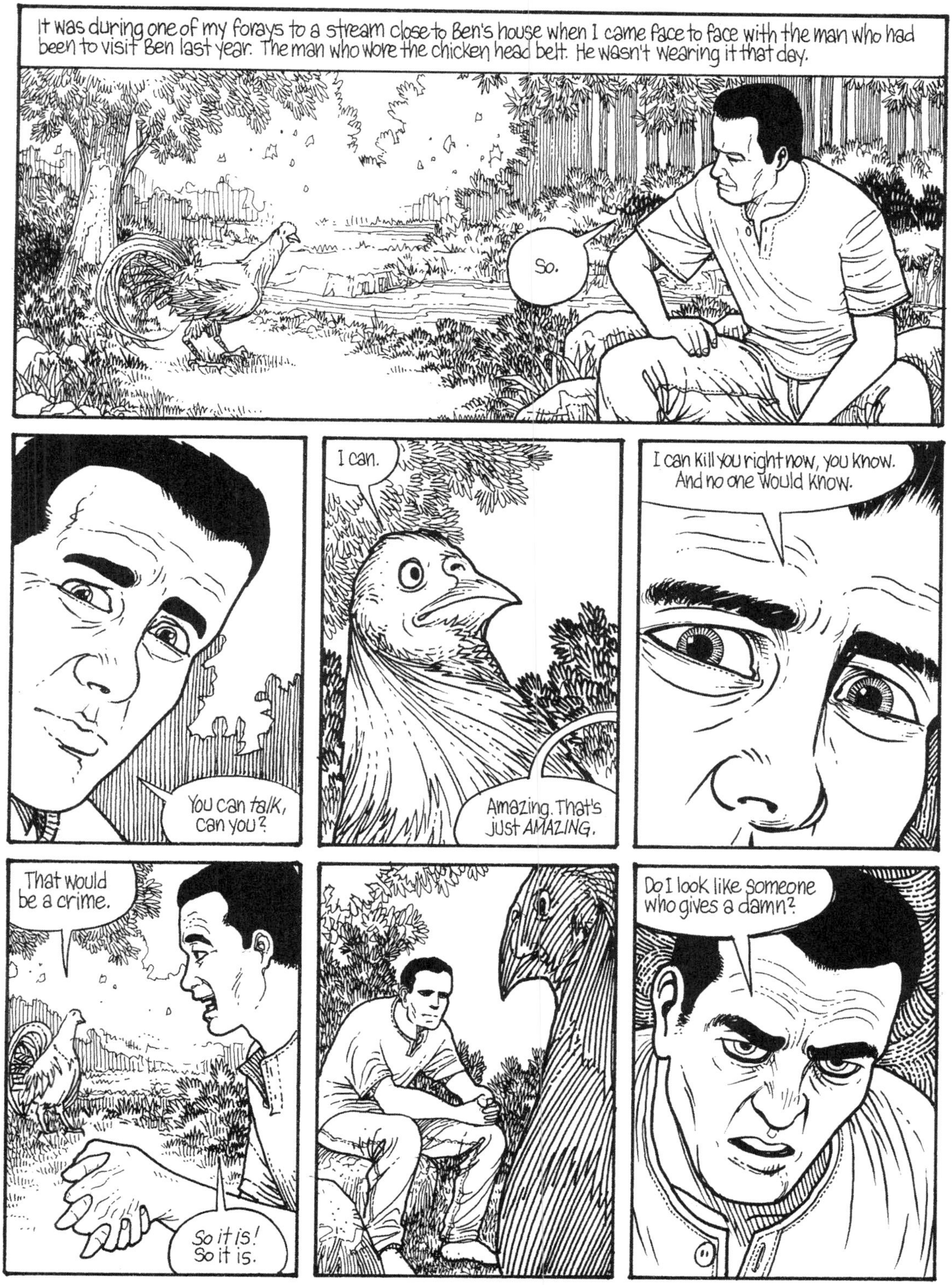
It was during one of my forays to a stream close to Ben's house when I came face to face with the man who had been to visit Ben last year. The man who wore the chicken head belt. He wasn't wearing it that day.
So.
You can *talk*, can you?
I can.
Amazing. That's just *AMAZING*.
I can kill you right now, you know. And no one would know.
That would be a crime.
So it is! So it is.
Do I look like someone who gives a damn?

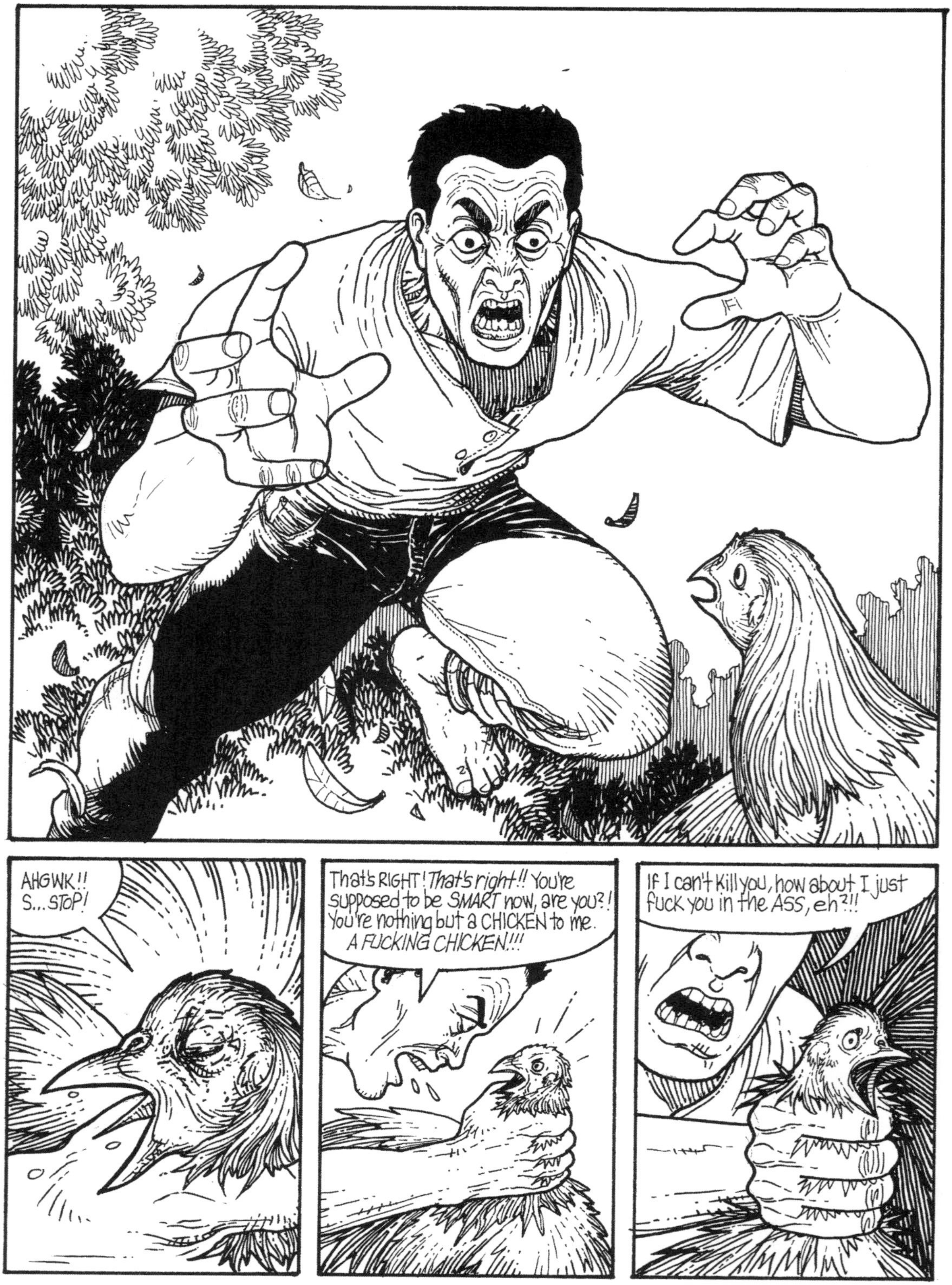
AHGWK!!
S...STOP!
That's RIGHT! That's right!! You're supposed to be SMART now, are you?! You're nothing but a CHICKEN to me.
A FUCKING CHICKEN!!!
If I can't kill you, how about I just fuck you in the ASS, eh?!!

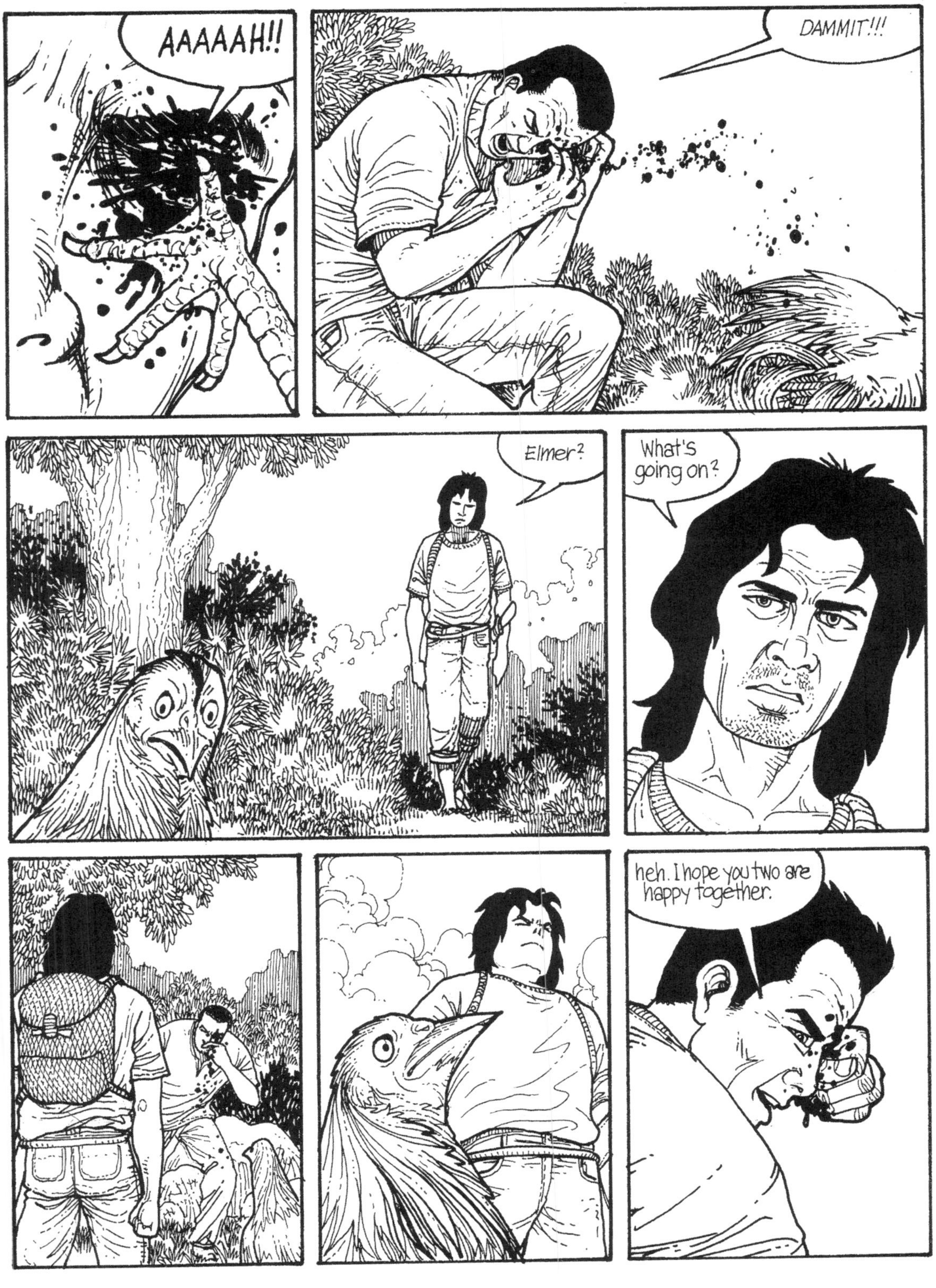
AAAAAH!!
DAMMIT!!!
Elmer?
What's going on?
heh. I hope you two are happy together.

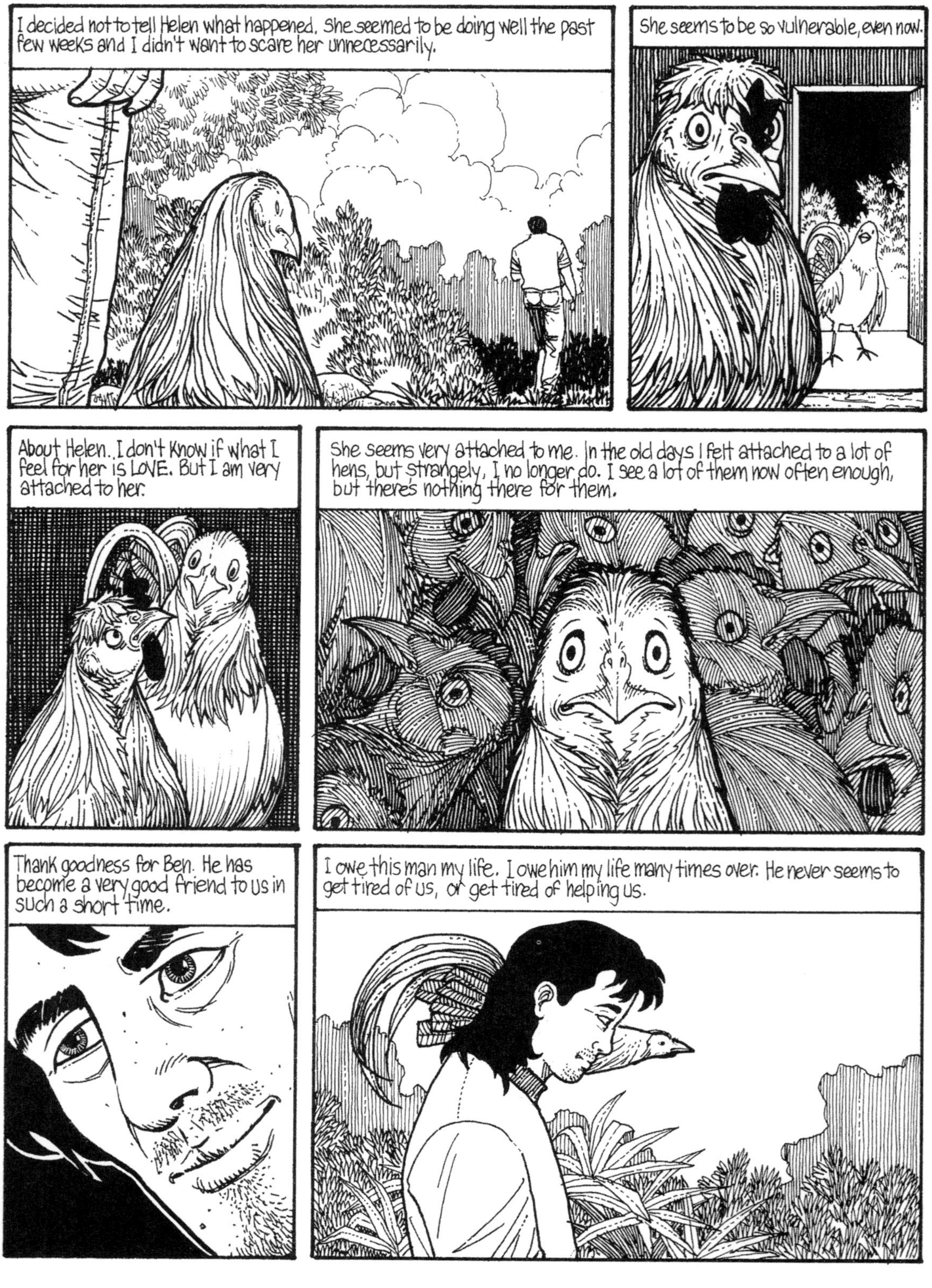
I decided not to tell Helen what happened. She seemed to be doing well the past few weeks and I didn't want to scare her unnecessarily.
She seems to be so vulnerable, even now.
About Helen.. I don't know if what I feel for her is LOVE. But I am very attached to her.
She seems very attached to me. In the old days I felt attached to a lot of hens, but strangely, I no longer do. I see a lot of them now often enough, but there's nothing there for them.
Thank goodness for Ben. He has become a very good friend to us in such a short time.
I owe this man my life. I owe him my life many times over. He never seems to get tired of us, or get tired of helping us.

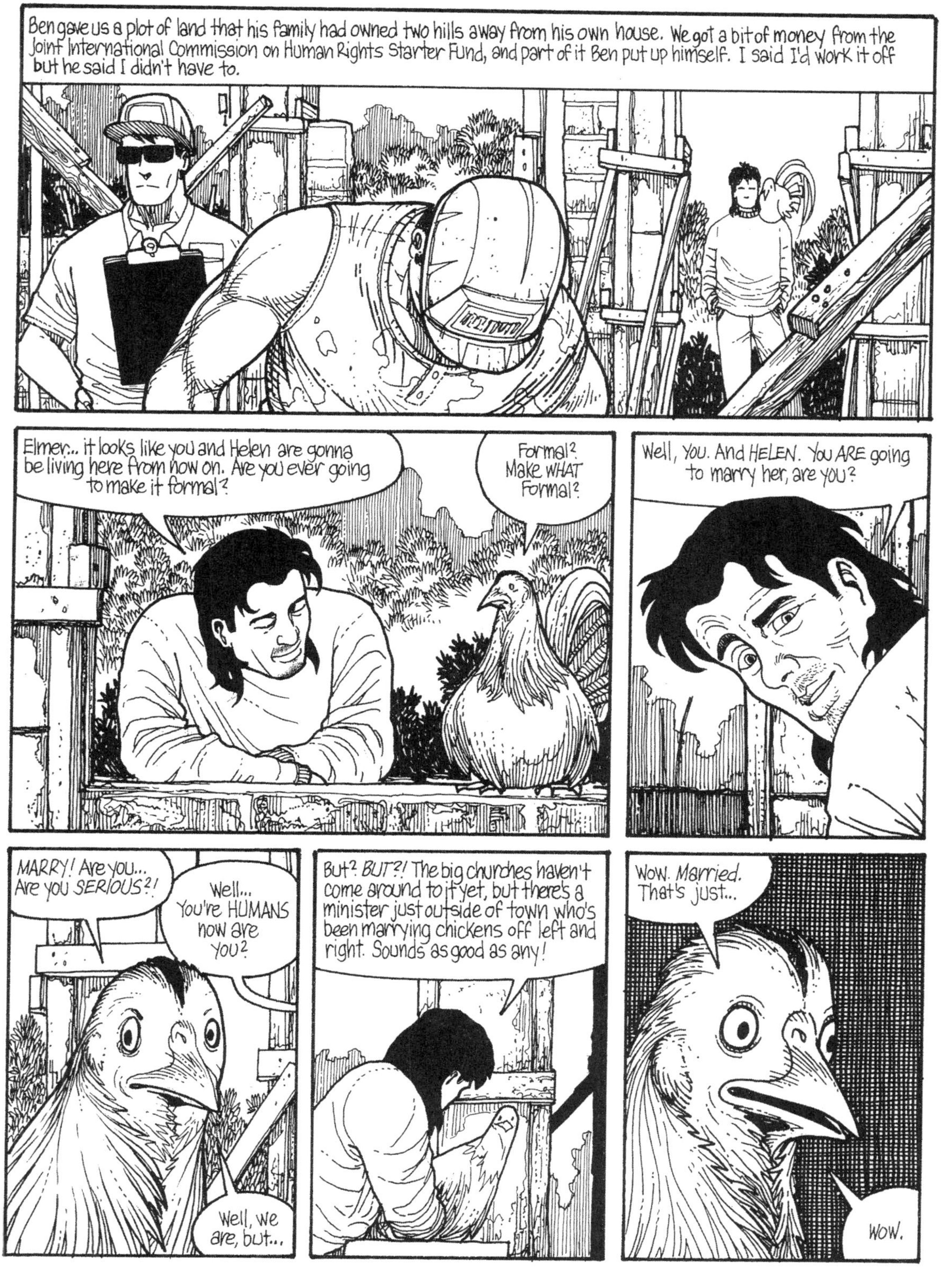
Ben gave us a plot of land that his family had owned two hills away from his own house. We got a bit of money from the Joint International Commission on Human Rights Starter Fund, and part of it Ben put up himself. I said I'd work it off but he said I didn't have to.
Elmer... it looks like you and Helen are gonna be living here from now on. Are you ever going to make it formal?
Formal? Make WHAT Formal?
Well, YOU. And HELEN. You ARE going to marry her, are you?
MARRY! Are you... Are you SERIOUS?!
Well... You're HUMANS now are you?
Well, we are, but...
But? BUT?! The big churches haven't come around to it yet, but there's a minister just outside of town who's been marrying chickens off left and right. Sounds as good as any!
Wow. Married. That's just...
WOW.

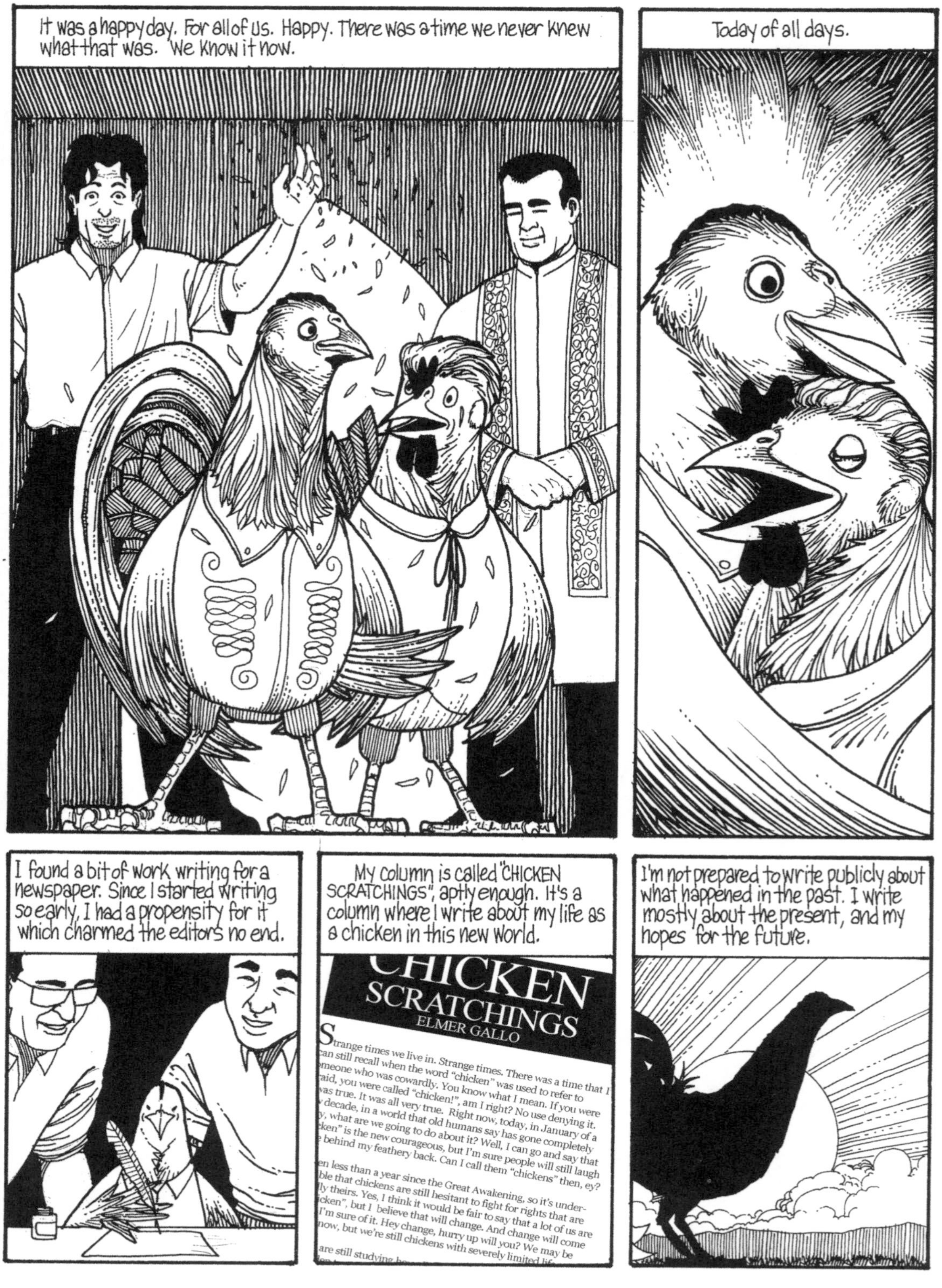
It was a happy day. For all of us. Happy. There was a time we never knew what that was. We know it now.
Today of all days.
I found a bit of work writing for a newspaper. Since I started writing so early, I had a propensity for it which charmed the editors no end.
My column is called "CHICKEN SCRATCHINGS", aptly enough. It's a column where I write about my life as a chicken in this new World.
CHICKEN SCRATCHINGS
ELMER GALLO
Strange times we live in. Strange times. There was a time that I
can still recall when the word "chicken" was used to refer to
meone who was cowardly. You know what I mean. If you were
aid, you were called "chicken!", am I right? No use denying it.
as true. It was all very true. Right now, today, in January of a
decade, in a world that old humans say has gone completely
y, what are we going to do about it? Well, I can go and say that
ken" is the new courageous, but I'm sure people will still laugh
behind my feathery back. Can I call them "chickens" then, ey?
en less than a year since the Great Awakening, so it's under-
ble that chickens are still hesitant to fight for rights that are
ly theirs. Yes, I think it would be fair to say that a lot of us are
cken", but I believe that will change. And change will come
I'm sure of it. Hey change, hurry up will you? We may be
now, but we're still chickens with severely limited
are still studying
I'm not prepared to write publicly about what happened in the past. I write mostly about the present, and my hopes for the future.

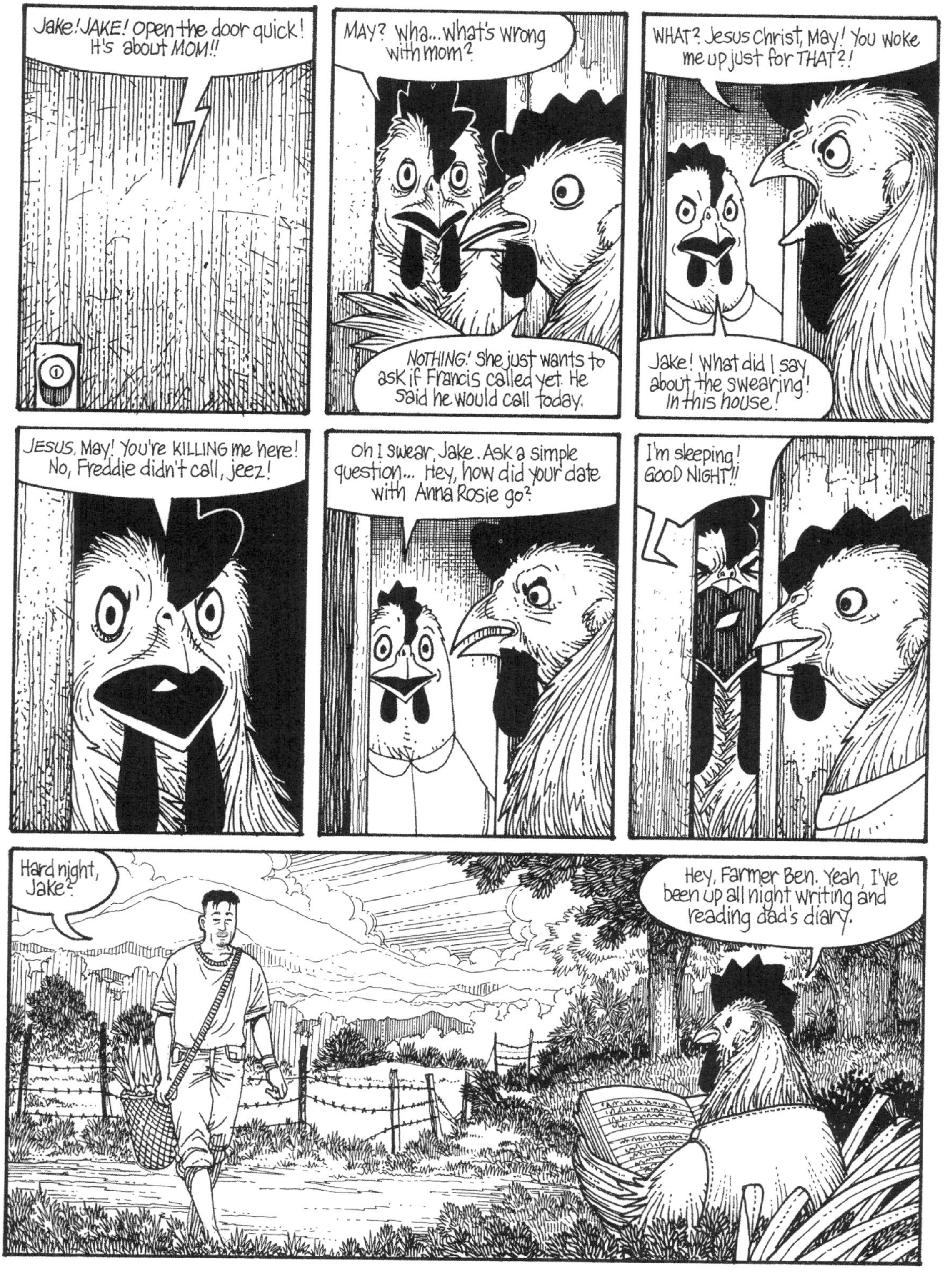
Jake! JAKE! Open the door quick! It's about MOM!!
MAY? Wha... what's wrong with mom?
NOTHING! She just wants to ask if Francis called yet. He said he would call today.
WHAT? Jesus Christ, May! You woke me up just for THAT?!
Jake! What did I say about the swearing! In this house!
JESUS, May! You're KILLING me here! No, Freddie didn't call, jeez!
Oh I swear, Jake. Ask a simple question... Hey, how did your date with Anna Rosie go?
I'm sleeping! GOOD NIGHT!!
Hard night, Jake?
Hey, Farmer Ben. Yeah, I've been up all night writing and reading dad's diary.

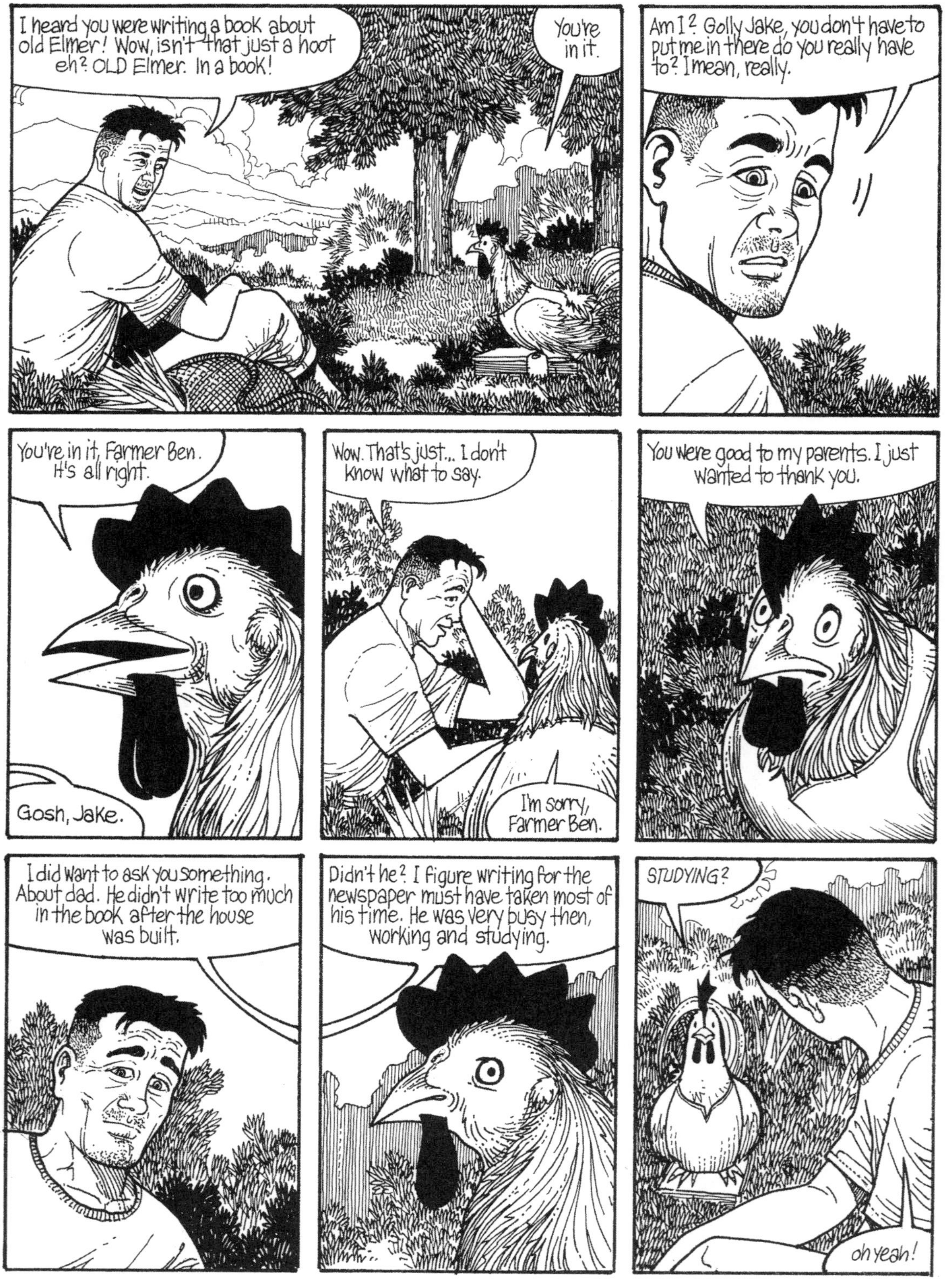
I heard you were writing a book about old Elmer! Wow, isn't that just a hoot eh? OLD Elmer. In a book!
You're in it.
Am I? Golly Jake, you don't have to put me in there do you really have to? I mean, really.
You're in it, Farmer Ben. It's all right.
Gosh, Jake.
Wow. That's just... I don't know what to say.
I'm sorry, Farmer Ben.
You were good to my parents. I just wanted to thank you.
I did want to ask you something. About dad. He didn't write too much in the book after the house was built.
Didn't he? I figure writing for the newspaper must have taken most of his time. He was very busy then, working and studying.
STUDYING?
oh yeah!

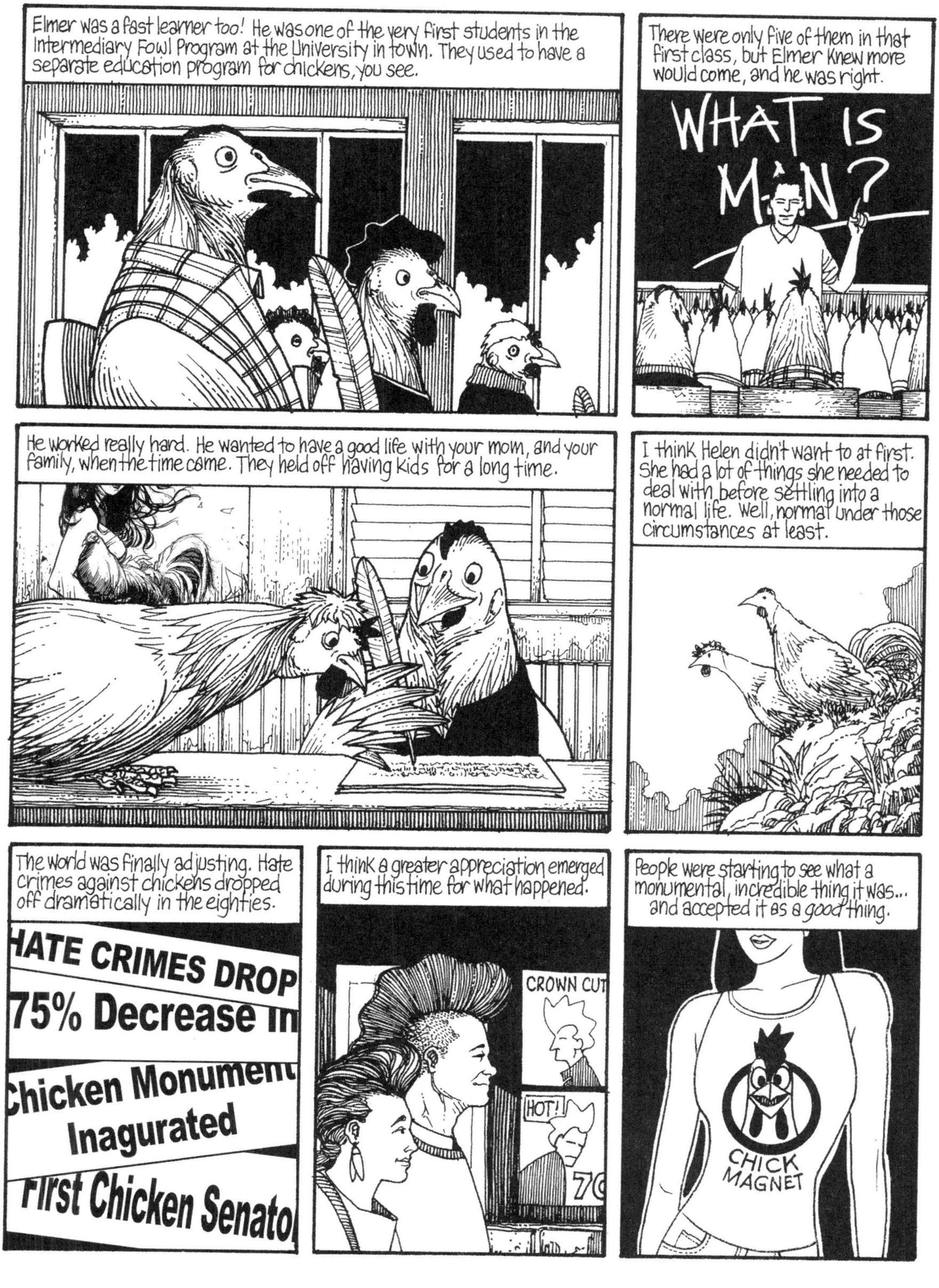
Elmer was a fast learner too! He was one of the very first students in the Intermediary Fowl Program at the University in town. They used to have a separate education program for chickens, you see.
There were only five of them in that first class, but Elmer knew more would come, and he was right.
WHAT IS MAN?
He worked really hard. He wanted to have a good life with your mom, and your family, when the time come. They held off having kids for a long time.
I think Helen didn't want to at first. She had a lot of things she needed to deal with before settling into a normal life. Well, normal under those circumstances at least.
The world was finally adjusting. Hate crimes against chickens dropped off dramatically in the eighties.
HATE CRIMES DROP
75% Decrease in
Chicken Monument
Inagurated
First Chicken Senato
I think a greater appreciation emerged during this time for what happened.
CROWN CUT
HOT!
People were starting to see what a monumental, incredible thing it was... and accepted it as a *good* thing.
CHICK MAGNET

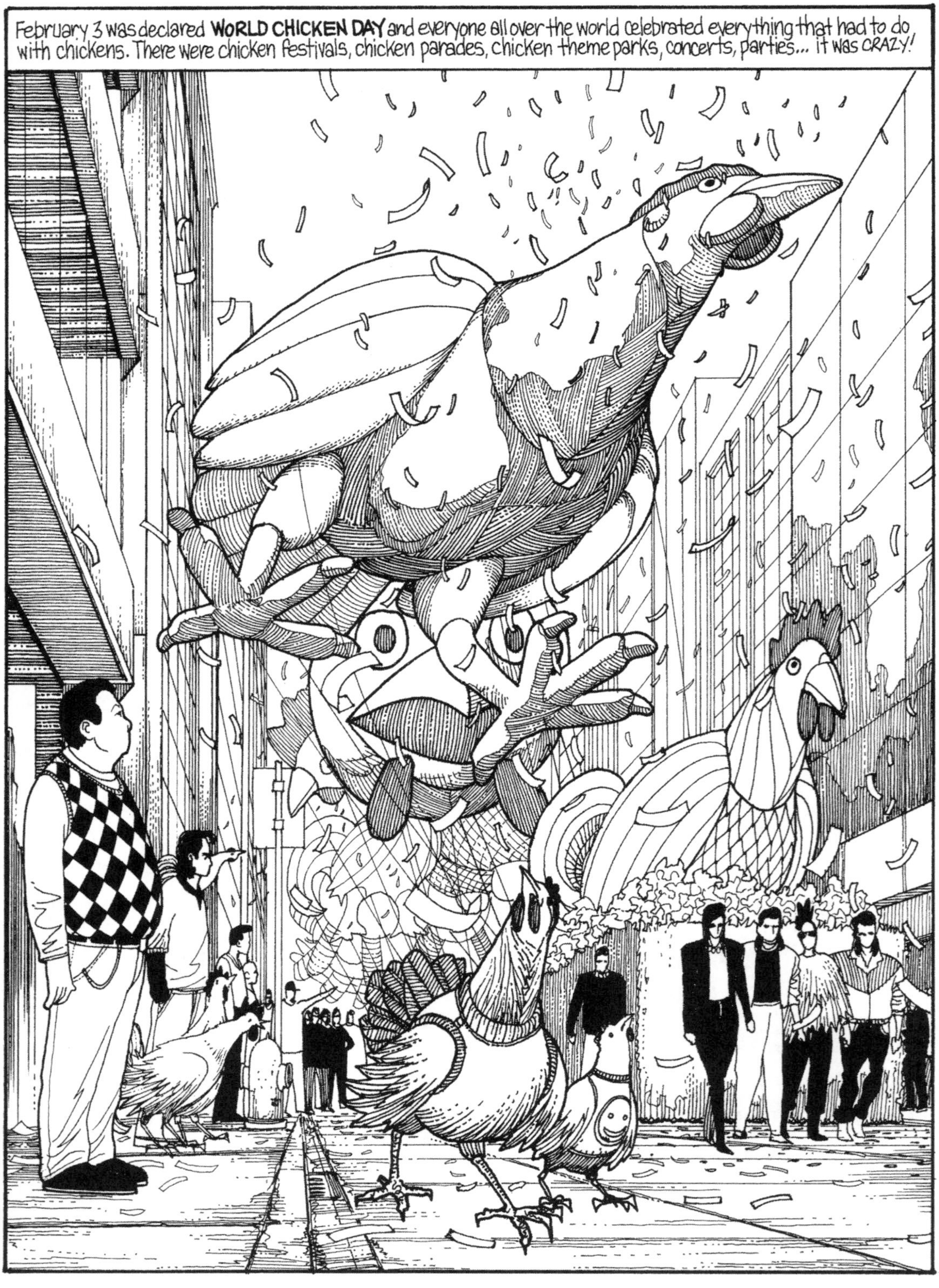
February 3 was declared **WORLD CHICKEN DAY** and everyone all over the world celebrated everything that had to do with chickens. There were chicken festivals, chicken parades, chicken theme parks, concerts, parties... it was CRAZY!

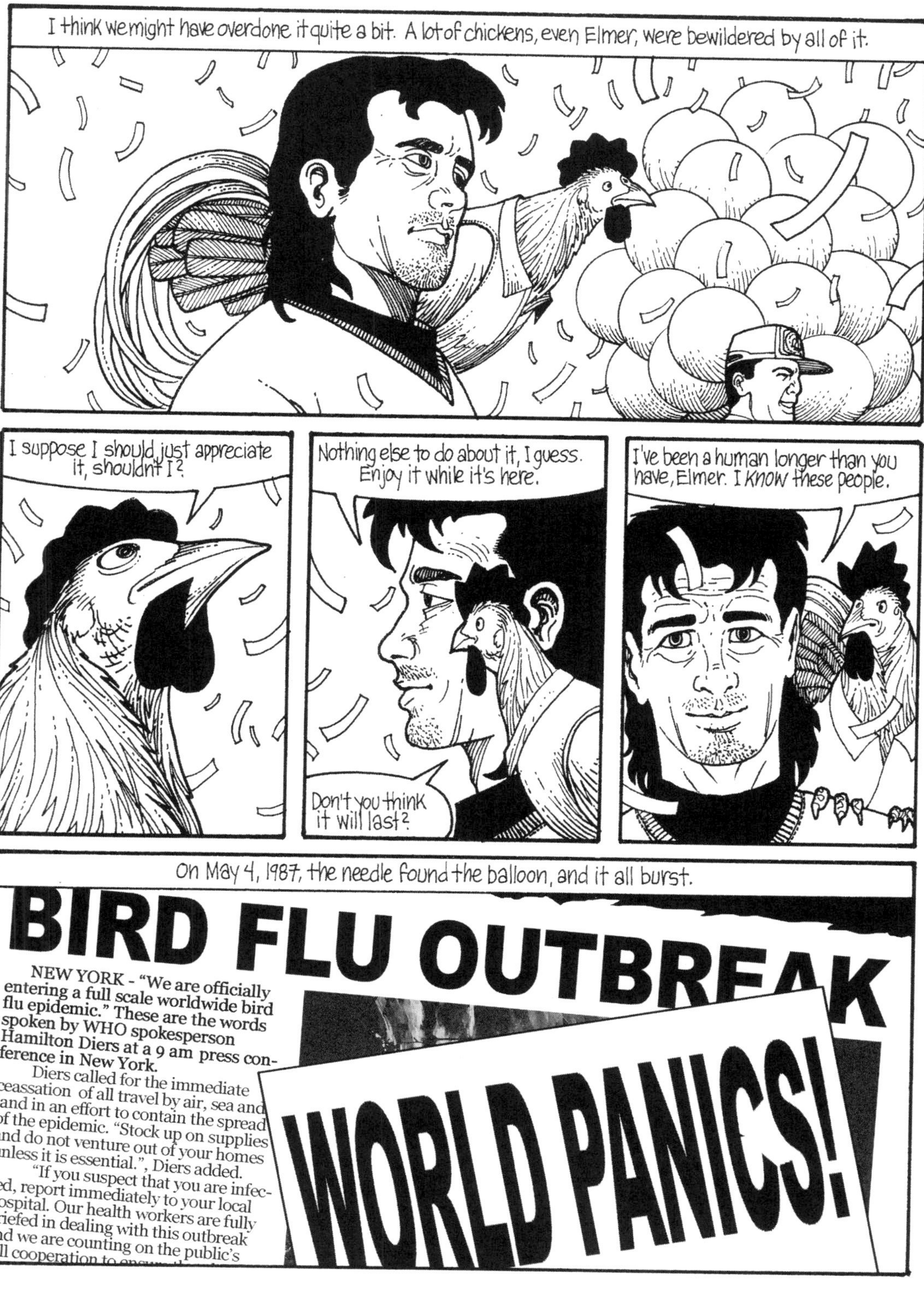

I think we might have overdone it quite a bit. A lot of chickens, even Elmer, were bewildered by all of it.
I suppose I should just appreciate it, shouldn't I?
Nothing else to do about it, I guess. Enjoy it while it's here.
Don't you think it will last?
I've been a human longer than you have, Elmer. I *know* these people.
On May 4, 1987, the needle found the balloon, and it all burst.
BIRD FLU OUTBREAK
NEW YORK - "We are officially entering a full scale worldwide bird flu epidemic." These are the words spoken by WHO spokesperson Hamilton Diers at a 9 am press conference in New York.
Diers called for the immediate ceassation of all travel by air, sea and land in an effort to contain the spread of the epidemic. "Stock up on supplies and do not venture out of your homes unless it is essential.", Diers added.
"If you suspect that you are infected, report immediately to your local hospital. Our health workers are fully briefed in dealing with this outbreak and we are counting on the public's full cooperation to
WORLD PANICS!

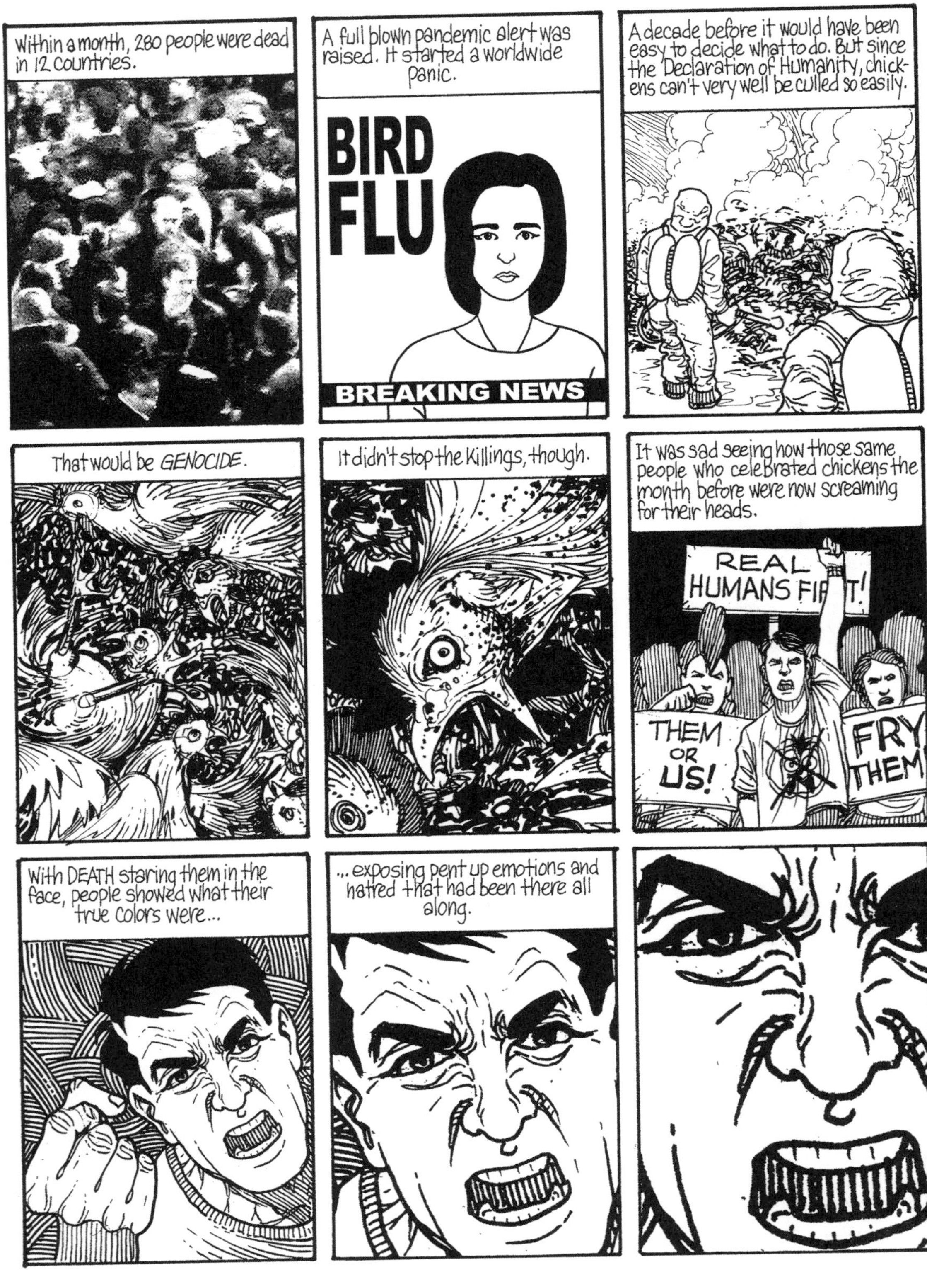

Within a month, 280 people were dead in 12 countries.
A full blown pandemic alert was raised. It started a worldwide panic.
BIRD FLU
BREAKING NEWS
A decade before it would have been easy to decide what to do. But since the Declaration of Humanity, chickens can't very well be culled so easily.
That would be GENOCIDE.
It didn't stop the killings, though.
It was sad seeing how those same people who celebrated chickens the month before were now screaming for their heads.
REAL HUMANS FI T!
THEM OR US!
FRY THEM
With DEATH staring them in the face, people showed what their true colors were...
...exposing pent up emotions and hatred that had been there all along.

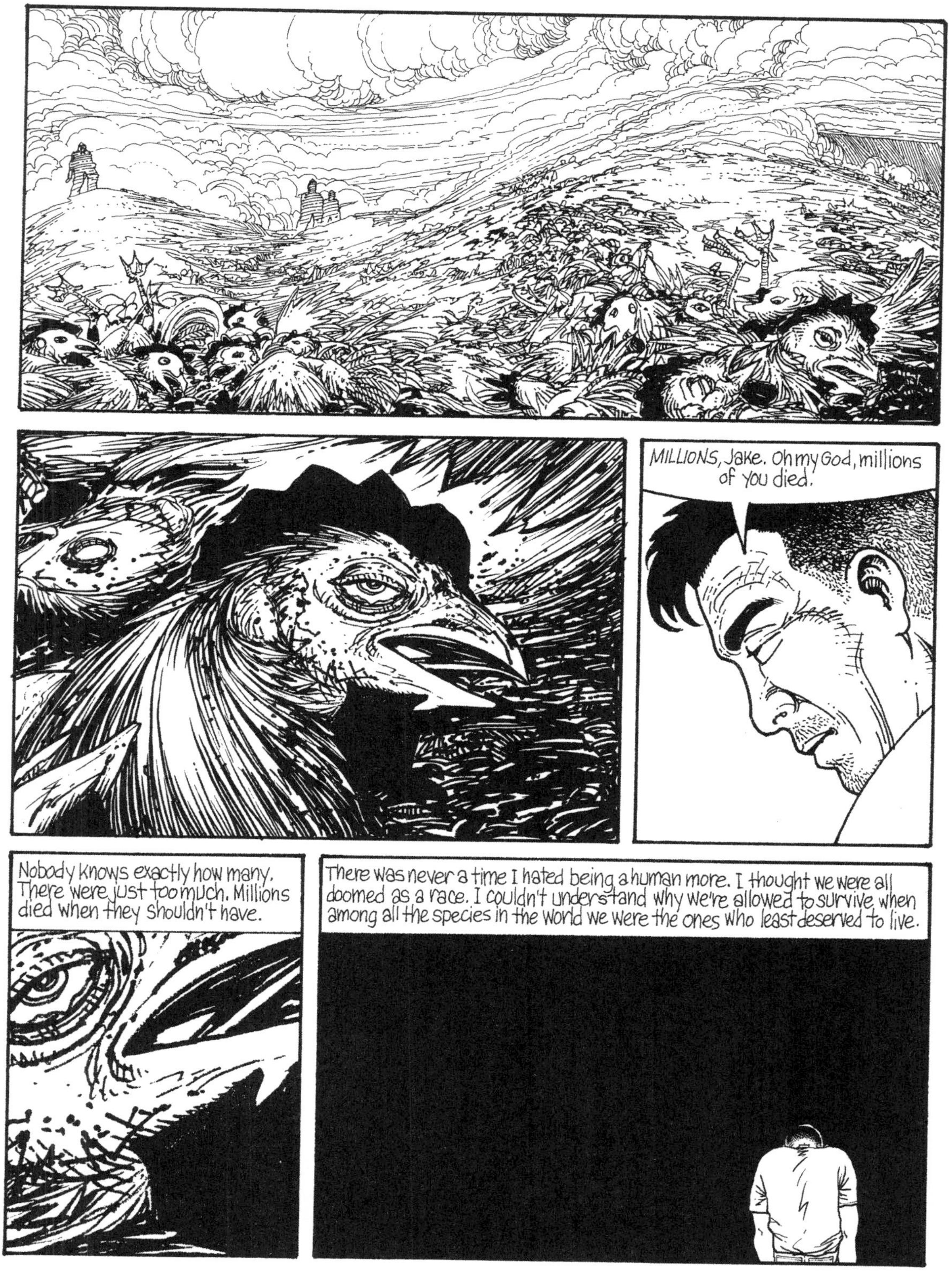
MILLIONS, Jake. Oh my God, millions of you died.
Nobody knows exactly how many. There were just too much. Millions died when they shouldn't have.
There was never a time I hated being a human more. I thought we were all doomed as a race. I couldn't understand why we're allowed to survive when among all the species in the world we were the ones who least deserved to live.

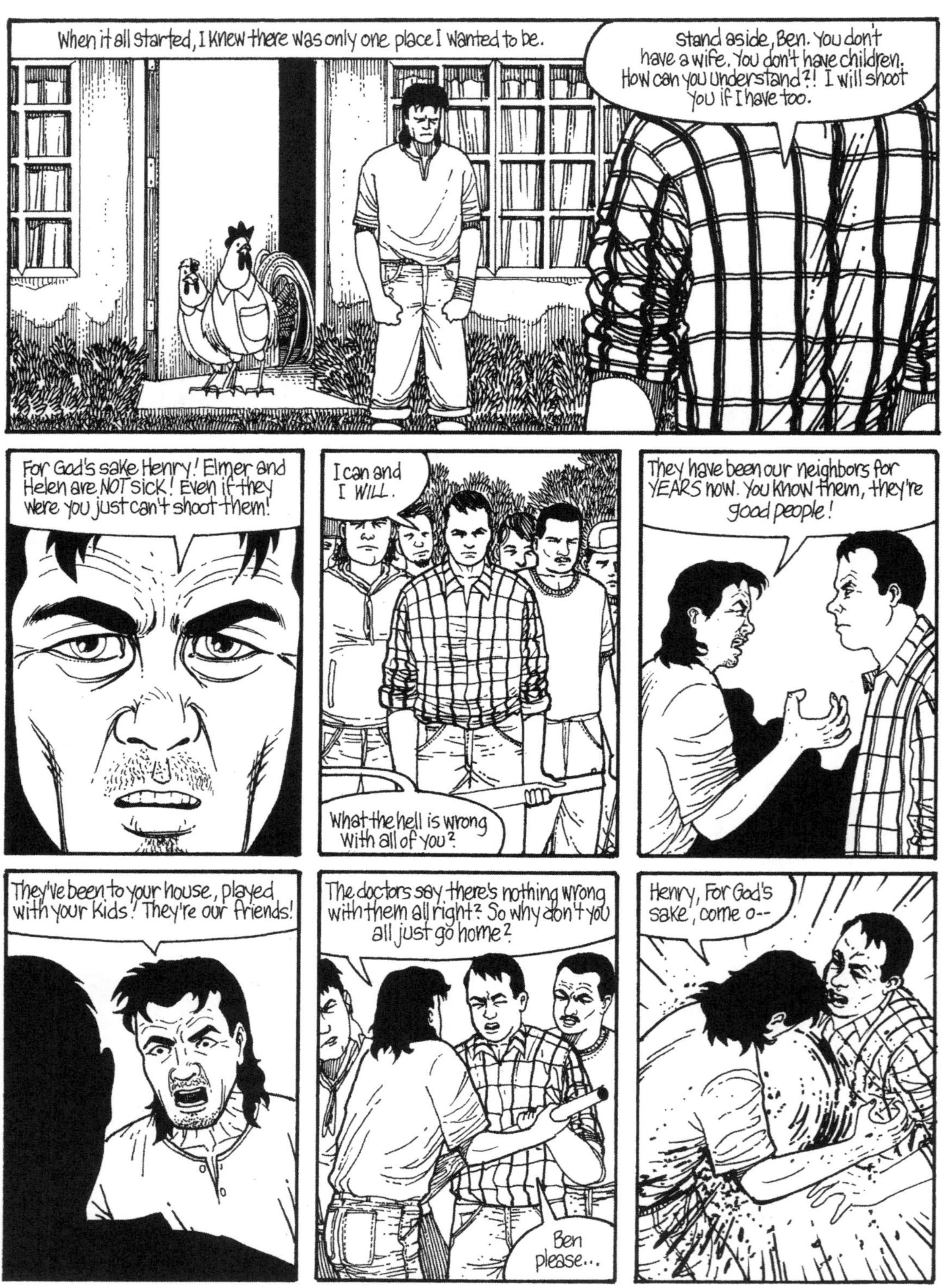
When it all started, I knew there was only one place I wanted to be.
Stand aside, Ben. You don't have a wife. You don't have children. How can you understand?! I will shoot you if I have too.
For God's sake Henry! Elmer and Helen are NOT sick! Even if they were you just can't shoot them!
I can and I WILL.
What the hell is wrong with all of you?
They have been our neighbors for YEARS now. You know them, they're good people!
They've been to your house, played with your kids! They're our friends!
The doctors say there's nothing wrong with them all right? So why don't you all just go home?
Ben please...
Henry, For God's sake, come o--

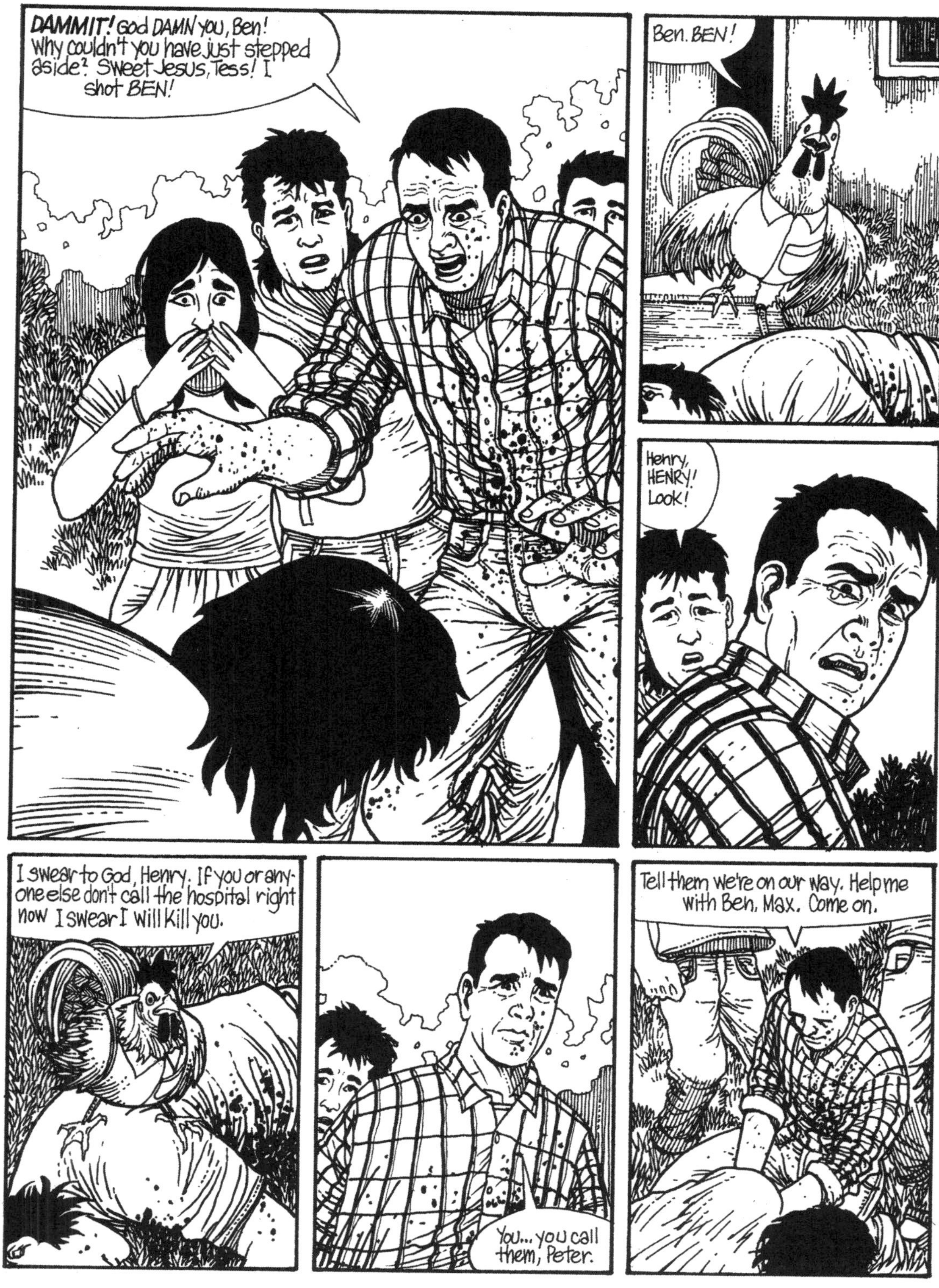
DAMMIT! God DAMN you, Ben! Why couldn't you have just stepped aside? Sweet Jesus, Tess! I shot BEN!
Ben. BEN!
Henry, HENRY! Look!
I swear to God, Henry. If you or anyone else don't call the hospital right now I swear I will kill you.
You... you call them, Peter.
Tell them we're on our way. Help me with Ben, Max. Come on.

Ungh...

Now how did I know it was you sitting his ass on me?

This is getting to be too much of a habit, Ben.

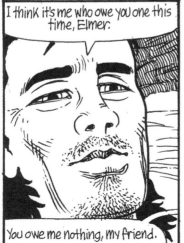

I think it's me who owe you one this time, Elmer.

You owe me nothing, my friend.

Nothing at all.

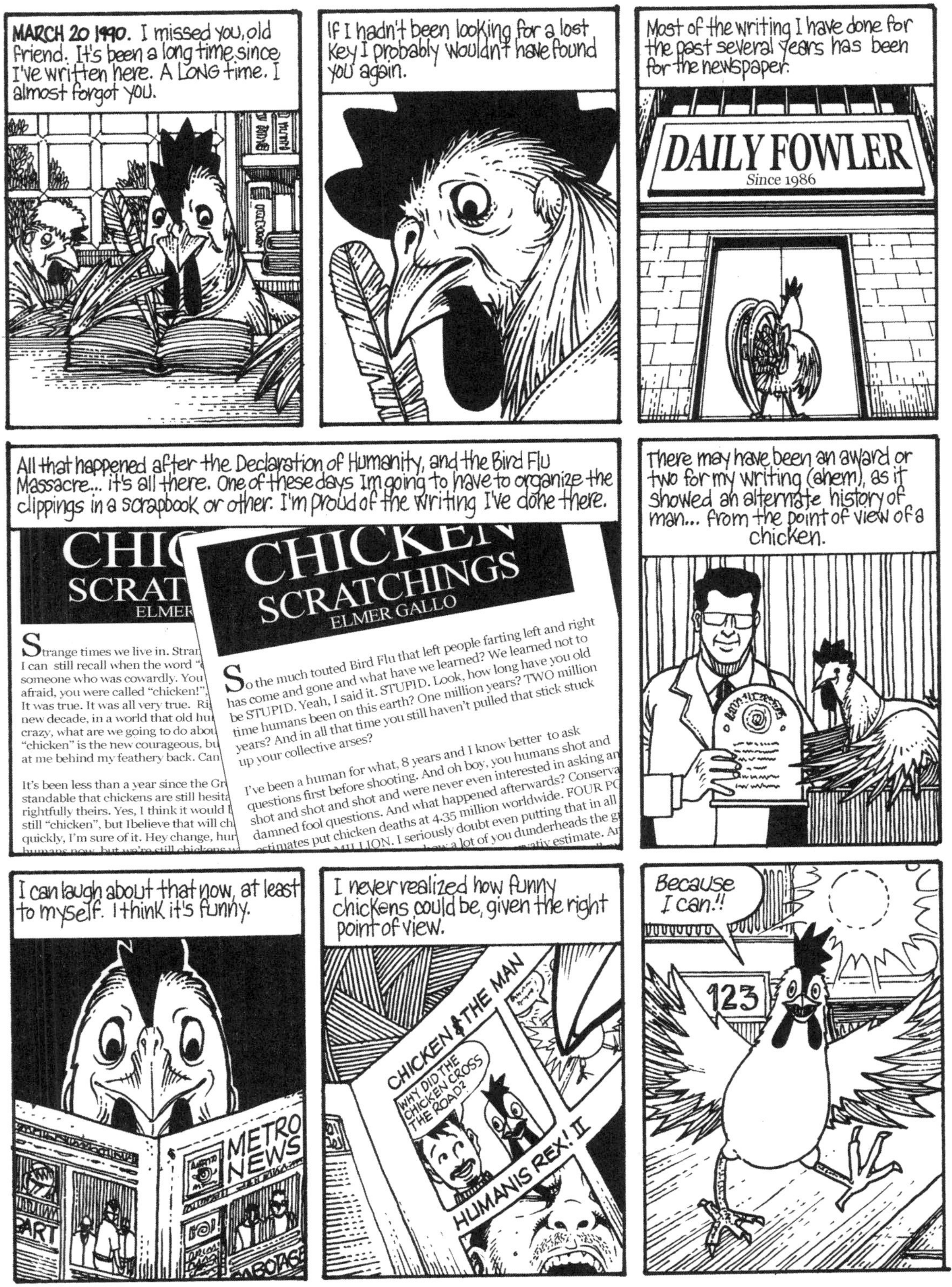
MARCH 20 1990. I missed you, old friend. It's been a long time since I've written here. A LONG time. I almost forgot you.
If I hadn't been looking for a lost key I probably wouldn't have found you again.
Most of the writing I have done for the past several years has been for the newspaper.
DAILY FOWLER
Since 1986
All that happened after the Declaration of Humanity, and the Bird Flu Massacre... it's all there. One of these days Im going to have to organize the clippings in a scrapbook or other. I'm proud of the writing I've done there.
CHIC
SCRAT
ELMER
Strange times we live in. Stran
I can still recall when the word "c
someone who was cowardly. You
afraid, you were called "chicken!",
It was true. It was all very true. Rig
new decade, in a world that old hu
crazy, what are we going to do abou
"chicken" is the new courageous, bu
at me behind my feathery back. Can
It's been less than a year since the Gr
standable that chickens are still hesita
rightfully theirs. Yes, I think it would b
still "chicken", but Ibelieve that will ch
quickly, I'm sure of it. Hey change, hur
CHICKEN
SCRATCHINGS
ELMER GALLO
So the much touted Bird Flu that left people farting left and right has come and gone and what have we learned? We learned not to be STUPID. Yeah, I said it. STUPID. Look, how long have you old time humans been on this earth? One million years? TWO million years? And in all that time you still haven't pulled that stick stuck up your collective arses?
I've been a human for what, 8 years and I know better to ask questions first before shooting. And oh boy, you humans shot and shot and shot and were never even interested in asking an damned fool questions. And what happened afterwards? Conserva estimates put chicken deaths at 4.35 million worldwide. FOUR PO
There may have been an award or two for my writing (ahem), as it showed an alternate history of man... from the point of view of a chicken.
I can laugh about that now, at least to myself. I think it's funny.
METRO NEWS
SABOTAGE
I never realized how funny chickens could be, given the right point of view.
CHICKEN & THE MAN
WHY DID THE CHICKEN CROSS THE ROAD?
HUMANIS REX! II
Because I can!!
123

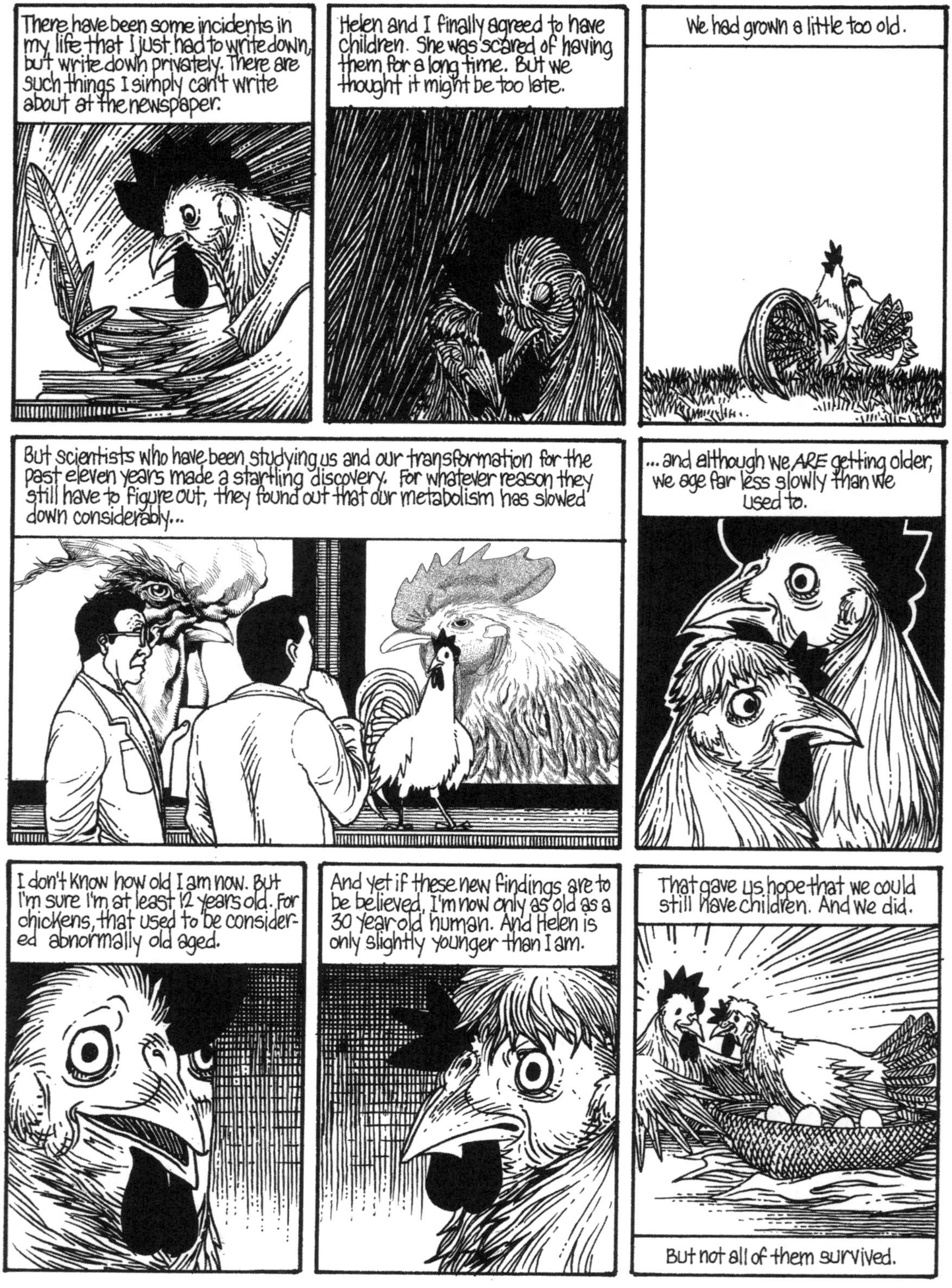

There have been some incidents in my life that I just had to write down, but write down privately. There are such things I simply can't write about at the newspaper.
Helen and I finally agreed to have children. She was scared of having them for a long time. But we thought it might be too late.
We had grown a little too old.
But scientists who have been studying us and our transformation for the past eleven years made a startling discovery. For whatever reason they still have to figure out, they found out that our metabolism has slowed down considerably...
...and although we ARE getting older, we age far less slowly than we used to.
I don't know how old I am now. But I'm sure I'm at least 12 years old. For chickens, that used to be considered abnormally old aged.
And yet if these new findings are to be believed, I'm now only as old as a 30 year old human. And Helen is only slightly younger than I am.
That gave us hope that we could still have children. And we did.
But not all of them survived.

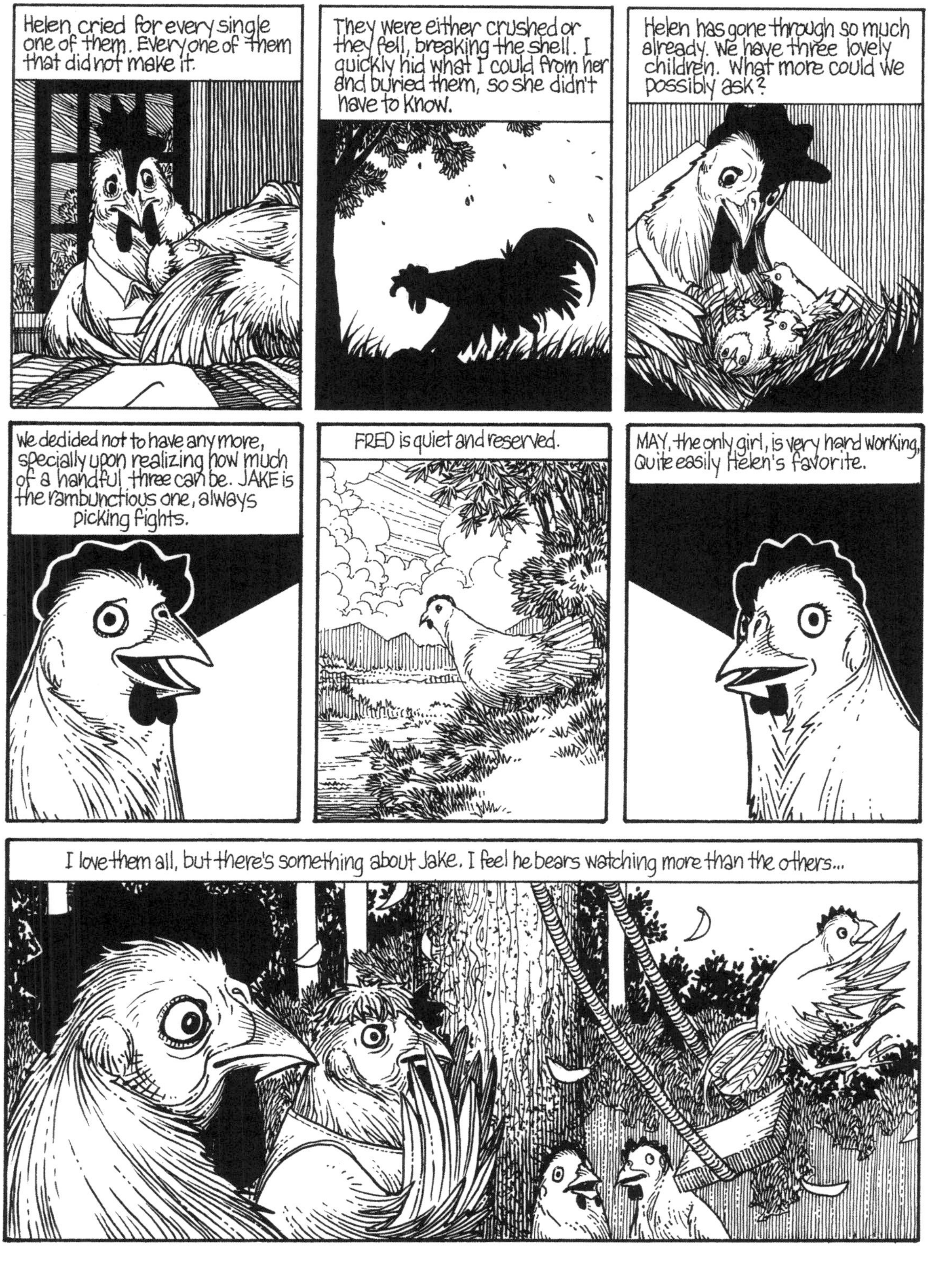
Helen cried for every single one of them. Every one of them that did not make it.
They were either crushed or they fell, breaking the shell. I quickly hid what I could from her and buried them, so she didn't have to know.
Helen has gone through so much already. We have three lovely children. What more could we possibly ask?
We dedided not to have any more, specially upon realizing how much of a handful three can be. JAKE is the rambunctious one, always picking fights.
FRED is quiet and reserved.
MAY, the only girl, is very hard working, Quite easily Helen's favorite.
I love them all, but there's something about Jake. I feel he bears watching more than the others...

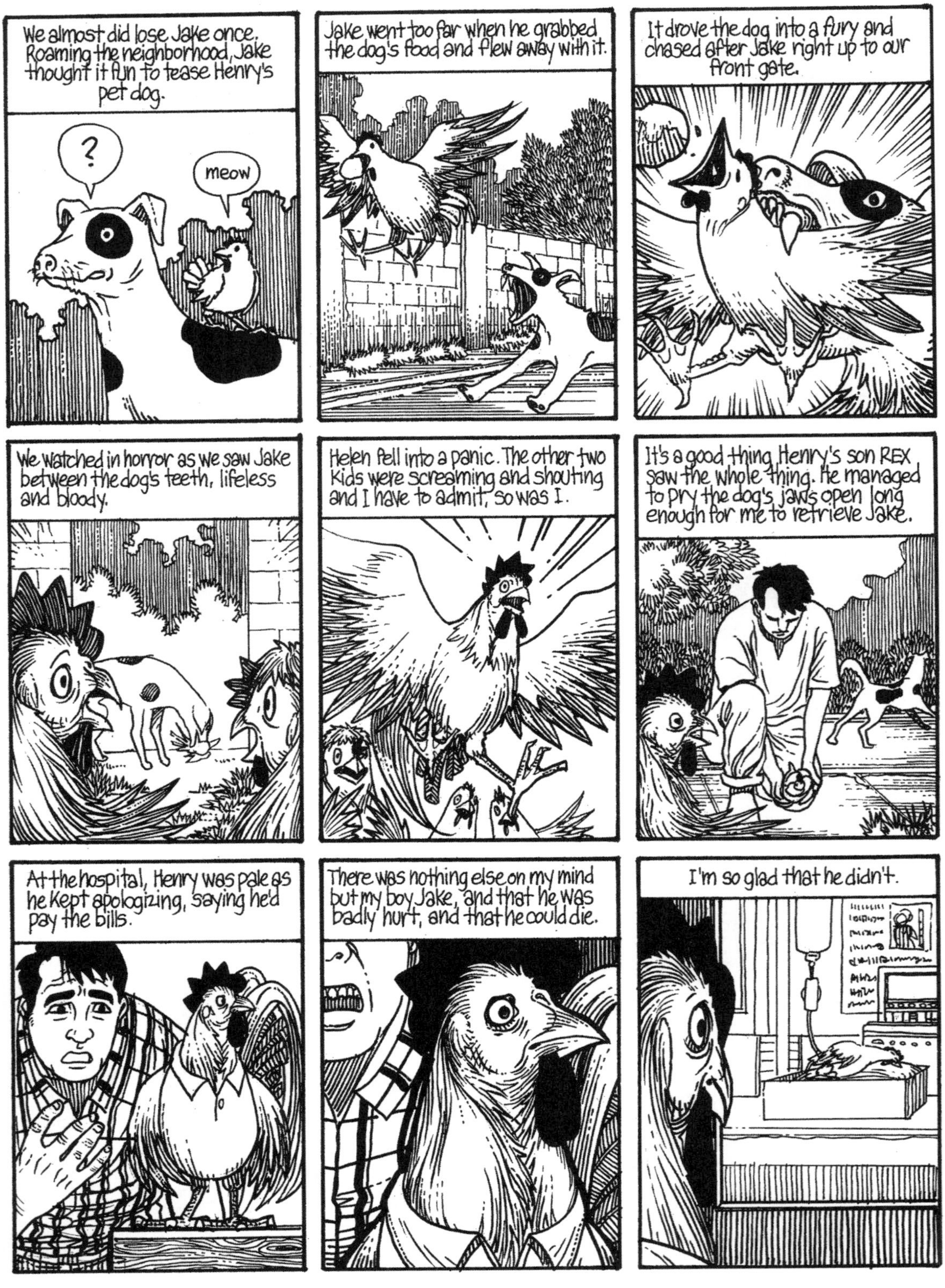
We almost did lose Jake once. Roaming the neighborhood, Jake thought it fun to tease Henry's pet dog.
?
meow
Jake went too far when he grabbed the dog's food and flew away with it.
It drove the dog into a fury and chased after Jake right up to our front gate.
We watched in horror as we saw Jake between the dog's teeth, lifeless and bloody.
Helen fell into a panic. The other two kids were screaming and shouting and I have to admit, so was I.
It's a good thing Henry's son REX saw the whole thing. He managed to pry the dog's jaws open long enough for me to retrieve Jake.
At the hospital, Henry was pale as he kept apologizing, saying he'd pay the bills.
There was nothing else on my mind but my boy Jake, and that he was badly hurt, and that he could die.
I'm so glad that he didn't.

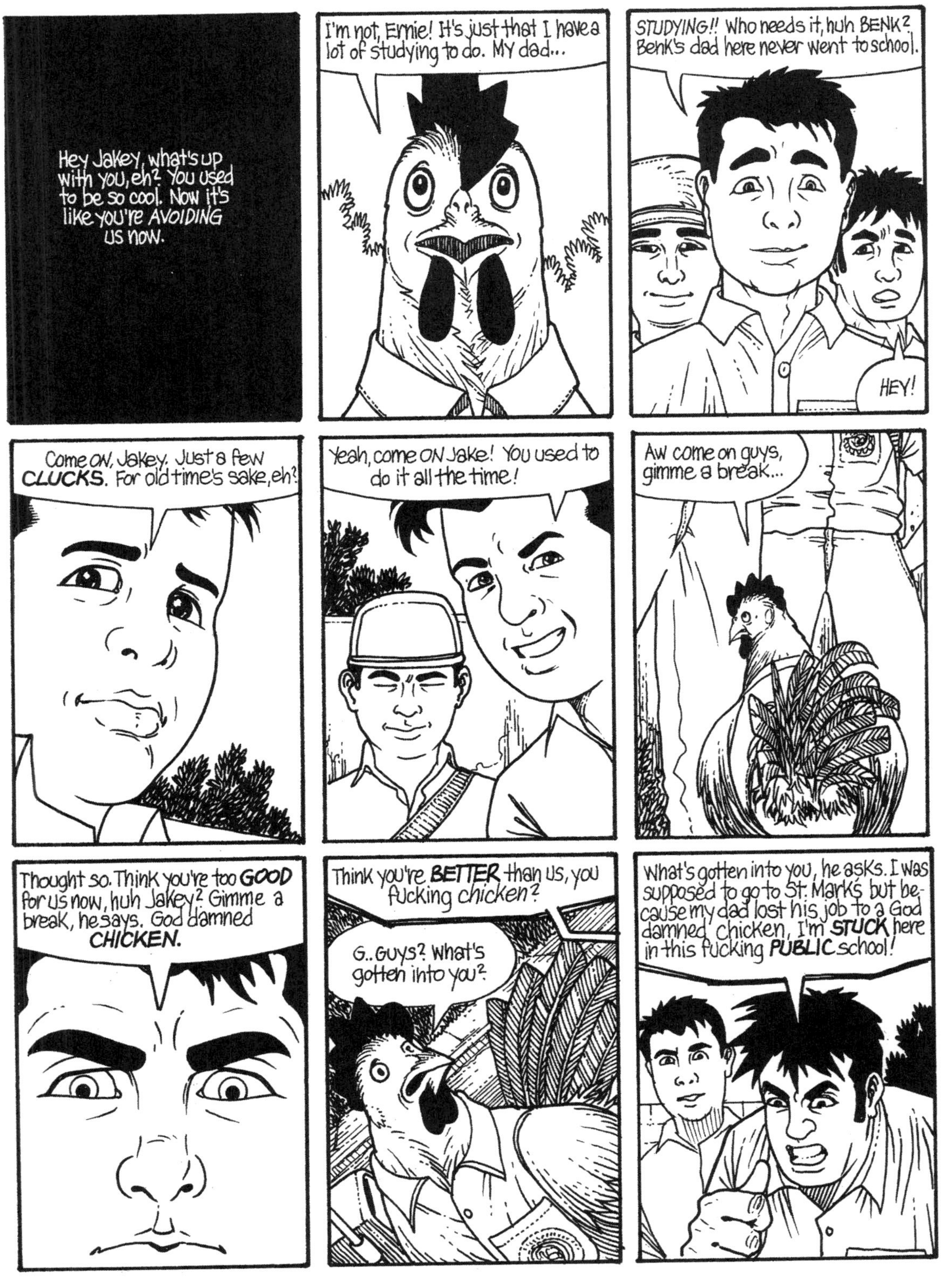
Hey Jakey, what's up with you, eh? You used to be so cool. Now it's like you're AVOIDING us now.
I'm not, Ernie! It's just that I have a lot of studying to do. MY dad...
STUDYING!! Who needs it, huh BENK? Benk's dad here never went to school.
HEY!
Come ON, Jakey. Just a few CLUCKS. For old time's sake, eh?
Yeah, come ON Jake! You used to do it all the time!
Aw come on guys, gimme a break...
Thought so. Think you're too GOOD for us now, huh Jakey? Gimme a break, he says. God damned CHICKEN.
Think you're BETTER than us, you fucking chicken?
G.. GUYS? What's gotten into you?
What's gotten into you, he asks. I was supposed to go to St. Mark's but because my dad lost his job to a God damned chicken, I'm STUCK here in this fucking PUBLIC school!

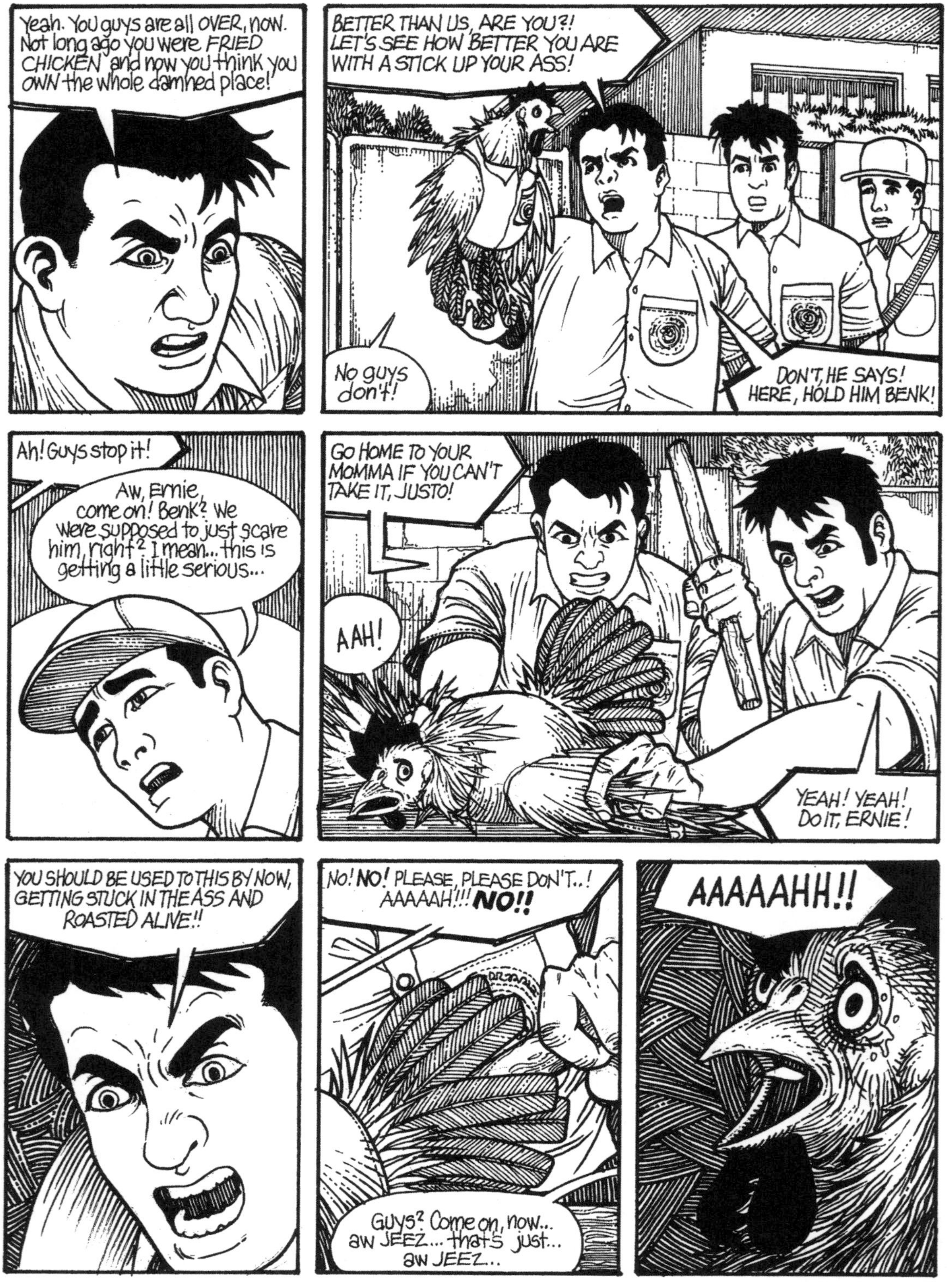

Yeah. You guys are all OVER, now. Not long ago you were FRIED CHICKEN and now you think you own the whole damned place!
BETTER THAN US, ARE YOU?! LET'S SEE HOW BETTER YOU ARE WITH A STICK UP YOUR ASS!
No guys don't!
DON'T, HE SAYS! HERE, HOLD HIM BENK!
Ah! Guys stop it!
Aw, Ernie, come on! Benk? We were supposed to just scare him, right? I mean... this is getting a little serious...
GO HOME TO YOUR MOMMA IF YOU CAN'T TAKE IT, JUSTO!
AAH!
YEAH! YEAH! DO IT, ERNIE!
YOU SHOULD BE USED TO THIS BY NOW, GETTING STUCK IN THE ASS AND ROASTED ALIVE!!
No! NO! PLEASE, PLEASE DON'T..! AAAAAH!!! NO!!
Guys? Come on, now... aw JEEZ... that's just... aw JEEZ...
AAAAAHH!!

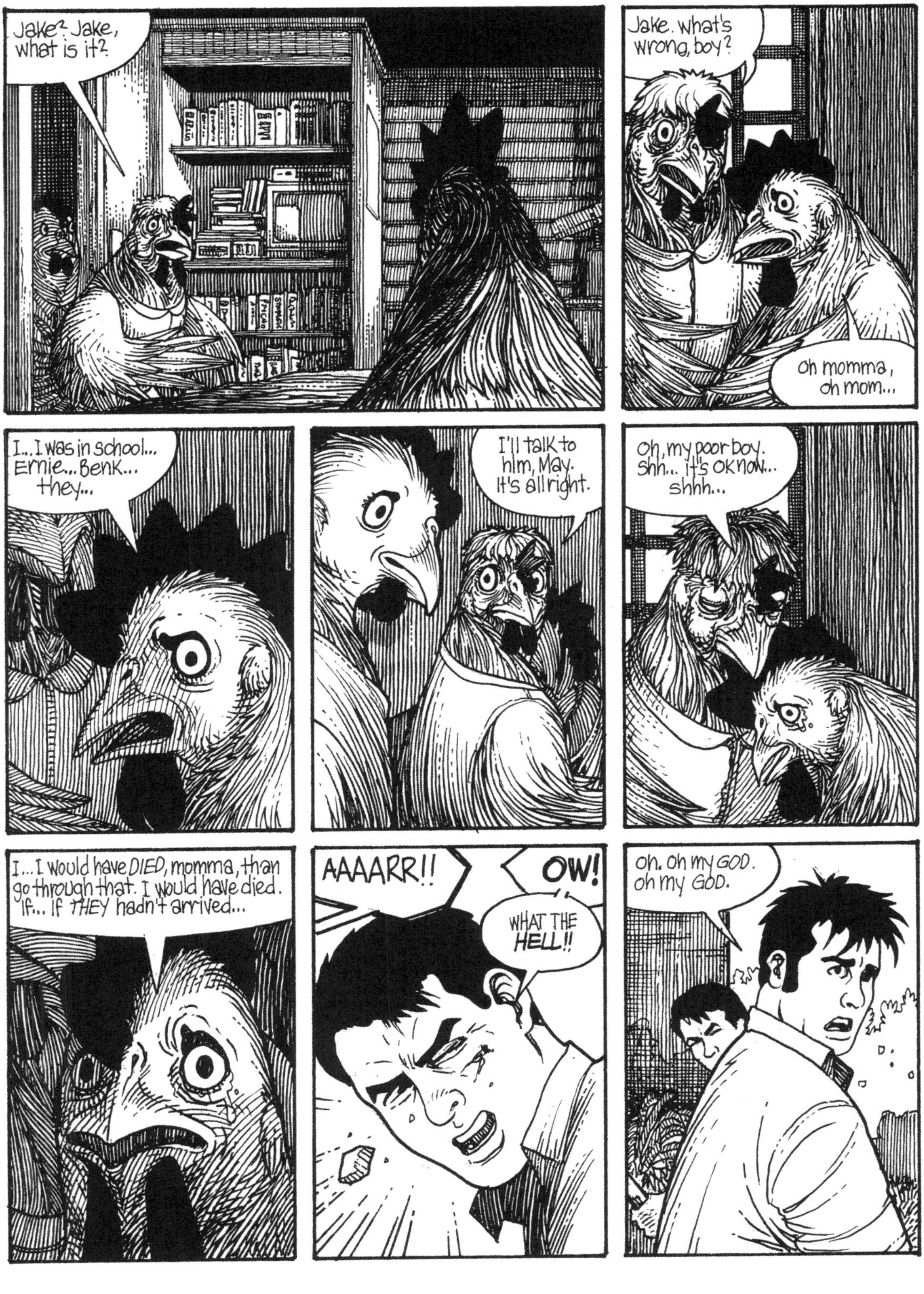
Jake? Jake, what is it?
Jake. what's wrong, boy?
Oh momma, oh mom...
I... I was in school... Ernie... Benk... they...
I'll talk to him, May. It's all right.
Oh, my poor boy. Shh... it's OK now... shhh...
I... I would have DIED, momma, than go through that. I would have died. If... If THEY hadn't arrived...
AAAARR!!
OW!
WHAT THE HELL!!
Oh. Oh my GOD. Oh my GOD.

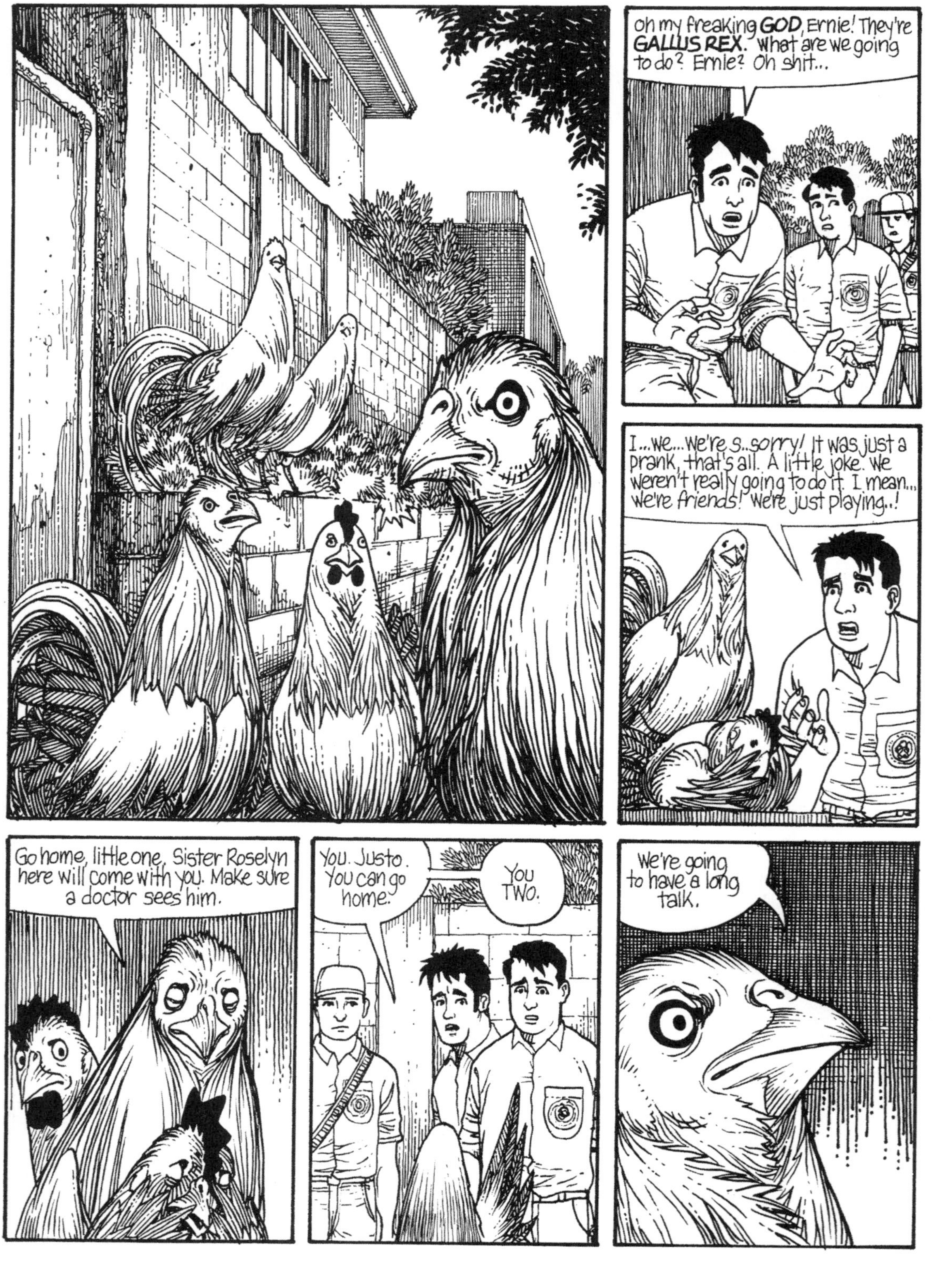
Oh my freaking GOD, Ernie! They're GALLUS REX. What are we going to do? Ernie? Oh shit...
I...we...we're s..sorry! It was just a prank, that's all. A little joke. We weren't really going to do it. I mean... we're friends! We're just playing..!
Go home, little one. Sister Roselyn here will come with you. Make sure a doctor sees him.
You. Justo. You can go home.
You TWO.
We're going to have a long talk.

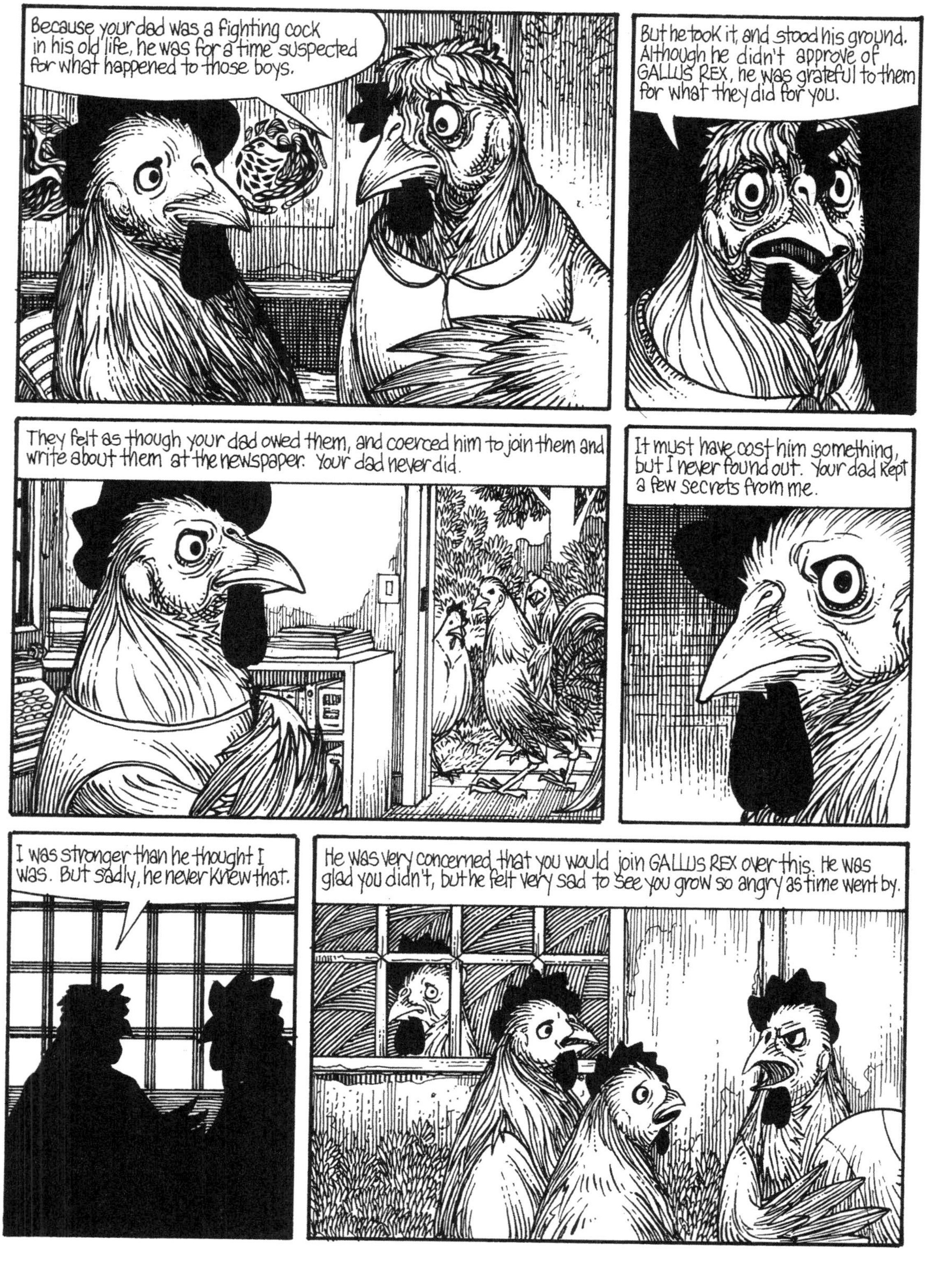
Because your dad was a fighting cock in his old life, he was for a time suspected for what happened to those boys.
But he took it, and stood his ground. Although he didn't approve of GALLUS REX, he was grateful to them for what they did for you.
They felt as though your dad owed them, and coerced him to join them and write about them at the newspaper. Your dad never did.
It must have cost him something, but I never found out. Your dad kept a few secrets from me.
I was stronger than he thought I was. But sadly, he never knew that.
He was very concerned that you would join GALLUS REX over this. He was glad you didn't, but he felt very sad to see you grow so angry as time went by.

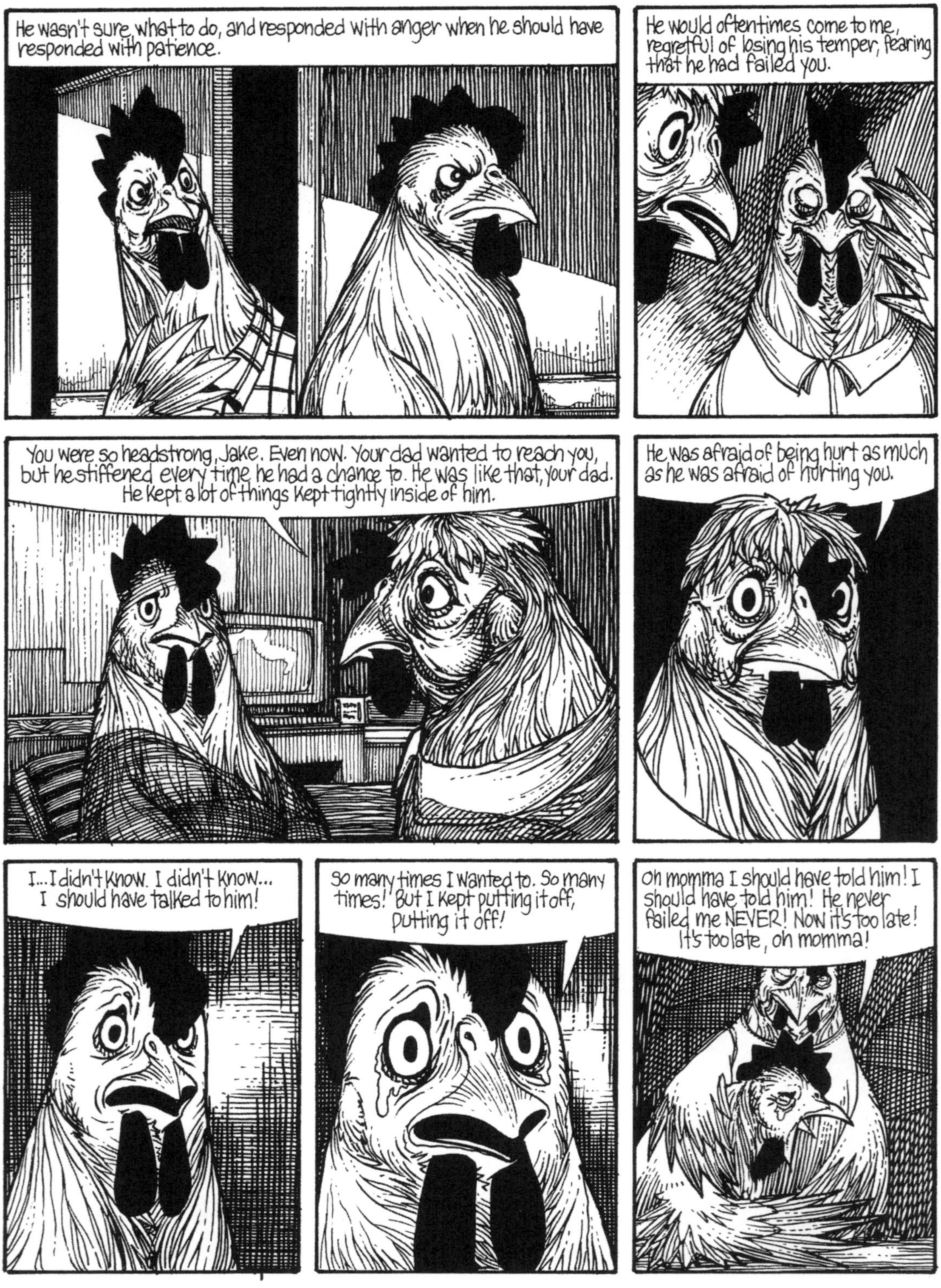
He wasn't sure what to do, and responded with anger when he should have responded with patience.
He would oftentimes come to me, regretful of losing his temper, fearing that he had failed you.
You were so headstrong, Jake. Even now. Your dad wanted to reach you, but he stiffened every time he had a chance to. He was like that, your dad. He kept a lot of things kept tightly inside of him.
He was afraid of being hurt as much as he was afraid of hurting you.
I... I didn't know. I didn't know... I should have talked to him!
So many times I wanted to. So many times! But I kept putting it off, putting it off!
Oh momma I should have told him! I should have told him! He never failed me NEVER! Now it's too late! It's too late, oh momma!

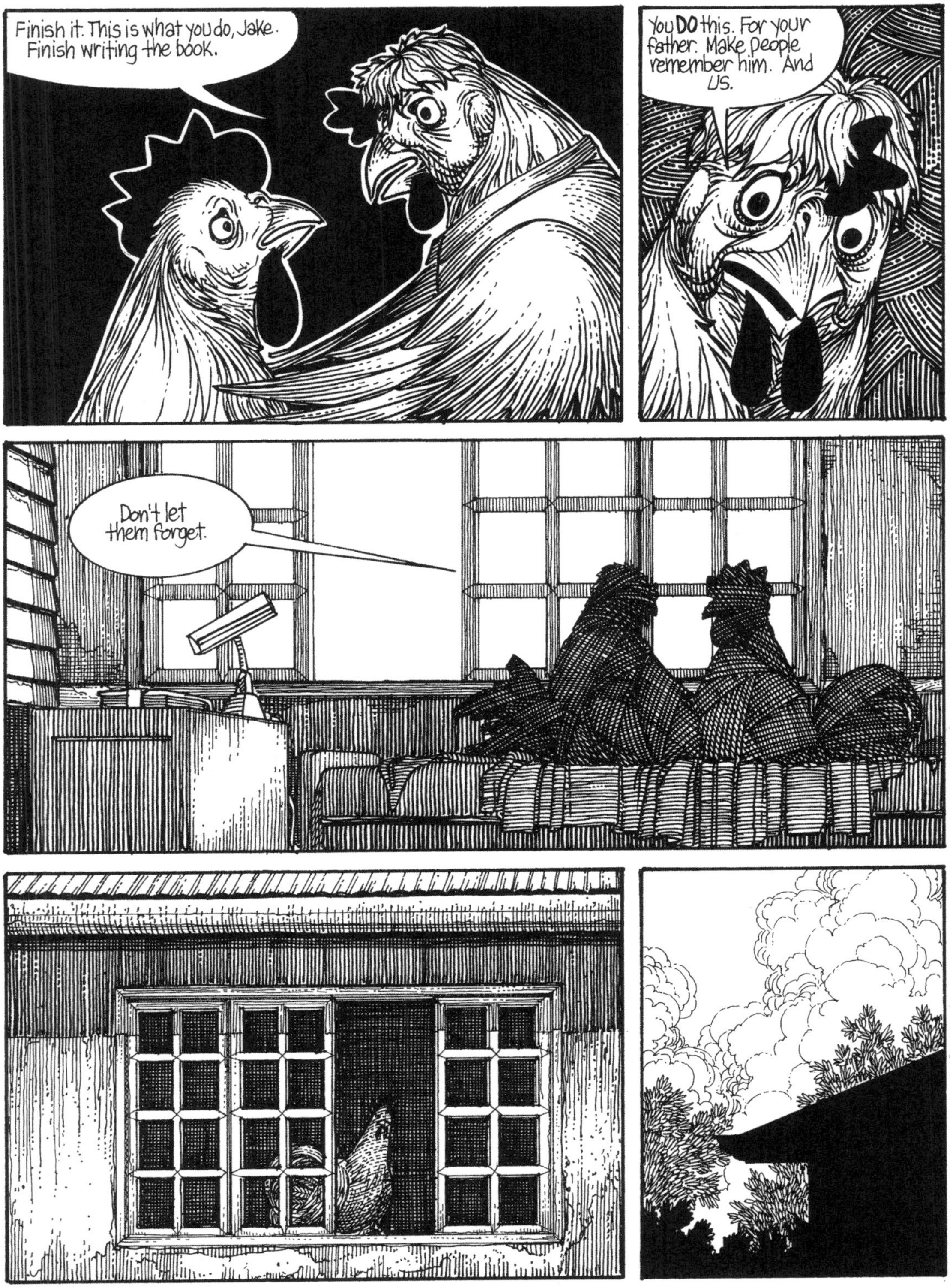
Finish it. This is what you do, Jake. Finish writing the book.
You DO this. For your father. Make people remember him. And US.
Don't let them forget.

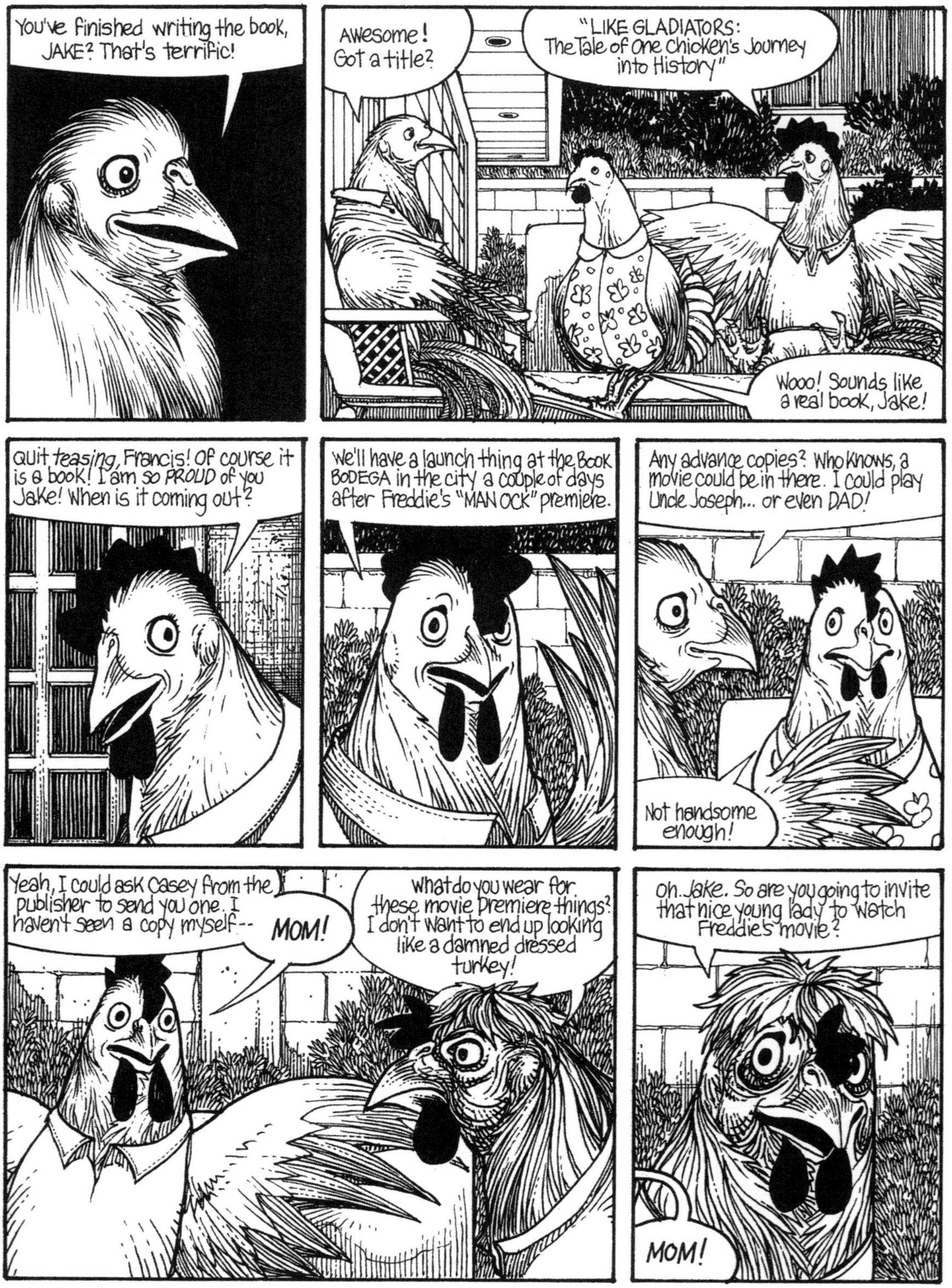

You've finished writing the book, JAKE? That's terrific!
Awesome! Got a title?
"LIKE GLADIATORS: The Tale of One Chicken's Journey into History"
Wooo! Sounds like a real book, Jake!
QUIT teasing, Francis! Of course it is a book! I am so PROUD of you Jake! When is it coming out?
We'll have a launch thing at the Book BODEGA in the city a couple of days after Freddie's "MAN OCK" premiere.
Any advance copies? Who knows, a movie could be in there. I could play Uncle Joseph... or even DAD!
Not handsome enough!
Yeah, I could ask Casey from the publisher to send you one. I haven't seen a copy myself--
MOM!
What do you wear for these movie premiere things? I don't want to end up looking like a damned dressed turkey!
Oh..Jake. So are you going to invite that nice young lady to watch Freddie's movie?
MOM!

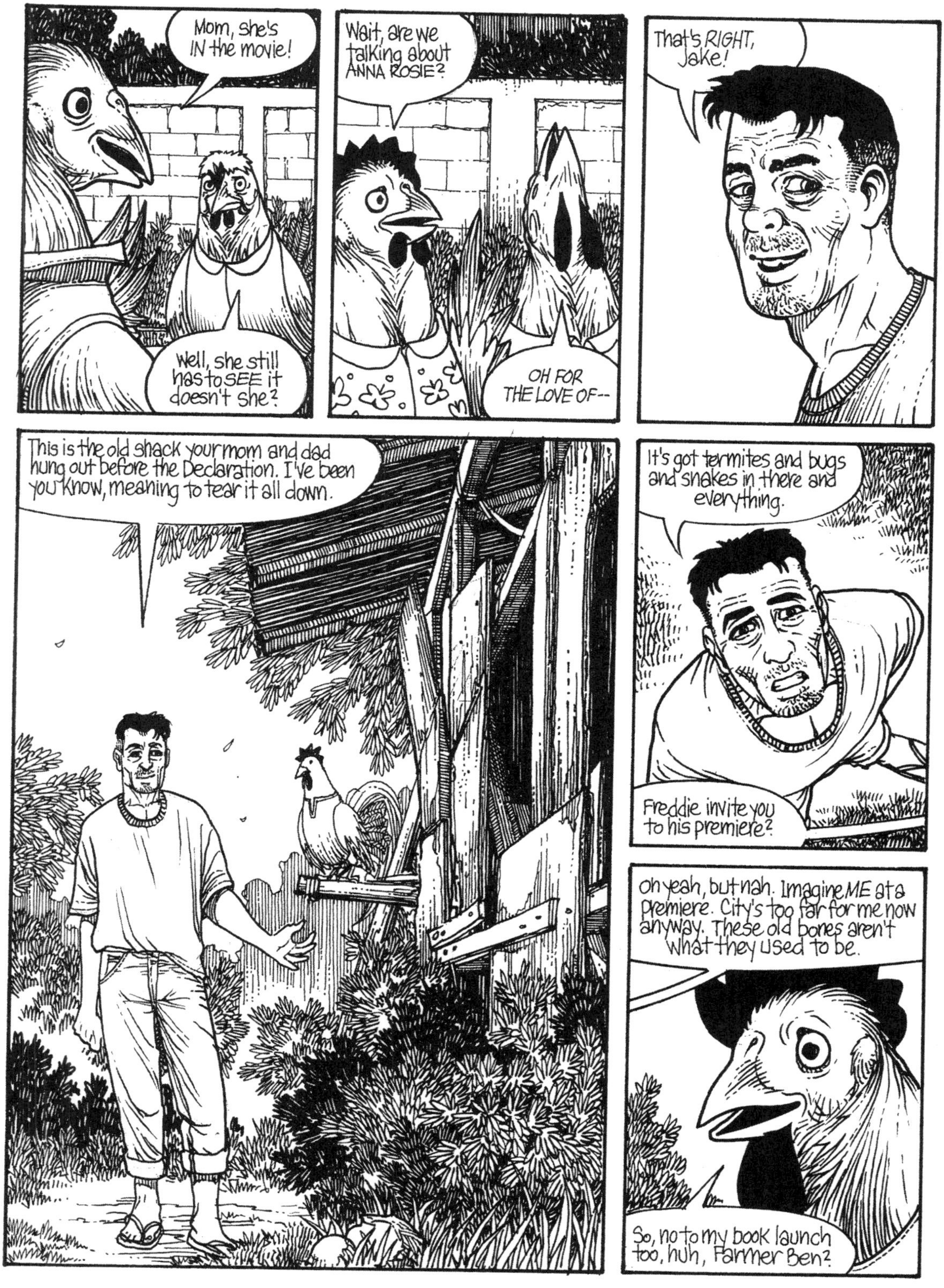
Mom, she's IN the movie!
Well, she still has to SEE it doesn't she?
Wait, are we talking about ANNA ROSIE?
OH FOR THE LOVE OF--
That's RIGHT, Jake!
This is the old shack your mom and dad hung out before the Declaration. I've been you know, meaning to tear it all down.
It's got termites and bugs and snakes in there and everything.
Freddie invite you to his premiere?
Oh yeah, but nah. Imagine ME at a premiere. City's too far for me now anyway. These old bones aren't what they used to be.
So, no to my book launch too, huh, Farmer Ben?

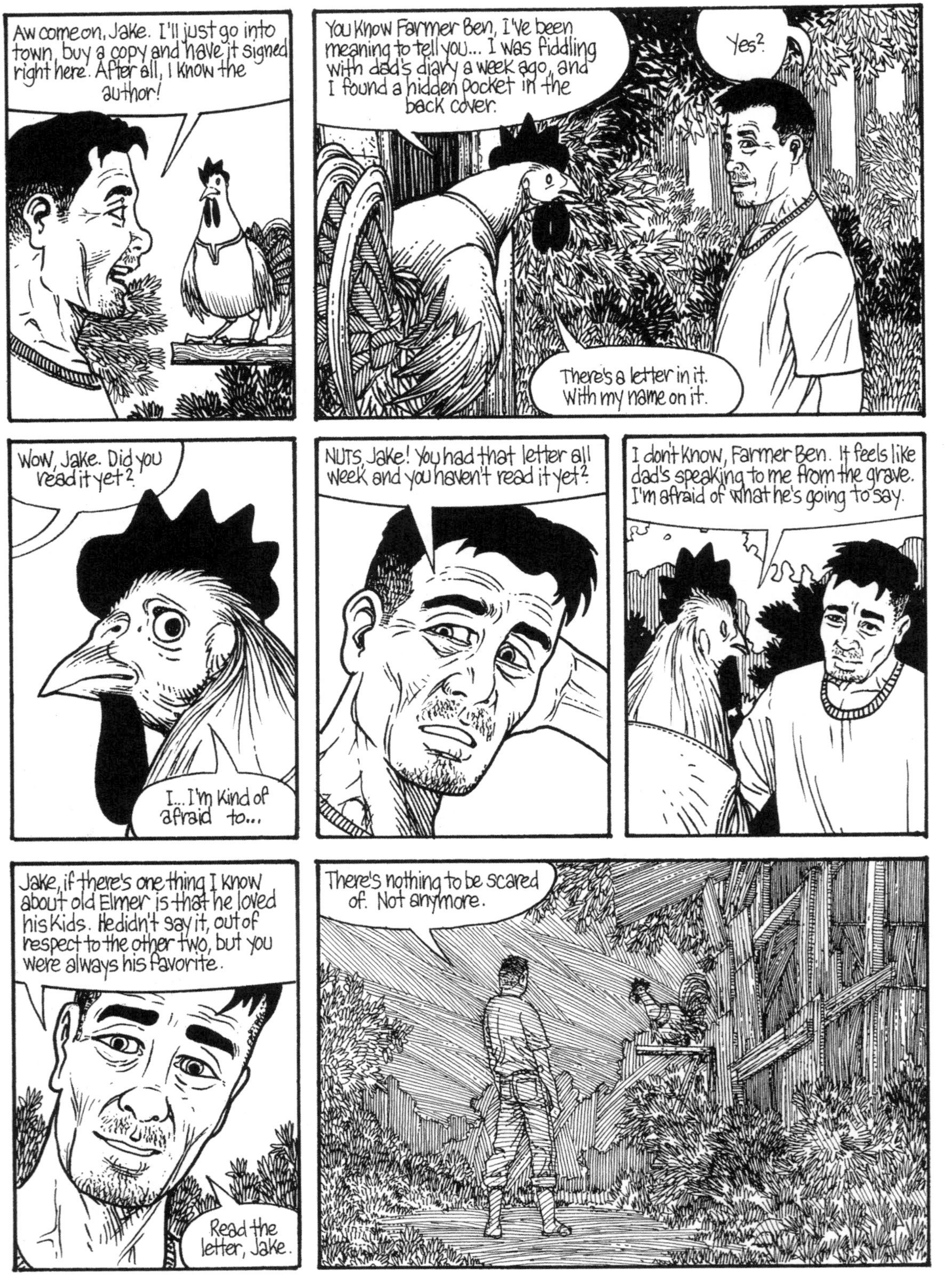

Aw come on, Jake. I'll just go into town, buy a copy and have it signed right here. After all, I know the author!
You know Farmer Ben, I've been meaning to tell you... I was fiddling with dad's diary a week ago, and I found a hidden pocket in the back cover.
Yes?
There's a letter in it. With my name on it.
Wow, Jake. Did you read it yet?
I... I'm kind of afraid to...
NUTS, Jake! You had that letter all week and you haven't read it yet?
I don't know, Farmer Ben. It feels like dad's speaking to me from the grave. I'm afraid of what he's going to say.
Jake, if there's one thing I know about old Elmer is that he loved his kids. He didn't say it, out of respect to the other two, but you were always his favorite.
Read the letter, Jake.
There's nothing to be scared of. Not anymore.

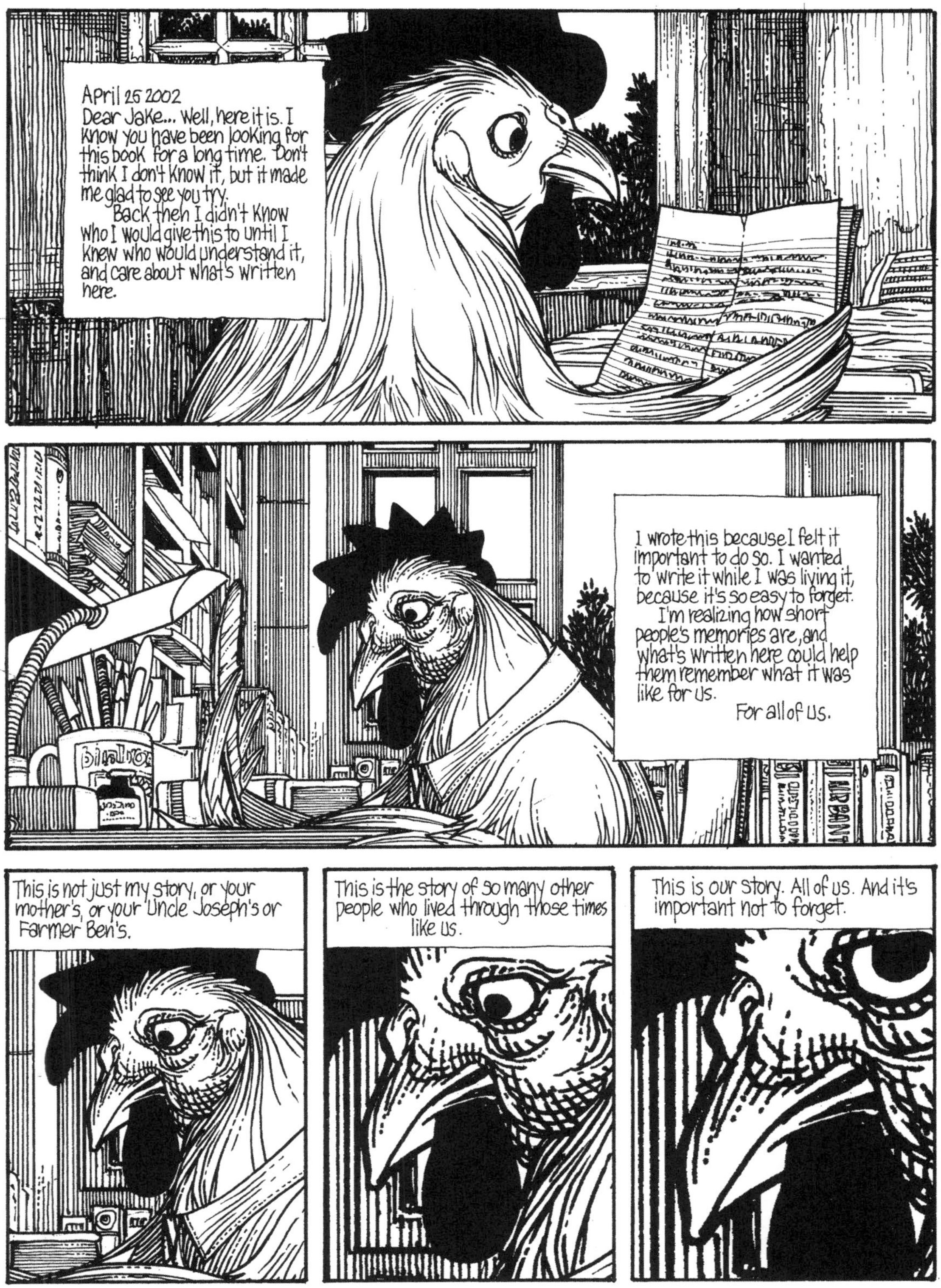
April 25 2002
Dear Jake... Well, here it is. I know you have been looking for this book for a long time. Don't think I don't know it, but it made me glad to see you try.
Back then I didn't know who I would give this to until I knew who would understand it, and care about what's written here.
I wrote this because I felt it important to do so. I wanted to write it while I was living it, because it's so easy to forget.
I'm realizing how short people's memories are, and what's written here could help them remember what it was like for us.
For all of us.
This is not just my story, or your mother's, or your Uncle Joseph's or Farmer Ben's.
This is the story of so many other people who lived through those times like us.
This is our story. All of us. And it's important not to forget.

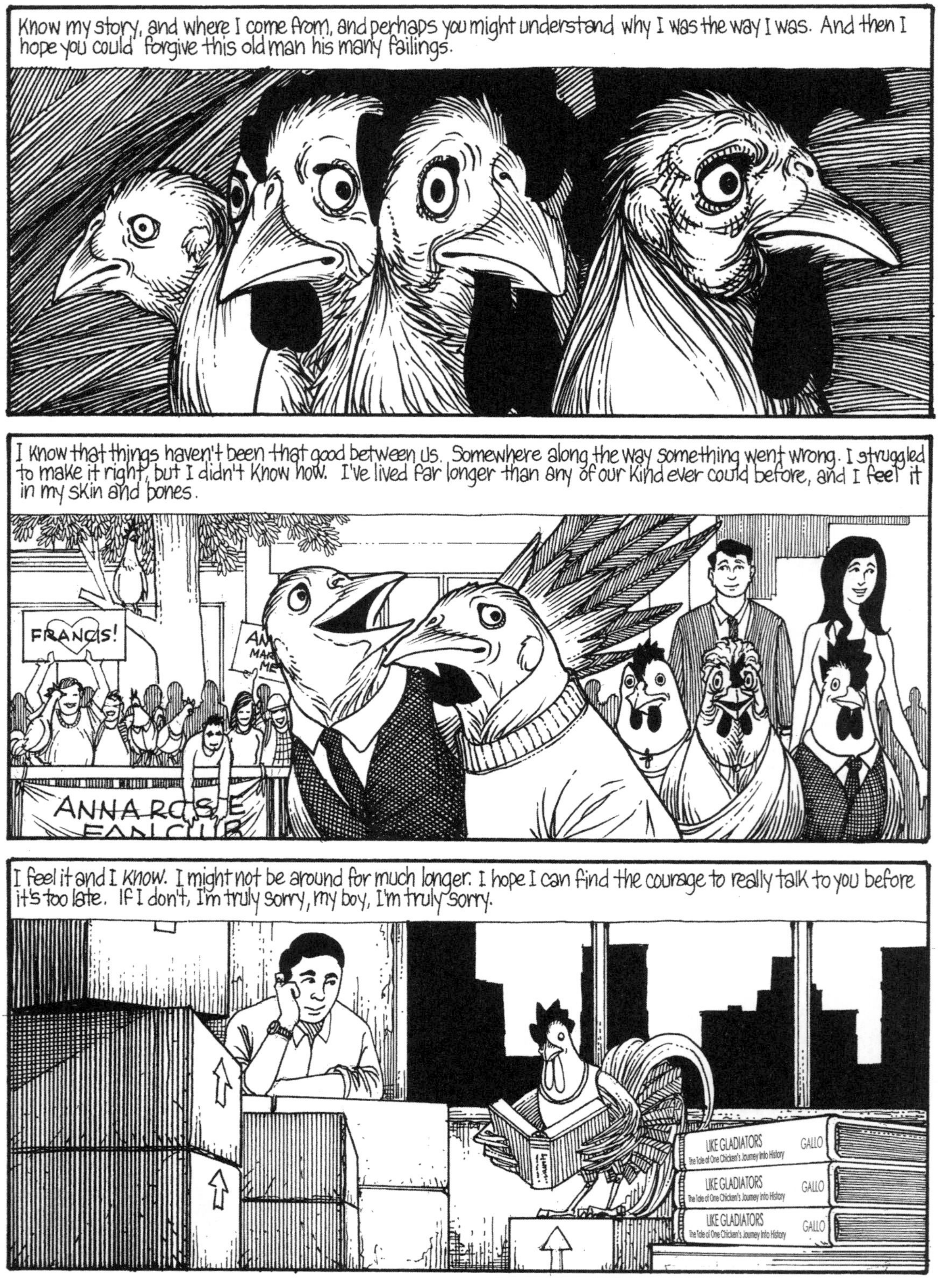
Know my story, and where I come from, and perhaps you might understand why I was the way I was. And then I hope you could forgive this old man his many failings.
I know that things haven't been that good between us. Somewhere along the way something went wrong. I struggled to make it right, but I didn't know how. I've lived far longer than any of our kind ever could before, and I feel it in my skin and bones.
FRANCIS!
ANNA ROSE
I feel it and I know. I might not be around for much longer. I hope I can find the courage to really talk to you before it's too late. If I don't, I'm truly sorry, my boy, I'm truly sorry.
LIKE GLADIATORS
The Tale of One Chicken's Journey Into History
GALLO
LIKE GLADIATORS
The Tale of One Chicken's Journey Into History
GALLO
LIKE GLADIATORS
The Tale of One Chicken's Journey Into History
GALLO

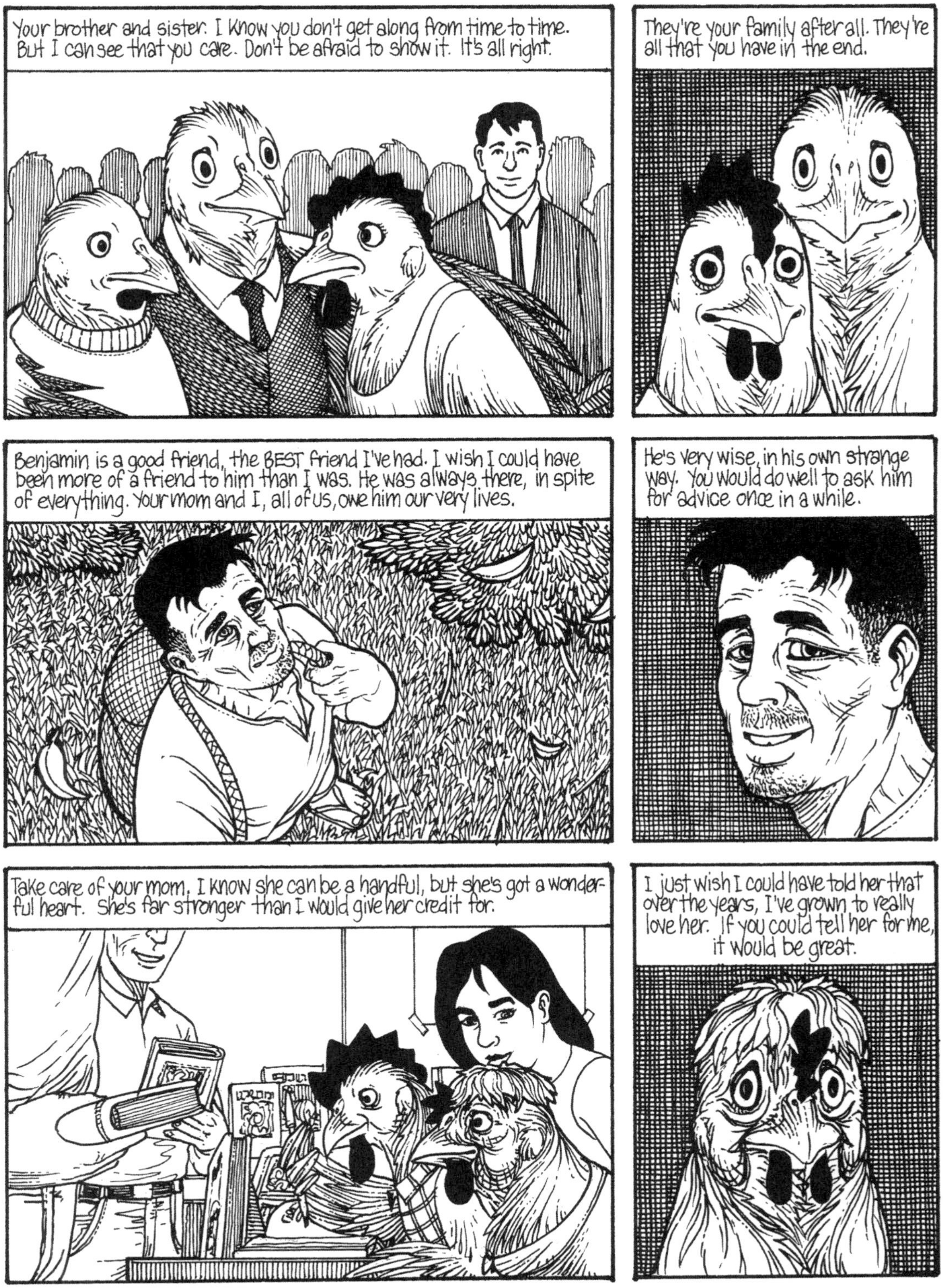
Your brother and sister. I know you don't get along from time to time. But I can see that you care. Don't be afraid to show it. It's all right.
They're your family after all. They're all that you have in the end.
Benjamin is a good friend, the BEST friend I've had. I wish I could have been more of a friend to him than I was. He was always there, in spite of everything. Your mom and I, all of us, owe him our very lives.
He's very wise, in his own strange way. You would do well to ask him for advice once in a while.
Take care of your mom. I know she can be a handful, but she's got a wonderful heart. She's far stronger than I would give her credit for.
I just wish I could have told her that over the years, I've grown to really love her. If you could tell her for me, it would be great.

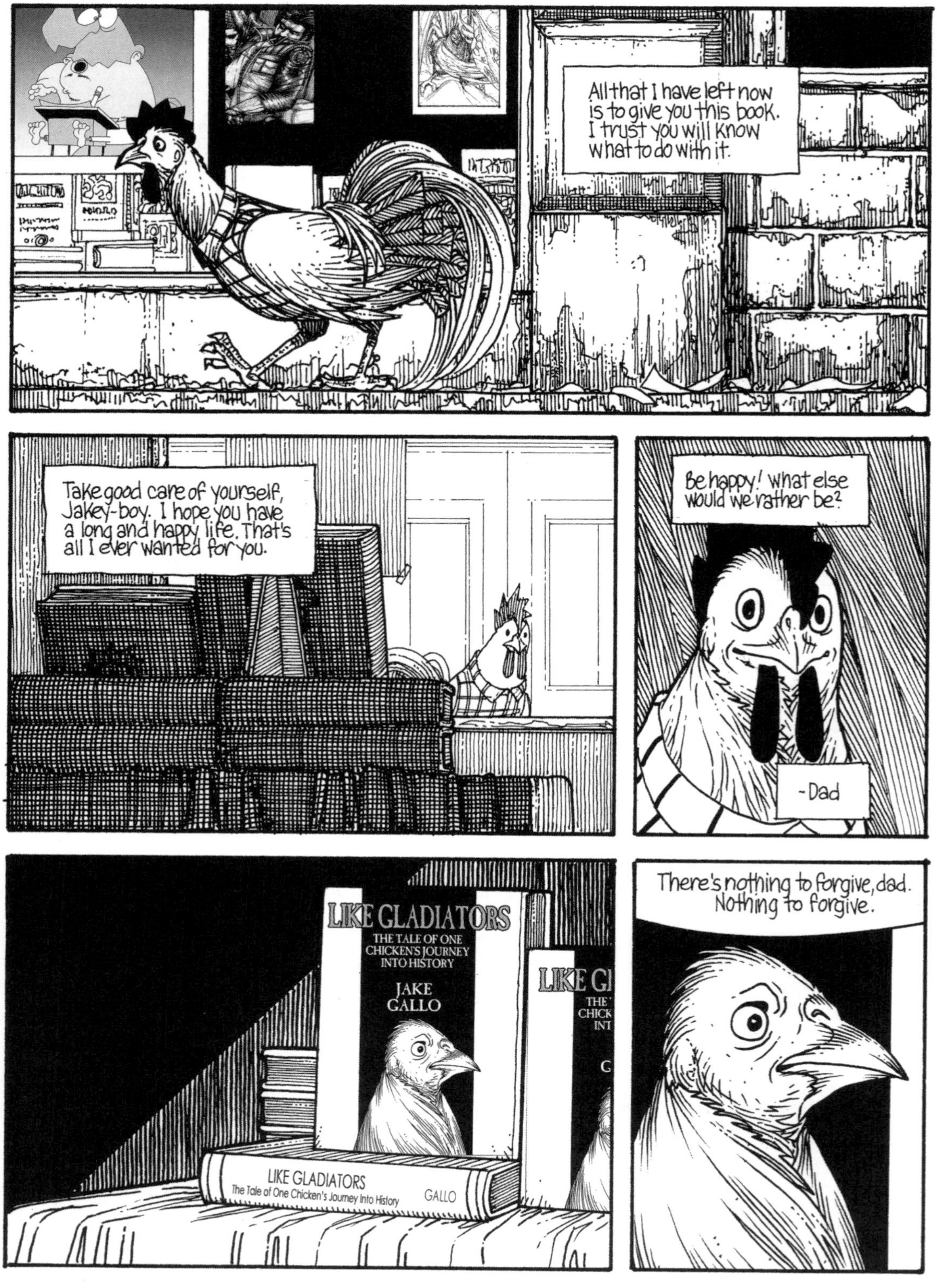
All that I have left now is to give you this book. I trust you will know what to do with it.
Take good care of yourself, Jakey-boy. I hope you have a long and happy life. That's all I ever wanted for you.
Be happy! What else would we rather be?
-Dad
LIKE GLADIATORS
THE TALE OF ONE CHICKEN'S JOURNEY INTO HISTORY
JAKE GALLO
LIKE GLADIATORS
The Tale of One Chicken's Journey Into History
GALLO
There's nothing to forgive, dad. Nothing to forgive.

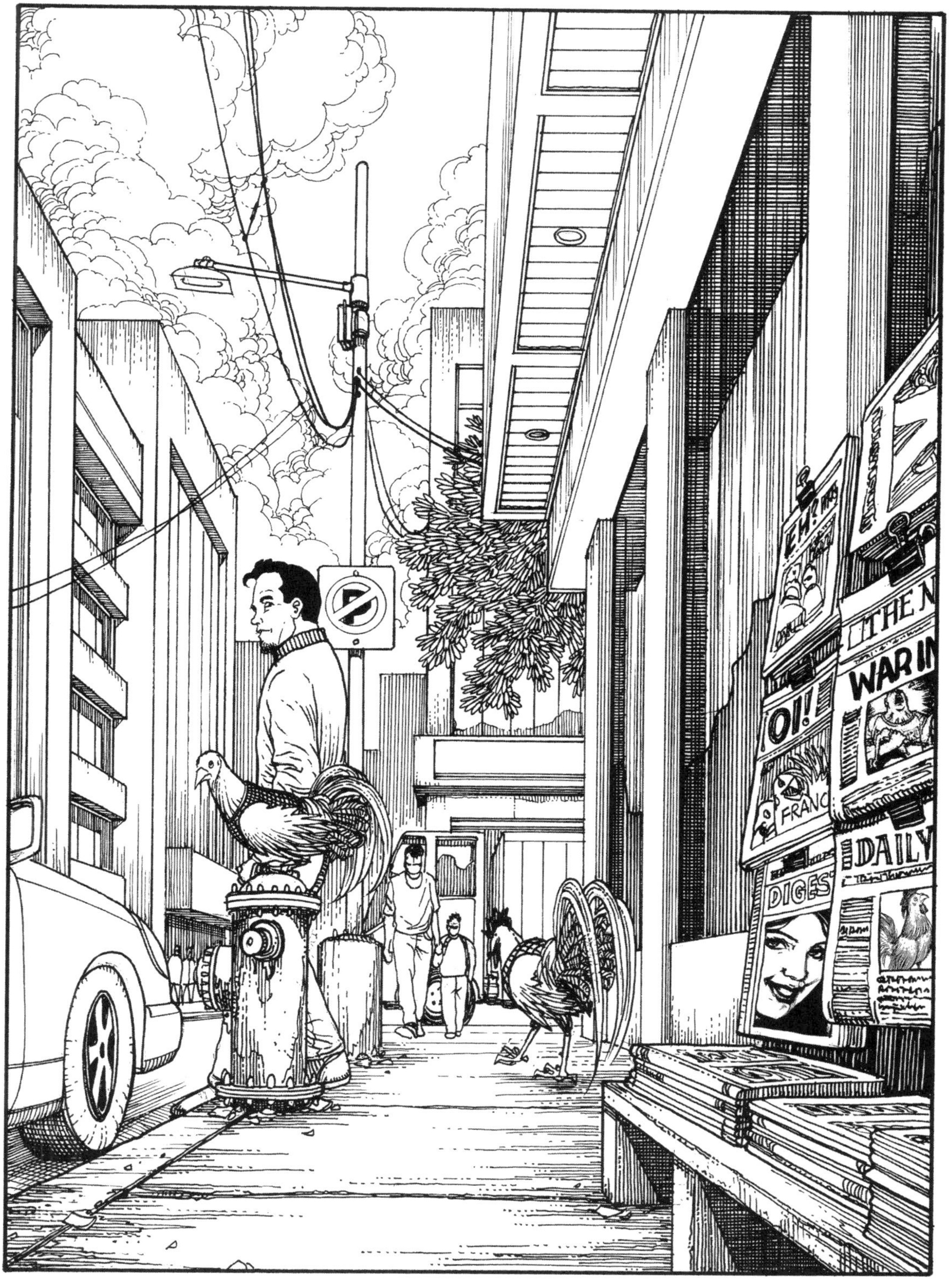
EH?
THE N
WAR IN
OI!
FRANC
DAILY
DIGES

Y ou have no idea how glad I am that you bought this book, and I am no less glad even if you simply borrowed it. What matters is that this book is in your hands and that you are reading it. Thank you. Thank you very much for giving me the opportunity to share my stories with you.

For those of you who may be familiar with my name, I am indeed the same Gerry Alanguilan who have been toiling behind the scenes as an inker on many comic books for Marvel, DC and Image beginning in 1995. To tell you the truth, I had wanted to be a superhero artist but having undergone training with Whilce Portacio, I realized my strengths perhaps lay elsewhere. It turned out inking was one of my strengths and it was a role I accepted gladly, specially since I got to work with the best superhero artists in the business including Whilce himself, Roy Allan Martinez and Leinil Francis Yu.

For the next 10 years I was involved with some of terrific books like New X-men, Wolverine, X-Force, Batman/Danger Girl, Darkness, Iron Man, and the inking work I'm proudest of: Superman: Birthright. But after doing it for so long I realized I had been suppressing my own creative impulses. Even before I started inking, I was already writing and drawing my own comics and self-publishing them as photocopied mini-comics. It is through those efforts that I realized that one of my other strengths lay in writing. I wanted to write and I wanted to draw. I had been getting all these ideas for stories for many years and I've dutifully written them all down in a little black book I always carried with me. And as I turned the pages of that book, the ideas kept screaming at me to get made.

In 2005, I took a leap of faith and quit my steady inking job and dove headlong into writing and drawing my own stories. In just a few years I was able to complete several projects which I did for other local publishers and through my own Komikero Publishing. Most significant of these projects were **"Humanis Rex!"**, a science fiction war story, **"Timawa"**, my attempt at a non-powered superhero, **"Johnny Balbona"**, humor with lots of hair, **"Where Bold Stars Go To Die"**, my attempt at comics for adults, and finally **"ELMER"**, my ultimate chicken story.

"Why Chickens?" I'm often asked. I've had a life long fascination for chickens. I love to observe them and play with them. It's easy because I've always been surrounded by chickens. In fact, a pack of them just grazed past my front gate, clucking and pecking as they went. They look funny and they act funny. Their jittery paranoid manner is always a source of great amusement for me. While out for a walk one day I began to speculate and wonder about what these chickens were thinking about when they see me walk by. They clucked and chattered nervously (or angrily?) whenever I ventured too close. Being human, I absolutely had no comprehension what these chickens were thinking.

But what if they could think? What if they could think like us and be as intelligent as us? What if they could talk? What would they say? What would they do? Would they be angry upon the realization thatwe have enslaved them, eaten them, and cheered on as we allowed them to fight each other to the death?

That seemed to trigger an avalanche of ideas that came gushing out like water from a broken pipe. KFCs and other fried and barbecue chicken places would have to close. Religions would have to deal with chickens wanting to get married, even those wanting to get married to two legged humans. They would have their own political groups, their own Cluck Cluck Klans, their own church and their own nation. They would take offense to the word "chicken" as a word for cowardice, and chickens crossing the road jokes would be considered cheap and politically incorrect. It just went on and on. Even after I had written the final draft to the story, more ideas seemed to want to join in.

So I decided on a way to contain and streamline all the ideas by telling the story through the life experience of just one family of chickens, the Elmer Gallo family.

After posting a four page preview online from the first issue, I was surprised by the reaction I got from my fellow artists. Chicken fan art came pouring in from talented amateurs, pros and even seasoned comics veterans. Because the Elmer universe was so huge, I felt that whatever chicken illustration that was sent to me would fit in somehow, somewhere in the reality of the comic book. To honor the beautiful illustrations that I have received, I resolved to incorporate them into the artwork as background graffiti, posters, graphs, paintings, screen projections, and T-shirt designs. Some that didn't fit I placed in full color on the inside back covers and letters pages of the individual issues.

Elmer was initially released through Komikero Publishing as four issues from 2006-2008, and then compiled into one volume in October 2009.

Since I had no steady job, my savings slowly dwindled . Me and my family survived through sales of Elmer and my other comics, as well sales of my inked original artwork from Marvel and DC. By the end, I have had to take out a loan from a couple of my good friends just to get the collected edition out in time for Komikon 2009, the 5th Annual Philippine Komiks Convention.

Having seen some interest for Elmer from a few places abroad, I began sending Elmer out to retailers and reviewers in the US and UK to further gauge what kind of reception this story would have. I had intentionally tried to keep settings and proper names as generic as possible in an effort to give the impression that this could happen anywhere. Being Filipino and a strong advocate of the Filipino identity in art, I guess I couldn't help show it in the drawings that I have done.

Although I was never fully daunted by the challenge, I ultimately decided that distributing my books from the Philippines to countries abroad would be too expensive and the logistics too difficult to surpass. I resolved to find a publisher for it who would be willing to include Elmer in their publishing roster. For the next few months I sent copies of Elmer to every conceivable independent comic book publisher, as well as to editors I knew here and there. There were a few positive nibbles here and there but there was nothing definite. I was beginning to think of giving up looking for a publisher, reconsidering distribution by myself once again when SLG Publishing came back with a whoppingly huge and definite-sounding "YES".

This book represents the culmination of half a decade's worth of work, sacrifice, and love. This book is in your hands because a lot of people made it possible. Thanks to all those who sent artwork that appears in this book or on the website. Thanks to all the letters of thoughtful feedback including those who helped me proofread the text including Jaime Arroyo and Teddy Pavon. Thanks to Ryan Toledo for his technical expertise. Thanks to all those who wrote about, promoted and helped me sell the book including Adam David, Kenny Penman, Joe Gordon, Ruel de Vera, Budjette Tan, Sandy Sansolis, Felix Cua, Mike Simbulan, Bill Nichols, Wesley Green, Tom Spurgeon, Steven Grant, Neil Gaiman, Warren Ellis, Matt Hawes, Andrew Wheeler and so much more that I couldn't possibly write it all down.

Thanks to Dan Vado and Jennifer De Guzman at SLG Publishing for taking the risk with my book.

Special thanks to Leinil Francis Yu, Jamie Bautista and Serge Ewenczyk .

And most special thanks to my wife Ilyn, who stuck with me for richer and for poorer, in sickness and in health. Not a fan of mine, she's a constant critic, a constant needle in my balloon, and a constant magnet that keeps my feet planted firmly on the ground. Her contribution to my work and my creative state of mind is something I cannot possibly measure. Without her, I'm literally bugnuts.

Although by 2010 I have returned full time to inking (today I'm currently working on the second issue of Superior by Mark Millar and Leinil Yu), I have resolved to continue working on my own personal projects. Whenever inking permits, I continue work on my next comic book entitled **"The Marvelous Adventures of the Amazing Doctor Rizal"**, an all ages full color and large format graphic novel that will be released as soon as I finish it. When that will be I have no idea. But I'm confident I will get there eventually.

Gerry Alanguilan
San Pablo City, Philippines
September 1, 2010

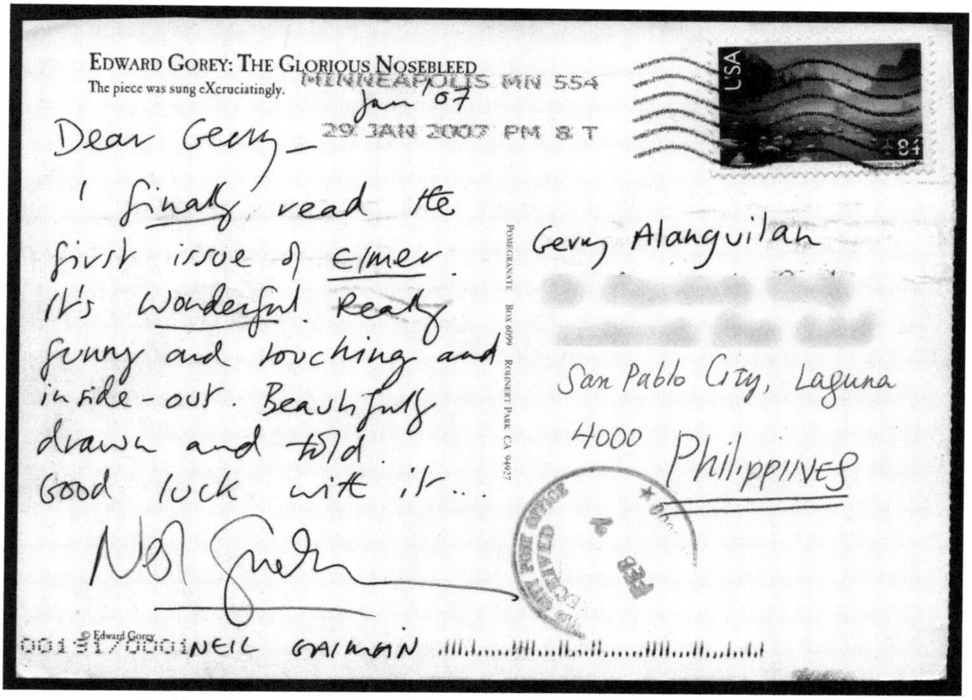
EDWARD GOREY: THE GLORIOUS NOSEBLEED
The piece was sung eXcruciatingly.

MINNEAPOLIS MN 554
Jan 07
29 JAN 2007 PM 8 T

Dear Gerry –
I finally read the first issue of Elmer. It's wonderful. Really funny and touching and inside-out. Beautifully drawn and told.
Good luck with it...
Neil Gaiman

POMEGRANATE BOX 6099 ROHNERT PARK CA 94927

Gerry Alanguilan
San Pablo City, Laguna
4000 Philippines

© Edward Gorey
0013170001 NEIL GAIMAN

My thanks to Mr. Neil Gaiman. I'm absolutely gobsmacked.

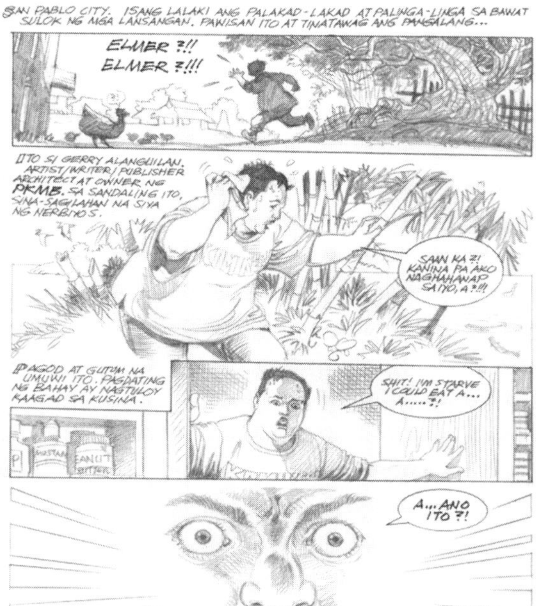
SAN PABLO CITY. ISANG LALAKI ANG PALAKAD-LAKAD AT PALINGA-LINGA SA BAWAT SULOK NG MGA LANSANGAN. PAWISAN ITO AT TINATAWAG ANG PANGALANG...
ELMER ?!!
ELMER ?!!!
ITO SI GERRY ALANGUILAN. ARTIST/WRITER/PUBLISHER ARCHITECT AT OWNER NG PKMB. SA SANDALING ITO, SINA-SAGILAHAN NA SIYA NG NERBYOS.
SAAN KA ?! KANINA PA AKO NAGHAHANAP SA'YO, A ?!!!
PAGOD AT GUTOM NA UMUWI ITO. PAGDATING NG BAHAY AY NAGTULOY KAAGAD SA KUSINA.
SHIT! I'M STARVE I COULD EAT A... A.....?!
A...ANO ITO ?!

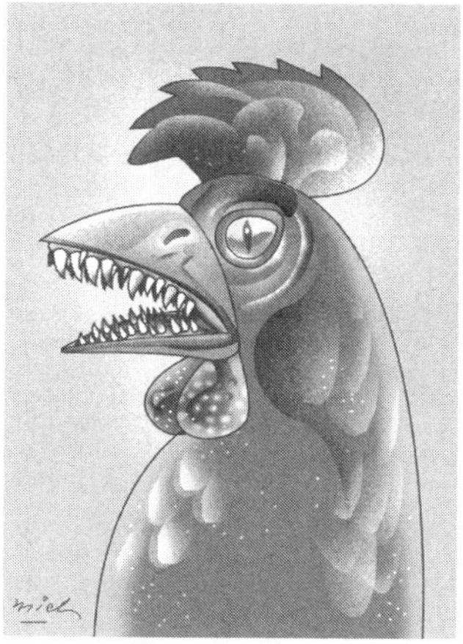
miel

Elmer by the awesome
Deng Coy Miel

Veteran Filipino comics illustrator Romeo Tanghal, popularly known for inking George Perez on Teen Titans, did this strip of Elmer and me. I was laughing for days. Thank you sir, I am very much honored!

I'm truly happy that ELMER seems to have sparked the creativity and imagination of some of today's best comics artists. **Arnold Arre** (right), popularly known for his graphic novels Andong Agimat, Mythology Class, Martial Law Babies, etc., offers this hysterical image of a chicken's revenge.

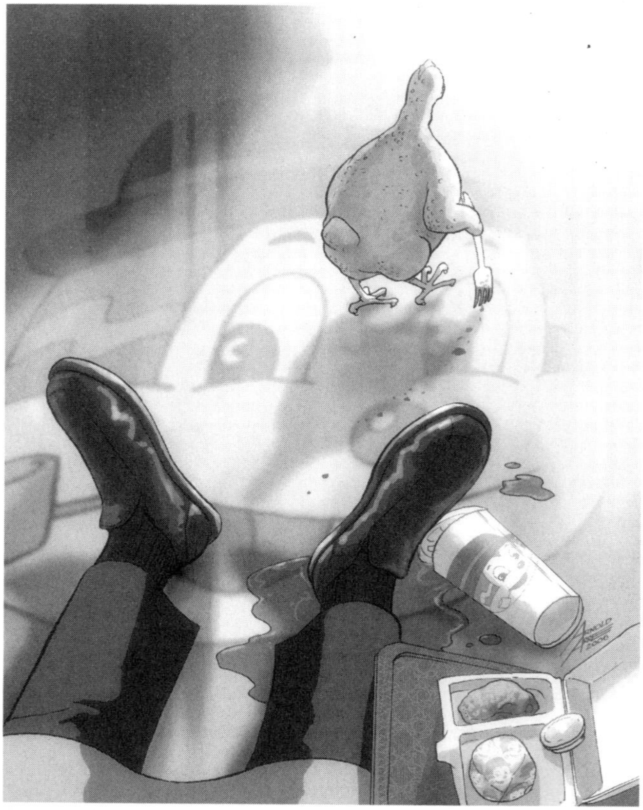

Leinil Francis Yu, undoubtedly one of the most popular comic book artists worldwide, just so happens to be a pal of this shameless name dropper, and he gives this awesome image of chickens against all odds.

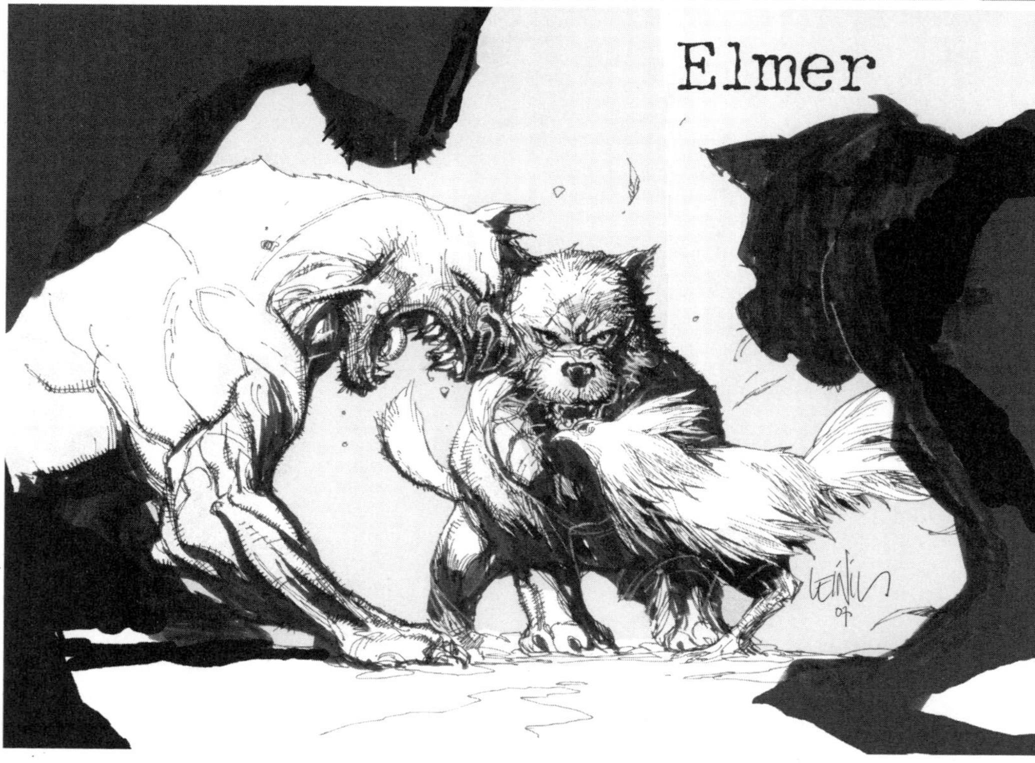
Elmer